BASIC HISTORY OF
AMERICAN CONSERVATISM

by
Robert Muccigrosso

AN ANVIL ORIGINAL
under the general editorship of
Hans L. Trefousse

KRIEGER PUBLISHING COMPANY
MALABAR, FLORIDA
2001

Original Edition 2001

Printed and Published by
KRIEGER PUBLISHING COMPANY
KRIEGER DRIVE
MALABAR, FLORIDA 32950

Library of Congress Cataloging-in-Publication Data

Muccigrosso, Robert.
    Basic history of American conservatism / Robert Muccigrosso.
        p.   cm.
    "An Anvil original."
    Includes bibliographical references and index.
    ISBN 1-57524-070-X (pbk. : alk. paper)
    1. Conservatism—United States—History. 2. Conservatism—United
States—History—Sources. I. Title.

JC573.2.U6 M83 2001
320.52'0973—dc21

                                                    00-059949

    10 9 8 7 6 5 4 3 2

For Maxine—Again

 **THE ANVIL SERIES**

Anvil paperbacks give an original analysis of a major field of history or a problem area, drawing upon the most recent research. They present a concise treatment and can act as supplementary material for college history courses. Written by many of the outstanding historians in the United States, the format is one-half narrative text, one-half supporting documents, often from hard to find sources.

CONTENTS

PREFACE AND ACKNOWLEDGMENTS

Some years ago William F. Buckley, Jr. noted that he invariably failed to satisfy an audience with a definition of conservatism. Like Joseph's fabled outerwear, conservatism is in fact a complex coat of many colors that defies exact description. Viewed historically, it has included ideas, attitudes, and adherents so diverse as at times to seem wholly incompatible.

But if consistency is not the hallmark of conservatism—or other "isms," for that matter—it does possess various distinguishing beliefs and values. Conservatives, for example, have tended to appeal to religion or at least to the presumed existence of a moral order to frame their beliefs. They traditionally have leaned toward rule by or at least guidance from an elite rather than place their faith in the masses, although more recently a current of conservative populism has come to the fore. Conservatives also are strongly inclined to look backward to the accumulated wisdom of the past for instruction. Further, they have placed a premium on the stability of the social order. As the eighteenth-century English "liberal" Adam Smith bluntly noted: "The peace and order of society is of more importance than even the relief of the miserable." (Not every conservative would go this far!) Change is not, assertions to the contrary, anathema to conservatives. But they do not generally embrace it eagerly and sometimes they seem to embrace it not at all. Yet on other occasions they do call for revised outlooks or legislation that would radically change the status quo, although admittedly in hope of restoring more cherished values and mores. The nineteenth-century British writer William Cobbett, while hardly a political conservative, subtly caught this distinction when he pointed out that "we want great alteration; but we want nothing new."

A preference for liberty over equality, when it is necessary to choose between the two, forms another characteristic commonly attributed to conservatives. Here, as elsewhere, the waters are often muddied. The conservative likes his/her liberty but at what cost and to what degree? How strong, if at all, is the affinity between conservatives and right-wing libertarians? Some from both camps have hotly denied any such affinity. Is individualism to be prized above the commonweal? And how far does the traditional distrust of the state by conservatives actually range? Far from being rugged individualists who deplored any intervention by the state or who slighted community values, many pre-Civil War conservatives embraced a philosophy at stark variance with numerous American conservatives of today. Further, conservatives historically have cherished, sometimes sanctified, property rights. Yet even here exceptions exist to what is one of the most pronounced characteristics of conservatism. Property yes, but unbridled capitalism? Once again a defining attribute calls for closer scrutiny and qualification.

The purpose of this study is to present a brief chronological history of American conservatism, emphasizing the ideas and individuals that have been most important in giving it substance and in reshaping it over time. The study makes no pretense of being all-inclusive: the extreme Right, for example, receives minimal attention. The book is, as it title indicates, a basic rather than a comprehensive work, and as such, is especially designed for the classroom as well as for the interested layperson. Similarly, restrictions of length preclude a host of relevant readings that otherwise might offer additional insights.

In writing this book and in compiling the documents herein, I have accumulated an author's customary debts. Hoping that I have not overlooked anyone, I would like to express my appreciation to various persons. I wish to thank Hans L. Trefousse, my editor, friend, and former colleague of many years, for having suggested this project and for his subsequent counsel. Thanks are also due Paolo Coletta and Mary-Jo Kline, two other long-time friends, for their useful suggestions. I am similarly grateful to the staffs of the Library of the University of Nevada, Las Vegas and the Clark County Summerlin Library for having provided invaluable assistance, and to Mary Roberts, Elaine Rudd, and the staff of Krieger for their help. Over the years the Brooklyn College students who took my course on American conservatism and others who also engaged me in serious discussions concerning conservatism—Naeem Din, Josh Feldstein, Jeff Medetsky, Allen Roth, Pat Russo, Hy Zamft—to name a warmly remembered few—provided a stimulus for writing this book. So, too, did my grandfather, Dominick Iannone, who revered Robert A. Taft and who seriously opened my young mind to the world of history. Last but certainly not least, I want to thank my loving and beloved wife, Maxine, for her warm encouragement and patience throughout this endeavor.

I offer the ritualized but sincere acknowledgment of sole responsibility for any factual errors.

PART I

HISTORY

CHAPTER 1

CONSERVATISM IN COLONIAL
AND EARLY AMERICA

Colonial Background. While certainly not the predominant tradition in American colonial life and thought—the newness of settlement and geographical distance from the mother country saw to that—conservatism did manage to implant seeds that sprouted and refused to die despite a climate that was more adverse than not. Conservatives in colonial America, whether they were the landed gentry of the southern colonies and upstate New York or urban merchants, constituted an elite that dominated colonial councils and that looked askance at the very notion of political participation by the masses. These conservatives, often linked through intermarriage and various degrees of kinship, preached that property was a prerequisite for the suffrage.

Colonial ministers were far more concerned with preaching the word of God than of debating the suffrage question, although this, too, was not neglected. Whatever their differences—and the differences that separated a Puritan divine from an Anglican one or from a follower of Roger Williams, Anne Hutchinson, or the preachers of the Great Awakening were enormous—most seemed to favor some form of hierarchy and to oppose the emotional excesses and anti-intellectual ferment that sporadically threatened to undermine order and stability. Relatedly, the nine colleges established during the colonial era—Harvard, William and Mary, Yale, New Jersey (Princeton), King's (Columbia), Philadelphia, Rhode Island (Brown), Queen's (Rutgers), and Dartmouth—functioned to inculcate traditional learning in both the scions of the upper class who were headed for the leisured life of the gentleman and for those who were headed for the ministry or statescraft.

Colonial conservatism found further expression in its admiration for balanced government, as exemplified by Great Britain with its tripartite division into monarchy, aristocracy, and commoners. Drawing upon the wisdom of the past as well as the example of the mother country, American conservatives lauded the principles of a government that promoted law and order while not stifling individual liberty. Whether Great Britain still embodied that fine balance in 1776 was, of course, a moot point, but for many it still did and they either departed America's shores or chose to remain and face the clouded prospects of a post-revolutionary new nation. Conservative values and traditions received a serious setback when an estimated hundreds of thousands of these Tories or Loyalists, as they more charitably deemed themselves, fled the thirteen colonies during the Revolution. Among them were counted such noteworthy figures as the lawyer Jared Ingersoll, the statesman Joseph Galloway, and the minister Jonathan Boucher, who, along with other émigrés, left behind a legacy that at least partially perdured.

More important for the continuation of the conservative legacy was the simple fact that many of those who had chosen to challenge British rule were themselves men of conservative principles and persuasion who regarded themselves as defenders of established rights rather than as radical transgressors of the established order. Admiration for a government that balanced liberty and order carried past their victorious quest for independence and into the founding of the new American nation. For some, however, postwar events threatened to snatch defeat from the jaws of victory. Problems of enforcing the Treaty of Paris peace provisions, unresolved territorial disputes, the disruption of trade and commerce, and ongoing friction between creditors and debtors that occasionally flared into such violence as Shays' Rebellion evoked concern and dismay. Dissatisfied with the limited ability of the central government to function under the Articles of Confederation, delegates ultimately convened in Philadelphia in 1787 to effect necessary changes. What they effected was nothing less than a dramatically new ordinance for governing. The call for reform had evoked a radical response, which, ironically, was to prove largely conservative in its final form. For while the Constitution defies neat categorization, its conservative elements underscored an overarching concern for order.

The Constitution. The new law of the land contained such largely conservative feaures as the separation of powers, a bicameral legislature, a strong president who possessed the power to veto legislation, an independent judiciary, and staggered terms of election. It also strove to protect property rights by denying states the power to impair contractual obligations. Further, the delegates made it extremely difficult to amend the Constitution. In sum, the Founding Fathers labored to secure a moderate republican form of government and to avoid a more radical direct democracy, as *The Federalist* would soon make abundantly clear.

Above all, questions of power—who shall have it and to what extent—

had occupied the framers of the historic document. James Madison in *Federalist* No. 10, the most famous of the *Federalist* papers, spelled out the need to control factions of citizens, which by their very nature "were averse to the rights of other citizens, or to the permanent and aggregate interests of the community." Fearful of a tyrannical central government, moreover, the framers followed the example of the British government as well as the ideas of the French Enlightenment philosopher Montesquieu to contrive a system of checks and balances among the branches of the central government. They also devised a federal system that divided power between the national and state governments—but not equally. Mindful of the weaknesses experienced through decentralization, the delegates to the Constitutional Convention increased the powers of the national government while diminishing those of the states. The former could now tax individuals and try them in national courts; the latter could not, as they had been able to do under the Articles of Confederation, issue currency, impose tariffs, or conduct their own foreign policy.

At the heart of the matter of power, its use and misuse, lay the question of human nature and the degree to which people could be trusted to exercise power responsibly. As Madison famously noted, if men were angels there would be no need for government. Madison well knew the limitations of human virtue and cited the "infirmities and depravities of the human character" and the "injustice and violence of individuals." Other Founding Fathers took an even dimmer view of human nature, at least that possessed by the masses of people. Alexander Hamilton referred to the general populace as a "Great Beast." Echoing this metaphor, Fisher Ames of Massachusetts deemed men "the most ferocious of all animals." Dour John Adams added his pessimistic observation that the record of humanity indicated that the masses were "as unjust, tyrannical, brutal, barbarous, and cruel as any king or senate possessed of uncontrollable power." Fearful, then, of the dark side of human nature, the Framers of the Constitution opted to restrict the suffrage and to create a form of government that would insure the rule of a (hopefully) virtuous and (hopefully) talented elite and to safeguard against shortsighted whims, popular passions, and political extremism of the mob. Liberty, yes; democracy, surely not.

Influence of Edmund Burke. Rule by all the people would also have been anathema to a contemporary British advocate of balanced government, Edmund Burke. It seems ironic that any history of American conservatism begins with this Irish-born member of Parliament, but irony must give way to necessity. Rich in both its boldness and nuance of thought, his philosophy has provided conservatives with ideas and guidelines from the eighteenth century to the present, although some liberals have also laid claim to Burkean convictions.

Like the bulk of conservatives both then and since, Burke saw dangers in the ideas advocated by Enlightenment philosophers, particularly those of the French Enlightenment (Montesquieu excepted). He did not deny that natural rights, the cornerstone of Enlightenment political thought, existed. Indeed, he revered the ideas of John Locke and his like-minded Anglo-Saxon brethren as much as did the American framers of the Declaration of Independence. But he stressed the limitations of natural rights. Their existence was an abstraction that offered but limited guidance in the day-to-day conduct of human affairs and actually presented substantial obstacles to the realization of human needs. "The science of constructing a commonwealth, or renovating it, or reforming it," he claimed, "is . . . not to be taught *a priori*." Instead, governance must be based on practical considerations, and practical considerations must take into account tradition, tradition in general and tradition as it pertained to individual peoples and states. Change was necessary, of course, but the acquired wisdom of the ages dictated that its pace be gradual and that it take into account the unwritten imperative that linked past, present, and future generations into an organic whole. For Burke, society represented a permanent contract, "a clause in the great primeval contract of primeval society, linking the lower with the higher natures, connecting the visible and invisible world." Like most conservatives, Burke grounded his philosphy in a transcendent moral order that necessitated a strong role for religion in secular society.

As a conservative, Burke feared too rapid change, specifically revolution, which threatened to undermine the permanent contract of society. He noted in his *Reflections on the Revolution in France* (1790) that "it is with infinite caution that any man ought to venture upon pulling down an edifice which has answered in any tolerable degree for ages the common purposes of society, or on building it up again without having models and patterns of approved utility before his eyes." To be sure, Burke as a Whig did approve of the English Glorious Revolution of 1688 beause the revolutionaries, in his opinion, had been defending their traditional rights against a tyrannical monarch. Relatedly, he had sympathized with American colonists before their break with the mother country since King George III and his Tory allies in Parliament had needlessly flaunted authority and had proved intransigent to justifiable colonial concerns. Rebellious Frenchmen of 1789, in contrast, were revolting without due cause. An early and insistent opponent of their actions, Burke denounced the French onslaught against their traditional rulers and values. Intoxicated by the heady brew of Enlightenment promises, they had sold their birthright for the proverbial mess of pottage that would end, he correctly foresaw, in military dictatorship.

Burke's fulminations against the French Revolution brought together the major threads of his conservative thought: a limited government presided over by a responsible monarch and hereditary aristocracy that avoids both absolute monarchy and absolute democracy; the importance of religion; the severe limitations of human reason and human nature; the dangers stemming from abrupt change; the central importance of tradition as the vital adhesive that holds society together. To one extent or another, these threads would also be woven into the tapestry of American conservatism.

The Federalists. Broad questions of politics and economics that divided Americans during the early national period gave specific form to conservative ideas and tendencies. Reflecting this division, a well-defined two-party system arose during the presidency of George Washington, despite the great patriot hero's hope that the nation would be free of rancorous political partisanship. The Federalist party by and large represented the interests and ideas of the conservatives of those days, although not all those of subsequent times. (The Federalists, by advocating a strong national government, anticipated the position of twentieth-century liberals. Conversely, the Republican, or Democratic-Republican as they are sometimes called, foes of the Federalists, led by Jefferson and Madison, the latter having developed second thoughts about a strong central government, staunchly supported states' rights and limited powers for the national government. These became staples of the antebellum South and an integral part of the conservative movement two centuries later.) Ranging widely in temperament, geographical locale, and specific agendas, the Federalists contributed in a variety of ways to the conservative cast of early politics and to the shaping of the American conservative tradition. Above all others, two Federalists especially helped to fashion both the intellectual and practical dimensions of this early American conservatism: Alexander Hamilton and John Adams.

The Hamiltonian legacy to American conservatism remains moot. For some historians of this tradition Alexander Hamilton was not a legitimate conservative or at most was a very questionable one. Their objections and reservations notwithstanding, certain of his views strongly underscore his mainstream conservative thinking. Fear of the masses and the need for an elite to rule punctuated his writings and public utterances throughout his career. Perhaps more fearful than most of the dangers presented by democracy, he suggested but did not press the point during debates on the Constitution that the United States become a monarchy. (And yet he did urge universal male suffrage for elections to the House of Representatives.) For Hamilton, who admired the British form of government as an appropriate model for others, a balance between liberty and order was vital: "As too much power leads to despotism, too little leads to anarchy, and both, eventually, to the ruin of the people." Well aware that liberty and order never rested in perfect equilibrium, he, like most Federalists, inclined toward order. That meant entrusting the national government with powers that the Antifederalists, who had opposed the Constitution, and the subsequent Republicans were loath to do. Under a federal system of government such as Americans had opted for, Hamiltonians were not concerned that the national government would forge the chains of tyranny, at least not as long as the right people exercised power. Rather, they feared that the individual states would render the central government impotent. In his *Opinion as to the Constitutionality of the Bank* (1791), Hamilton refuted Jefferson's argument for a narrow reading of the powers granted the national government by the Constitution and argued instead for a broad construction. (*See Document No. 1.*)

An unyielding opposition to the French Revolution also placed Hamilton solidly within the parameters of late eighteenth-century American conservatism. "The Great MONSTER," as he termed the upheaval in France, was a "disgusting spectacle" brought about by "unprincipled reformers." Liberty had yielded to anarchy, a stable system of hierarchy to a leveling egalitarianism, religion to atheism, salubrious moderation to unbridled passion. Jeffersonian Republicans, at least until the heyday of Robespierre and the Jacobin Terror, might see the Revolution as a glorious quest for human freedom. For Hamilton, for the Federalists, for Edmund Burke, for most conservatives everywhere, it was an unmitigated disaster.

Still, the question of whether Hamilton and his like-minded brethren were true conservatives remains vexatious and ultimately may depend more on the eye of the beholder than any agreed-upon definition. An active, forceful government, after all, would not always seem a blessing to people—states' righters, laissez-faire advocates, others—who have called themselves conservatives. For such, the Jeffersonian distrust of government represents a compelling vision of politics, and for them, the nation's third president, who believed but did not always practice the maxim that that government which governs least governs best, might seem the genuine conservative. But Hamilton's ideal of a forceful central government was truly conservative in the sense that he believed that only such a power could *conserve* and preserve the newly established nation. And above all, Hamilton was a nationalist.

For Hamilton, it seemed necessary to use what appeared as radical means to achieve his conservative ends of promoting nationhood. Sensing that the agrarian vision of Jeffersonians and the realities of a preponderant agricultural economy were ill-suited for the future, Washington's secretary of the treasury, in order to establish the credit of the United States, urged that the national government fund the nation's debt at full value and assume the debts incurred by the states during the Revolution. Successful in obtaining this objective, he also won the battle to establish a national bank. Not successful at the time was his bold proposal set forth in 1791 to encourage American manufactures by government assistance in the form of protective tariffs and bounties. For agrarians and others, the Hamiltonian program smacked of the mercantilism that England had imposed on the American colonies. Much worse, it seemed less like a visionary plan to promote a healthy nationalism and more like a barefaced scheme to fill the pockets of men of commerce and industry. Hamilton offered no apologies for the rich and well-born, whom he hoped through his economic proposals would be firmly attached to the central government and would thereby provide protection against detrimental democratic inroads. Some later conservatives would denounce Hamilton for sowing and watering the seeds of an unhealthy industrialism and the creation of a harmful plutocracy. For one contemporary—and a fellow Federalist (Noah Webster) at that—he was "the evil genius of this country." Yet Hamilton was hardly a pawn of the wealthy. His outspoken preference for tariffs on luxuries and taxes on inheritances drew no applause from that quarter. Nor did his opposition to poll taxes, which, when implemented, skewed political power ever more decisively in favor of the upper classes. For Hamiltonians, then and now, Washington's secretary of the treasury was a wise conservative who knew that guided change was a prerequisite for preservation and that this change must come from a benevolent national government composed of the wise, the wealthy, and the virtuous.

In comparison with those of Hamilton, the *bona fides* of John Adams's conservatism have received no real challenge. Quite the contrary. For many, this sturdy statesman seemed America's first great conservative thinker and doer, a defender of moderate republicanism. (*See Document No. 2.*) Like Hamilton, with whom he would bitterly clash at the time of his presidency, Adams had strong reservations about human goodness, the result, in no small measure, of the dark Calvinist legacy Puritans bequeathed his beloved New England. But some were more virtuous and talented than others, he claimed: "God Almighty has decreed in the creation of human nature an eternal aristocracy among men." A sharp although not rigid line of demarcation divided the aristocracy of the man from Quincy from that of Hamilton. For the former, intellect and character provided the necessary ingredients for a natural elite; for the latter, wealth was also a powerful factor. (In Adams's darker moments—and there were many of them—such optimism flagged. He queried Thomas Jefferson in 1813: "What chance have talents and virtues in competition with wealth and birth and beauty?")

Further, while both of these Federalists justified property rights, they differed as to what essentially constituted "property." For Adams, much like the Jeffersonians, the term denoted land, tangible goods, and means of production; Hamiltonians, in contrast, included paper money and bills of credit in their definition. The speculator was welcome to Hamiltonians but not so to Adams and his cohorts. Rather like Jefferson, Adams sought to conserve the status quo: a republic of small property owners—farmers, tradesmen, skilled workers—who would remain more or less immune to the vicissitudes of an expanding commercial and industrial order that Hamilton simultaneously foresaw and encouraged.

Like other Federalists, Adams emphasized the need for a strong central government to protect property, preserve liberty, and maintain order. Above all he stressed the need for a balanced order that took into account human strengths and frailities. In his three-volume *Defence of the Constitutions of Government of the United States of America* (1787–1789), he posited the need for constant vigilance against the tyranny of a single individual, a few, or the many. Presuming that questions of property would always animate the haves and have-nots, he argued for an aristocratic Senate and a popular House to protect the interests of each. The ministrations of a chief executive with commensurate powers would help to preserve this balance to decide deadlocked questions. Somewhat like Bunthorne in Gilbert and Sullivan's *Patience* who was attached to "a not-too-French French bean," however, Adams desired a not-too-popular popular House of Representatives. And as late as 1821 he opposed extending the franchise in Massachusetts to the nonpropertied.

Adams regarded the national government as more than a restraining force against disorder. It should also serve to advance the well-being of people. This meant that it should, among other measures, promote education, which, he claimed, "makes a greater difference between man and man, than nature has made between man and the brute. The virtues and powers to which men may be trained, by early education and constant discipline, are truly astonishing and sublime." More controversially, especially in the light of subsequent historical experience, he believed that government should generally foster religion. Like Alexander Hamilton but so unlike Jefferson and Madison, he was a friend to established religion. Also like Washington's secretary of the treasury, this scion of New England Calvinism detested the French Revolution for its onslaughts against religion. Even before the anti-Church excesses of that upheaval became fully apparent, Adams lashed out against this "republic of thirty million atheists."

Decline of the Federalist Party. Having contributed so importantly to the shaping of early American conservatism, Adams and Hamilton unwittingly also contributed to the decline of its stalwart defender, the Federalist party. Substantial political differences reenforced a mutual personal coolness. Prickly and highly sensitive to slights, Adams was aware that some Hamiltonians, including Hamilton himself, had quietly maneuvered in 1796 to support another Federalist (Thomas Pinckney) rather than Adams for the presidency. After the latter's election some party members, even within the cabinet, patently continued to look to Hamilton for leadership. The French Revolution occasioned further discord among Federalists. The Hamiltonians called for war after the XYZ Affair in 1897, the Gallic affront which demanded bribes from three American commissioners sent to negotiate a settlement arising from French attacks on American ships. To their dismay, Adams resisted and in the end the matter with France was resolved peacefully.

Concern for radical events in France and for the support they received from some quarters in the United States occasioned the Federalist-sponsored Alien and Sedition Acts of 1798. This permitted Republicans, who denounced the harsh attack on personal liberties, to make political capital, and in a reasonably close election, Jefferson wrested the presidency from a harassed John Adams in 1800.

"We are all Republicans—we are all Federalists," counseled Jefferson in his First Inaugural Address. Few Federalists were swayed by this vision of consensus, and their antagonism to the new president never abated. Particularly anathema to them were his onslaughts against the judiciary, his decision to purchase Louisiana from France, and his vacillation in the face of both British and French violations of the nation's neutrality rights. As important, however, was their conviction that Jefferson had opened wide the doors to a pernicious democracy whose leveling effects would destroy the nation. Francis J. Grund, an Austrian visitor to the United States, recorded how Jefferson, even after his presidency had ended, was reviled as "that vile blasphemer!—that infidel scoundrel!—that godless father of democracy, who has ruined the country."

Conservative rather than reactionary, most Federalists were and remained republicans (sometimes reluctantly), but neither monarchists nor democrats. The high Federalist Fisher Ames of Massachusetts, a great admirer of Alexander Hamilton, spoke to that distinction: "Monarchy is a merchantman which sails well, but will sometimes strike on a rock, and go to the bottom, whilst a republic is a raft which would never sink, but then your feet are always in water." The election of Jefferson as president, however, convinced Ames that the nation was imperiled. Fearing that the republic could degenerate into anarchy followed by military despotism since the mob was to displace the "the wise and good and opulent," he exhorted his fellow Federalists to seek and consolidate power at the state level. Warned Ames: "A democracy is a volcano, which conceals the fiery materials of its own destruction. These will produce an eruption, and carry desolation in their wake."

Ames's exhortations notwithstanding, the popularity of Jefferson and his party grew at the expense of the Federalists, who increasingly became a sectional party of the Northeast, more especially New England. In 1804 a small number of ultra-Federalists headed by Thomas Pickering, who had served as secretary of state under both Washington and Adams, concocted the so-called Essex Junto to lead New England out of the union and into a separate confederacy. The plot failed, although it indirectly gave rise to the fatal and fateful duel between Hamilton and Aaron Burr. More serious and more injurious to Federalist fortunes was the Hartford Convention of late 1814 and early 1815. Its sessions convened in secrecy, the Convention, reflecting New England's strong opposition to the War of 1812, passed a number of resolutions designed to protect regional interests. Opponents unfairly circulated rumors that the delegates were plotting treason and secession. The force of these slanders, the public statements of extreme Federalists, and the end of the war brought irremediable discredit to the party. In 1816 James Monroe, the Republican presidential candidate, handily defeated Rufus King, his Federalist opponent. Not only had King lost badly, he proved to be the last Federalist candidate to aspire to the highest office in the land.

The death of the Federalist party soon after the War of 1812 did not herald the demise of conservatism in America. On the contrary. Though they failed to control the executive and legislative branches of the national government, conservatives fought tenaciously at the state level of government and found powerful allies in the judiciary at all levels. Joined by some old-time Republicans who had decided that they were not democrats, these conservatives continued to uphold a tradition of nationalism, balanced government, elitism, property rights, and economic stability that their forbears had seeded and enriched. Whether they could succeed in the face of rapid political, economic, and social change was another matter.

CHAPTER 2

CONSERVATISM IN THE AGE OF DEMOCRACY

What the Jeffersonians sowed the Jacksonians reaped. While the former retained certain elitist beliefs and defined democracy circumspectly, Andrew Jackson and his followers expanded the practice and rhetoric of democracy, though to what extent remains a moot point among historians. According to some, social and economic inequalities were actually increasing at this time. But whether the Jacksonians were more or less "democratic," and whatever the later, ever-changing interpretations of Jacksonianism, their contemporary conservative opponents perceived them as catering to the mob and endangering the nation's institutions and practices through the "spoils system." Convinced that Jacksonianism was a pernicious threat to the nation's welfare, the heirs of the Federalists and disabused Republicans sought to preserve and expand upon traditions established in the early years of the republic. Their far-flung efforts permeated the fields of law, politics and economics, social mores, culture and religion.

The Marshall Supreme Court. No person played a more important role in the preservation of Federalist values and concerns than did John Marshall. Born on the Virginia frontier in 1755, he was the first of fifteen children and a distant relation of Thomas Jefferson, who would become his bitter enemy. A Revolutionary patriot, Marshall hero-worshipped George Washington, with whom he served at Valley Forge. Wartime experience proved instrumental in shaping his future outspoken nationalism. That experience, he professed, was "where I was confirmed in the habit of considering America as my country, and Congress as my government." In the postwar years Marshall achieved prominence within the Federalist party first on a state level and then on the national scene. He declined an appointment as attorney general from President Washington, served as a delegate to France in 1798 at the time of the XYZ Affair, and won election to the House of Representatives in 1799. President Adams appointed him secretary of state the following year, but it was his appointment—again by Adams—as chief justice of the Supreme Court in early 1801 that brought him eminence and gave distinct shape to the nation's judicial system. By the time of his death in 1835, Marshall and the Court had established the principle of judicial review and had invoked the supremacy of federal laws over state laws. They had also advanced the protection of private property and fostered economic development. Looking back on his elevation of Marshall to the highest court in the land, Adams termed it "the pride of my life."

Constitutionally speaking, the Supreme Court transcends partisan politics. In reality, both then and now, it reflects, sometimes subtly, sometimes not, the attitudes and assumptions of its individual justices. A staunch Federalist formed from the Hamiltonian mold, John Marshall dominated his Court through compelling arguments and a persuasive personality. Having asserted the right of judicial review for the Court in the famous *Marbury* v. *Madison* case in 1803—a right that did not go unquestioned by Republicans—the chief justice proceeded to exercise the Court's newly won constitutional powers in a series of remarkable decisions. In 1795, for example, the legislature of Georgia had awarded huge land grants to various companies. When it came to light that numerous legislators had accepted bribes from the companies, the next Georgia legislature rescinded their predecessors' handiwork in an effort to undo these notorious Yazoo land frauds. Lawsuits followed, ultimately reaching the Supreme Court, which in 1810 struck down the annulment of the land grants in *Fletcher* v. *Peck*. Speaking for the Court, Marshall noted that Georgia "is a member of the American Union; and that Union has a constitution the supremacy of which all acknowledge, and which imposes limits to the legislatures of the several states, which none claim the right to pass." Deftly, Marshall had strenghtened the Court's power of judicial review and had extended its scope to apply to laws passed by states, whereas in the *Marbury* case only federal matters were at hand. But *Fletcher* v. *Peck* was not only a victory for nationalism, for by defending the right of contract it also underscored the Court's resolve to protect private property howsoever odorous may have been its origins.

The Marshall Court expanded its rulings on the sanctity of contracts and the primacy of federal over state laws in a series of decisions, the most notable of which occurred between 1819 and 1824. In *Sturgis* v. *Crowninshield* the Court in 1819 struck down a New York state bankruptcy law. That same year in *Dartmouth College* v. *Woodward* it ruled that a New Hampshire legislature had acted unconstitutionally in its attempt to convert Dartmouth into a public college, an act, the Court decreed, that violated the terms of an earlier colonial period charter. Marshall and his fellow justices handed down yet a third major decision in 1819, one that was even more far-reaching in importance: *McCulloch* v. *Maryland*. The powerful Second Bank of the United States, established in 1816 as a successor to the First Bank of the United States whose charter had expired five years earlier, posed a serious threat to some state banks. In response Maryland enacted an annual tax on the national bank, which in turn flatly refused to pay. The Supreme Court sided with the national bank. Marshall pronounced that "the power to tax involves the power to destroy," and no state could destroy an institution created by the national government. Read in its entirety, Marshall's argument evoked strong shades of Alexander Hamilton's argument for the legality of the First Bank of the United States and for the authority of nationalism.

In 1821 in *Cohens* v. *Virginia* Marshall, drawing upon legal reasoning earlier used by Joseph Story, his Court colleague, warm admirer, and fellow conservative, wrote the majority opinion for two brothers who were tried and convicted in a state court for having sold lottery tickets in violation of a Virginia statute. (*See Document No. 3.*) Agreeing that the defendants had not been protected by a federal law of 1802 that had authorized a lottery, the Chief Justice extended the scope of the High Court's powers over state courts by allowing a defendant to take his case to the Court even when the plaintiff was the state and as long as the defendant did not initiate the suit. In *Gibbons* v. *Ogden* (1824), the Court invalidated a statute that had granted a monopoly on steamboat company service between New York and New Jersey. Marshall based the Court's ruling on a sweeping interpretaton of the commerce clause of the Constitution. According to Marshall, commerce included "every species of commercial intercourse," and Congress's right to regulate it "may be exercised to its utmost extent, and acknowledges no limitations other than are prescribed in the Constitution."

The Marshall Court, to the approval of conservatives, had extended the powers of the central government and had helped to safeguard private property. Its decisions had channeled change into as much order as possible in a society where whirl increasingly held dominion. Not even the Court, however, could contain the niagara of democratic ideas and practices.

Attempts to Limit Democracy. It was evident by the 1820s, even before the election of Andrew Jackson, that the forces of democracy had gained substantial momentum. No longer willing to accept the elitism of the early republic, rank-and-file Americans pushed for fuller participation in politics. Their demands included the popular election of the president as well as various judges, and the amendment of state constitutions to reflect democratic sentiments. To achieve their goals they focused on the elimination of property qualifications for voting and holding office.

With the recent demise of their party on the national level, Federalists looked to state politics to stem the rising tide of democracy. Some of their former Republican foes, among them the Virginians James Madison, James Monroe, and John Randolph, shared their concern. Only property owners, they contended, had a sufficient economic stake in society to preserve it. They also predicated their arguments on the assumption that only such men possessed sufficient wisdom, character, and impartial judgment. Whatever the proportions of high ideals and self-interest that infused their contentions, historical antecedents and forceful rhetoric buttressed their cause. During the 1820s these conservative opponents of mass suffrage took their stand at state conventions held in Massachusetts (1820–1821), New York (1821), and Virginia (1829–1830). Perhaps none spoke so adamantly against extending the franchise as did Chancellor James Kent of New York, a prominent jurist and a member of the state's supreme court who warned that "the tendency of universal suffrage, is to jeopardize the rights of property, and the principles of liberty." (*See Document No. 4.*) The majority of delegates at the constitutional convention rejected Kent's counsel and rescinded most property qualifications for the suffrage. The constitutional conventions in Massachusetts and Virginia responded in similar fashion.

Even before the last convention votes were tallied in Virginia it had become clear that the day of the old Federalists and their recently apostate Jeffersonian allies had faded into twilight and was inexorably about to turn into the oblivion of night. The new day would belong to democrats in the main but not entirely since a new generation of conservatives would strive to maintain their heritage. Yet enormous circumstantial changes in American life and society had deprived these newer conservatives of the strict principles and more or less coherent program that had characterized their Federalist forebears. Less secure in an age that augured the enthronement of democracy, they added a flexibility to the firm guideposts laid down by the Federalists and made their compromises with their times. Partly pragmatic, partly opportunistic, they plied their own brand of conservatism in an age of democracy and strong economic expansion.

National Conservativism. Less conservative in many respects than his father, John Quincy Adams adapted his convictions to fit emerging needs. Fundamental for him was the need to employ the powers of the federal government to foster the nation's development. In his First Annual Message to Congress, delivered on December 6, 1825, President Adams went far beyond the nationalistic spirit so dear to his father and other Federalists. To achieve material benefits second to none, he called upon Congress to promote agriculture, commerce, and manufacturing, as well as education, science, and the arts. He envisioned, among other items, a national university, an astronomical observatory, a public ship to explore the Pacific Northwest, and the establishment of a uniform standard of weights and measures. Overly ambitious for its time and caught in the snarls of partisan politics, Adams's program went unaccepted.

More successful in the immediate future than the broad agenda outlined by President Adams was to be the "American System" trumpeted by his secretary of state, Henry Clay. Although he unsuccessfully sought the presidency in three elections, Clay was a titan among politicos during the "middle period" of the nation's history. A one-time Jeffersonian who in 1811 had opposed the rechartering of the Bank of United States as unconstitutional, Clay performed an about-face and, like the Hamiltonians, advocated an active national government to spur the economy. Noting the diverse economic interests, strengths, and weaknesses of the nation's geographic sections, he claimed that his American System would benefit all by erecting tariffs, building roads and canals, and preserving a sound currency through a second national bank. The mercantile East would gain protection from foreign goods through the imposition of tariffs and would readily find new markets in the West as a result of federally aided transportation improvements. The West, in return, would benefit by shipping its raw materials eastward and also would enjoy more consumer goods.

Clay gained strong support for the American System from the Philadelphia publisher and publicist Matthew Carey, his son Henry Carey, who was the first true professional economist in the United States, and from the immigrant German economist Friedrich List. How beneficial the American System would be to the South, which was increasingly becoming a single-staple economy, was problematic, as numerous southerners vociferated. Still, the American System lay at the heart both of the National Republican party of Adams and Clay during the 1820s and its sucessor, the Whig party, which coalesced the enemies of Andrew Jackson the following decade.

Daniel Webster, who along with Clay and John C. Calhoun formed a triumvirate of dominant congressional figures during this era, also breathed new life into the nationalist precepts of Hamilton and his Federalist party. Unlike Clay, the New Hampshire-born Webster did not have to foreswear any early political convictions to embrace a neo-Federalism: he was a staunch Federalist from the start. As a young schoolteacher he wrote in 1802 that "the path to despotism leads through the mire and dirt of uncontrolled democracy." Leaving the schoolroom for the courtroom, Webster gained fame. His successful representations for the plaintiff in *Dartmouth* v. *Woodward*, *McCulloch* v. *Maryland*, and *Gibbons* v. *Ogden* cemented his reputation as one of the nation's leading constitutional lawyers and underscored his commitment to the Federalist principles written into judicial decisions by Chief Justice Marshall. Time did not dissipate his distrust of the masses. He opposed the popular election of state senators at the Massachusetts constitutional convention in 1820; in 1848 he successfully defended the established Rhode Island state government against the popular government that the insurgent Thomas Dorr and his followers had briefly established several years earlier. It was, he admonished, a "great conservative principle" to protect against "the sudden impulses of mere majorities."

Webster's economic views initially diverged from those of Hamilton. He opposed the rapid growth of manufacturing and the protective tariffs of 1816 and 1824, fearing that they would destroy the commerce and shipping upon which New England's well-being then rested. Sectional impoverishment, the loss of an essentially rural way of life that he cherished, and the conversion of independent farmers into deracinated factory hands loomed large. By the late 1820s, however, he had changed his mind. New England had become by that time a powerful center for manufacturing, its factories the marvel of the nation. Webster, who had relocated to Boston, now gladly supported the protective tariff of 1828 and by the next decade had warmly embraced Clay's American System.

Skeptics and enemies, of whom there were many, questioned the sincerity of Webster's changing economic views. Politically highly ambitious, the Massachusetts senator, they charged, possessed an opportunism matched only by his greed for money, which had become nearly legendary. Webster may have bent his views to catch the prevailing popular winds, at least on some occasions, but when the preservation of the Union was called into question he stood steadfast. In 1830 most outside the South applauded his long reply to Senator Robert Y. Hayne of South Carolina in which he skillfully shredded the latter's argument for the right of states to nullify national legislation. Twenty years later, however, he was widely vilified in both the North and the South for having championed the highly controversial Compromise of 1850, which in retrospect postponed the Civil War by a decade. Vilification notwithstanding, Daniel Webster had enjoyed one of his finest hours as a statesman and national conservative.

The inexorable march of democracy during the first half of the nineteenth century affected the nation's social mores and culture no less than it did its politics and economics. The primary yardstick by which both opponents and proponents of democracy gauged these changes was, as it had been ever since the colonial era, Europe and, more especially, England. The call for a distinctly American way of life and culture separate from that of the Old World had been gaining momentum ever since the Revolution until by the Jacksonian era it had become virtually an article of faith for numerous democrats. Declared Ralph Waldo Emerson in his Phi Beta Kappa address at Harvard College in 1837: "We have listened too long to the courtly muses of Europe. . . . We will walk on our own feet; we will speak our own minds." American conservatives strongly resisted the call for any thorough rejection of European ways, however, and in their struggle they drew sustenance from the critiques of contemporary transatlantic visitors. In retrospect, some of the most suggestive insights into the nature of American conservatism during the first half of the nineteenth century came from the observations of these travelers.

Foreign Critics of American Democracy. Eager to see at firsthand the developments in the New World, visitors from the Old World flocked to the United States during the first half of the nineteenth century. While some such as the Englishwoman Harriet Martineau and the Frenchman Michael Chevalier compared what they found here favorably with what they had temporarily left behind, others drew a mixed picture or limned their portraits in almost relentlessly negative hues.

Captain Frederick Marryat was one such naysayer. An English novelist popular with Americans for his *Mr. Midshipman Easy*, Marryat visited the United States in the 1830s. He thoroughly disliked the experience and candidly confessed later that the purpose of publishing his *Diary in America* (1839) was "to do injury to democracy." Atop his list of America's shortcomings was its unremitting greed and lack of respect for what should be cherished. The novelist was dismayed to learn that a railroad in Rhode Island ran through a cemetery. "They grind down the bones of their ancestors for the sake of gain," he lamented, "and consecrated earth is desecrated by the iron wheels, loaded with Mammon-seeking mortals." America was the land "where everything is sacrificed to time; for time is money."

Marryat's complaints that the land of democracy was the land of gross materialism and shocking disregard for the past can be attributed to the prejudices of an upper-class Briton born to the manner of tradition. But Charles Dickens, far from being a snob, chimed in with his own inventory of his transatlantic cousins' shortcomings. Dickens was the single most popular living foreign novelist at the time of his visit in 1842. It came as a surprise, and a rude one at that, when Dickens, who had been lionized and widely feted, proceeded, proverbially speaking, to bite the hands that had fed him. His *Martin Chuzzlewit* (1843–1844) satirized the American frontier, while *American Notes* (1850) scorned, among other traits of character, the unseemly and unrelenting pursuit of money by Americans and their lack of social graces. The latter work also suggested that Americans should continue to look to England and Europe for guidance in cultural matters.

Frances Trollope, mother of the novelist Anthony Trollope, had also castigated Americans for their seeming obsession with making money and their lack of good manners when she visited the United States in 1828. Her *Domestic Manners of the Americans* catalogued in detail what she deemed the shabby social behavior of her American cousins, which dwarfed in her estimation such laudable developments as the industriousness of common people and the opportunity for them to better their lot. Virtually everywhere, so it seemed to her, poor manners predominated. She reported so-called gentlemen in Kentucky picking their teeth with pocketknives, while in Cincinnati "the gentlemen spit, talk of elections and the price of produce, and spit again." Manners were no better in the nation's capital where a man "was seized with a violent fit of vomiting, which appeared not in the least to annoy or surprise his neighbors." Americans were simply too democratic for Mrs. Trollope's genteel tastes. She deplored "the wild scheme of placing all the power in the hands of the people." Moreover, she noted the hypocrisy of American democrats apropos indigenous people, more specifically, their eviction and subsequent forced migration of the Cherokee nation to undesired land across the Mississippi River: "They inveigh against governments of Europe, because, as they say, they favour the powerful and oppress the weak." She added scornfully: "You will see them one hour lecturing the mob on the indefeasible rights of man, and the next driving from their homes the children of the soil, whom they have bound to protect."

Alexis de Tocqueville lacked the haughty contempt for democratic America that Mrs. Trollope, Captain Marryat, and even Charles Dickens manifested. Yet this French aristocrat, who came to the United States in 1831 to study the nation's penal system, produced in *Democracy and America* the most remarkably astute insights into American institutions and social behavior of all the European visitors during the Jacksonian period. Indeed, to date many regard him as the single finest foreign observer of American life. Whether Tocqueville was a liberal conservative or a conservative liberal is as moot a point as is that of whether he was more or less in favor of democracy. The complexity of his perceptions renders these questions extraordinarily difficult to resolve. What does emerge from his work is his desire to allow Americans to understand the need to reconcile the best of their traditional values with the liberating forces of an ascendant democratic society: "Thus, the question is not how to reconstruct aristocratic society, but how to make liberty proceed out of that democratic state of society in which God has placed us."

Americans were "born free," according to Tocqueville. Lacking a feudal past and a rigid class structure to which Europeans were heirs, they happily were able to achieve liberty and assorted advantages denied to most. But these blessings came at a certain price. Preoccupied with making money and exuding a materialism that shocked Tocqueville as it did other European visitors, Americans had cut or were cutting themselves off from the past. "No one cares for what occurred before his time," he lamented. A restless people ever seeking something better,

Americans were like "an army in the field." Due to "the continual movement that agitates a democratic community, the tie that unites one generation to another is relaxed or broken; every man there readily loses all trace of the ideas of his forefathers or takes no care about them." The state of science and the arts in the United States also troubled the French visitor. "It must be acknowledged," he wrote, "that in few of the civilized nations of our time have the higher sciences made less progress than in the United States; and in few have great artists, distinguished poets, or celebrated writers, been more rare. Many Europeans . . . have looked upon it as a natural and inevitable result of equality; and they have thought that, if a democratic state of society and democratic institutions were ever to prevail over the whole earth, the human mind would gradually find its beacon-lights grow dim, and men would relapse into a period of darkness."

The uneasy relationship between liberty and equality underlay Tocqueville's concerns for America, much as it has for others from the earliest days of the republic to the present. Were liberty and equality compatible ideals? Did they offer an either/or, or a both/and proposition? Tocqueville never explicitly said, but he did put forth insights and caveats that implicitly could preserve freedom in its various guises from the seemingly unstoppable juggernaut of ideological and experiential democracy. Like other conservatives, Tocqueville feared mightily for liberty, not so much for liberty in the legal and civil sense—although he did have his concerns in these areas—but for liberty of thought and opinion. The would-be destroyer of liberty in a democracy would not necessarily be the iron fist of a despot or a coterie of despots, but, more insidiously, "the tyranny of the majority," which brooked no heterodoxy. "I know of no country in which there is so little independence of mind and real freedom of discussion as in America," observed Tocqueville. He did believe that "democratic communities have a natural taste for freedom." For equality, however, "their passion is ardent, insatiable, incessant, invincible . . . "

Domestic Critics of Democracy. Like Tocqueville, thoughtful American conservatives inveighed against what they considered the excesses and harmful effects of democratic practice while praising its positive achievements. Included among such conservatives were two of the nation's most prominent writers, James Fenimore Cooper and

Nathaniel Hawthorne. Further, as convinced Democrats rather than Whigs, these two underscored the difficulty of defining conservatism in an age of rapid change and dislocation.

The author of more than fifty novels and works of nonfiction, James Fenimore Cooper devoted considerable attention to the complexities and ambiguities of democracy. Like the title of his best known work of social and political criticism, he was himself the American democrat, albeit one with severe reservations. Like contemporary conservatives, he deplored how democratic society was inclining "in all things toward mediocrity." While applauding the right to property and its widespread proliferation as necessary components of civilization, he argued that this negated any equality of condition, which for some seemed a cornerstone of democratic ideology. "All that democracy means," the novelist cautioned, "is as equal a participation in rights as is practicable; and to pretend that social equality is a condition of popular institutions, is to assume that the latter are destructive of civilization, for, as nothing is more self-evident than the impossibility of raising all men to the highest standard of tastes and refinement, the alternative would be to reduce the entire community to the lowest."

American democracy needed a dedicated elite to preserve the old republican values of virtue, order, and decorum against those who, wittingly or not, were undermining them. Cooper, who considered and admired Andrew Jackson as an avatar of republican worth, directed his animus specifically against the Whigs, who, he charged, were engrossed in economic matters and preciously little else. As a result, the grasping financier and speculator, with their advocacy of easy money, were replacing the sound money men and the old landed gentry as represented by the Cooper family. (Unlike the "conservative" Whigs, Cooper strongly supported President Jackson in his successful battle to destroy the Second Bank of the United States.) Opinions and taste, subject to the whims of demagogues and the leveling influences of the untutored and unrestrained masses, had similarly degenerated, making life in democratic America a difficult proposition for both the true gentleman and the talented writer. As for the latter, complained Cooper, in democratic America "there is nothing to awaken fancy in that land of dull realities. No objects carry the mind back to contemplation of a remote antiquity. No moldering ruins excite interest in the history of the past. No memorials commemorative of noble deeds arouse enthusiasm and reverence. No traditions, legends, fables, afford material for poetry and romance."

The lament of James Fenimore Cooper for the plight of the American writer differed hardly a whit from that of Nathaniel Hawthorne (or, later, from Henry James). In his preface to *The Marble Faun* (1860), Hawthorne judged that "no author . . . can conceive of the difficulty of writing a Romance about a country where there is no shadow, no antiquity, no mystery, no picturesque gloomy wrong, not anything but a commonplace prosperity, in broad and simple daylight, as is happily the case with my dear native land. Romance and poetry, like ivy, lichens, and wall-flowers, need ruin to make them grow." The quotation from Hawthorne's late novel points to his fundamental love for America but also to his fear that materialism and monotony were stifling artistic creativity. His concerns, however, extend well beyond the esthetic. Like Cooper, who was his senior by fifteen years, he was a conservative Democrat by and large uneasy with democracy.

The years between the presidential election of Andrew Jackson and the outbreak of the Civil War witnessed enormously ambitious attempts to reform American society or sometimes even to transform it into a utopia. Abolition, women's rights, temperance, peace, education, penology, labor, socialism, religious revivalism—all found their zealous advocates and energy-laden organization. Hawthorne, like other conservatives of the era, was unable to share in this exuberant optimism. In *The Blithedale Romance* (1852) he good naturedly scoffed at the attempts of a group of New England Transcendentalists, several of whom he called friend, to establish a viable community along utopian lines. Earlier he had deflated utopian impulses in both "The Celestial Railroad" (1843) and "Earth's Holocaust" (1844), the latter a parable in which well-meaning reformers destroy everything valuable from the past in their benighted attempt to usher in an age of democratic perfection. Progressive ideas are predicated on the inherent goodness of human nature or at least its plasticity. For Hawthorne, human imperfection—sin, if you will—mocked the best laid plans of reformers and gnawed at their efforts. It was possible to improve the lot of humans, to be sure, but that improvement bumped against stony boundaries and came only after careful thought and wise guidance.

The Puritan heritage weighed heavily upon Hawthorne, who, like his Puritan forebears, stressed the darkness and mysteries of human nature that cast a pall over human activity and imposed limitations on good intentions. Nonetheless, the rigid Calvinist determinism and pessimism of the Puritans was yielding during Hawthorne's lifetime to Transcendentalism and the more liberal Unitarian and Universalist churches, which played down originanl sin and determinism. It was also giving way to the emotional revivalism of the "Second Great Awakening." Less liberal in their theology and preachings than Unitarians and Universalists, these reawakened Christians accepted humankind's innate depravity but at the same time stressed that salvation was possible. Transcendentalists, Unitarians, Universalists, and revivalists were all suitable components of a yea-saying democratic America that believed in progress. With the Calvinism of his Puritan ancestors receding but unable to accept the optimistic views of the newer sects, the agnostic Hawthorne, like Matthew Arnold in *Stanzas from the Grand Chartreuse*, stood suspended between a world that was dead and one that could not be born.

No such fate awaited the most noteworthy religious conservative of this era, Orestes Brownson. In his quest for certitude and order, this singular figure belongs to a long list of apostates, particularly from the twentieth century, who moved from the left to the right on the political spectrum. Born in rural Vermont in 1804, Brownson was struck by misfortune at age four when his impoverished widowed mother gave him to others to raise. His childhood insecurity well may have responsible for his later intellectual and emotional pursuit of an abiding faith. As a young man, the deeply religious Brownson tergiversated from Congregationalism to Presbyterianism to Universalism to Unitarianism and then in the mid-1830s to Transcendentalism. During these years young Brownson became a committed reformer, even somewhat of a radical. A staunch friend of labor, he persistently supported the cause of the working class in his work as a journalist, and praised the socialistic efforts of Fanny Wright and Robert Owen. Believing in the goodness and wisdom of the common man, he was buoyed by the prospects for democracy.

The presidential election of 1840 thoroughly disillusioned Brownson. Having excoriated the Whigs as the enemies of the working class, he was dumbfounded when the electorate heeded their blatant demagogic appeal to the sham symbols of a log cabin and hard cider and elected William Henry Harrison to the presidency. Later he bitterly rued: "Do not answer by referring us to the virtue and intelligence of the people. We . . . have no leisure to enjoy a joke, even if it be a good one." He added: "We have heard enough of liberty and the rights of man. It is high time to hear something of the duties of men and the rights of authority." In 1844 Orestes Brownson converted to Catholicism. At last finding a suitable spiritual and intellectual home after long years of search and abandonment, he remained a devout Catholic until his death in 1876. Brownson never surrendered his passionate youthful belief in the necessity for liberty and the benefits democracy could confer, although he had come to believe that equality should pertain solely to voting and legal rights. But a chastened, more sober Brownson saw in the example of the Church what he considered a salutary blend of freedom and order, and for more than thirty years he tried to educate his countrymen to accepting regulated freedom for themselves and their society. (*See Document No. 5.*) Liberty blended with authority generally suited conservatives, and nowhere more so than in the antebellum South.

CHAPTER 3

CONSERVATISM IN THE ANTEBELLUM SOUTH

Applying the word "conservative" to the antebellum South raises certain problems. Is "conservative" a fit epithet for a section of the nation that raised the specter of secession for nearly three decades before reifying that threat, or would "revolutionary" be more apt? And what does one make of the fact that the region's most celebrated political figure during this era, John C. Calhoun, has been called by one eminent historian (Richard Hofstadter) "the Marx of the Middle Class," and that the anticapitalist writings of other prominent southern polemicists gave aid and comfort to socialists? Definition once again proves troublesome. But not insurmountable, for the South in the years before the great fratricidal conflict was essentially a conservative society that drew upon conservative values, traditions, and arguments to preserve its distinctive way of life.

Conservatism took root in congenial southern soil during the colonial era. The rise of a landed gentry, which was more numerous and more influential than in other parts of the colonies with the possible exception of the great landowners along the Hudson River, abetted it, as did the presence of an established church in several southern colonies. But conservatism never predominanted in the South any more than it did in the North before the Revolution. This would change in the nineteenth century. While it would be gross reductionism to attribute this to the invention of the cotton gin, there is no doubt that this seemingly simple invention, which allowed a person to clean as much as fifty times more cotton than if done manually, had a galvanic effect. During the colonial era cotton was but one—and not the most important—of the region's agricultural staples. By the first half of the nineteenth century, however, cotton had become "king" and had wed the South, for better and, ultimately, for worse, to a one-staple economy. The cotton kingdom produced 150,000 bales at the time of the War of 1812; at the time of the Civil War that figure had soared to 4,500,000. More significantly, it reinvigorated slavery, whose numbers between 1800 and 1860 quadrupled to roughly four million. Inextricably linked, the rise of King Cotton and the expansion of slavery added new dimensions to conservatism in the antebellum South and tore apart the bonds of national union.

John C. Calhoun. No man more famously exemplified the twists and turns of conservatism in the antebellum South than did John C. Calhoun. His career in politics, which began in the South Carolina state legislature in 1809 and only ended with his death in 1850 in the midst of the passionate Senate debate over the Compromise of 1850, was studded with controversial positions that reflected a remarkable acumen as well as a remarkable change of direction. This is not to imply any cheap political opportunism on his part. Indeed, his contemporaries, both friend and foe alike, probably would have accepted Harriet Martineau's characterization of Calhoun as "the cast iron man who looks as if he had never been born, and could never be extinguished." Rigid in his principles—too rigid, for some—he changed his mind on matters only after deep reflection. His contemporary Ralph Waldo Emerson judged that consistency was the hobgoblin of small minds; and the mind of the contentious South Carolinian was not a small one.

Calhoun's political career and road to conservatism ran counter to that of Daniel Webster. Diametrically opposite "the godlike Daniel," who began as a Federalist and staunch defender of New England sectionalism, the plantation-bred Calhoun was a Jeffersonian Republican, a War Hawk who supported the War of 1812, and a proponent of the Second Bank of the United States. His career blossomed when he became secretary of war under President Monroe and then vice-president under first John Quincy Adams and then Andrew Jackson. Estranged from Jackson, in 1832 Calhoun resigned as vice-president and was elected United States senator by the South Carolina legislature. It was the nullification controversies of 1828 and 1832 rather than personal pique, however, that brought about the final rupture between the two giants and definitively changed the course of Calhoun's political career and thought.

The idea and implementation of a protective tariff pitted the North against the South, which lagged behind northern industrialization but which produced the nation's most valuable export, cotton. Not without reason southerners protested that while they generated national wealth they were punished by having to pay higher prices for imported goods. Reacting against the protectionist tariff of 1828, the so-called Tariff of Abominations, Calhoun wrote the *South Carolina Expostition and Protest*. Drawing upon Jefferson's Kentucky Resolutions of 1798 that had inveighed against the Federalist-inspired Alien and Sedition Acts, Calhoun argued that the United States Constitution was a compact made by sovereign states. States, therefore, could refuse to obey laws that were unconstitutional, and, to Calhoun, the tariff was unconstitutional since the Constitution empowered Congress to legislate tariffs for revenue but not for protection. People debated but did not act upon his argument. Four years later, however, the tariff of 1832, which failed to lower duties sufficiently to appease the South, engendered a crisis. A specially convened South Carolina convention voted to nullify the tariff and threatened to secede if the government attempted to enforce it; Andrew Jackson, who ironically wanted to see a lower tariff, threatened to hang Calhoun and to use force to bring the nullifiers to heel. A compromise tariff that passed the following year defused the situation—for the time being.

Calhoun developed his ideas on states' rights more fully in the years that followed the tariff and nullification controversy. Written in the 1840s but published only after his death in 1854, the *Disquisition on Government* represented the fruition of his thinking and offered a major and original contribution to American political theory and conservative thought. (*See Document No. 6.*) Like James Madison in his *Federalist Paper Number 10*, Calhoun posited competing interests vying for control of the government. Unlike Madison who believed that a system of checks and balances would inhibit this clash, the South Carolinian feared that a numerical majority would gain control of the government and impose its will on the hapless minority. To protect the latter, Calhoun devised his theory of the "concurrent majority," whereby a section or minority of the nation could exercise veto power to protect its vital concerns. The rigor of Calhoun's logic and the willingness to believe contributed strongly to the South's increasing inclination to put forth states' rights claims and to defy majoritarian democracy. Calhoun believed that his scheme to protect the minority interests of a section would alleviate the "strife and struggle" of contemporary problems and restore harmony to the nation. Paradoxically, by promoting this viewpoint, Calhoun and other states' rights advocates were contributing forcefully to the development of a strong southern nationalism and the very "strife and struggle" they wished to prevent. What an odd twist of fate for Calhoun, who had boasted that his beloved South was "the great conservative power, which prevents other portions [of the Union], less fortunately constituted, from rushing into conflict."

The line between sectionalism and nationalism was a blurred one in the antebellum South, for at what point did it feel that it was a section of the nation and at what point did it begin to consider itself a separate nation? Until secession there was no one exact time for this subtle but momentous transformation. Yet there was an abiding catalyst that gave the South a sense of uniqueness, encouraged it to extol its institutions, culture, and tradition, and provided an endless source of conflict with other parts of the nation: slavery.

Apologists for Slavery. The profitablility (at least for some) of slavery, its expansion into new states and territories, and the white South's dread of several million black slaves becoming unfettered—a dread exacerbated by the bloody uprising of Nat Turner in 1831—helped to determine that slavery would remain in place for an indefinite period of time. John C. Calhoun, while not originally noted primarily as an apologist for slavery, informed his fellow senators in 1837 that slavery was "instead of an evil, a good—a positive good." The occasion for his speech had been a flood of abolitionist petitions to Congress and an ensuing debate as to whether Congress should accept them. Fearful that the agitation of abolitionists would encourage slave insurrections, the alleged "Marx of the Middle Class" at different times suggested an informal alliance, or at least a quid pro quo, between northern capitalists and southern planters. The former, he urged, should restrain those who sought slavery's destruction; the latter, in return, would not incite northern workers by drawing attention to their deprivations. Right-thinking northerners, he pointed out, had a vested interest "in upholding and preserving the equilibrium of the slaveholding states." In short, Calhoun as a conservative was calling upon other conservatives to avoid turmoil and possible revolution.

Calhoun was but one of a growing number of southern apologists for slavery during the antebellum era. Unlike the South Carolinian whose advocacy of slavery, despite his protestation of its goodness, was more defensive than not, most of these apologists, particularly after the 1830s, found positive reasons for maintaining their "peculiar institution." It is impossible, of course, to determine the extent to which southerners truly believed that slavery was a positive institution or were applying an idealistic gloss to distract from its horrors as well as from the economics of cotton and the fear of race war. And although one does not take their arguments, or those of any defender of a cause, at full face value, it is important to consider them for what they can tell us as a construct and perhaps also as reality.

While some abolitionists denounced slavery as an affront to Christianity, slavery apologists invoked religion for support. Since Protestant Christianity thrived in the prewar South, one can infer that this defense of the peculiar institution carried considerable weight, particularly when put forth by skilled claimants. One such popular polemicist was Thornton Stringfellow, a Baptist minister from Virginia who culled both the Old and New Testaments to buttress his arguments.

A few defenders of slavery rested their case not on religion but on what they deemed to be irrefutable scientific truths. Most prominent among them was the physician and professor of anatomy at the University of Louisiana, Josiah Nott. A passionate ethnologist, Nott, to the dismay of clergymen, challenged the biblical depiction of human origins. Science had determined the existence of sufficient differences among the races, he argued, so as to prove the separate creation of each. Separate but not equal. And for Nott, the black race was inferior and suited to slave status, as he and his coauthor, George R. Gliddon, put forth in *Types of Mankind* (1856). Fittingly, Nott had earlier edited an English translation of Count Joseph Gobineau's *The Moral and Intellectual Diversity of Races*, a book that prefigured the Aryan pure race myths of Nazi Germany. And while the innate inferiority of blacks had been a widespread assumption among many white Americans since colonial times, it was only in the mid-nineteenth century that attempts were made to place such assumptions on a scientific basis.

Slavery apologists frequently invoked the secular past as well as or in place of religion and natural history to justify the present. The ancient world abounded with slavery, and justifiably so, argued Thomas R. Dew, a professor of history, political law, and metaphysics at William and Mary College, and after 1836 its president. A vital element in having made civilization possible, slavery, according to Dew, had alleviated some of the horrors of war, had helped to transform hunting economies into agricultural ones, and had advanced the position of women. Far from destroying republican institutions as some had protested, slavery made liberty possible, as Aristotle and others had claimed. Dew updated this seeming conundrum to claim that the South was more freedom-conscious than the North and also more egalitarian, at least in terms of white people: "Color alone is here the badge of distinction, the true mark of aristocracy, and all who are white are equal in spite of the variety of occupation." Apologists such as the novelists William Gilmore Simms and Chancellor William Harper of South Carolina imbibed these ideas, meshed them with their own, and asserted that the noble civilization of the South, like comparable high civilizations elsewhere in history, rested squarely upon slavery. Harper, in fact, went beyond Dew to conclude that slavery was the single cause of civilization.

Southern Romantic Nationalism. Besieged by abolitionists, dwarfed by the North in manufacturing and commerce, and threatened by hostile political forces especially after the rancorous debate surrounding the Compromise of 1850 and the divisive events of the fifties, the South increasingly turned inward to cultivate what it regarded as its own unique civilization. This romantic nationalism featured a blend of conservative and reactionary elements. Forged in the crucible of defensiveness, it sought inspiration, guidance, and justification from examples drawn eclectically from the ancient, medieval, and modern worlds. And from the crucible emerged a highly positive if distorted image of a singular society superior to its northern rival.

Exaggerations contain kernels of truth, and there may be more than a few such kernels in Mark Twain's pungent observation that Sir Walter Scott was so important in the shaping of southern character before the Civil War that he "in great measure was responsible for the War." Scott, along with Dickens (and despite the latter's condemnation of slavery), constituted the most popular quality novelists for southern readers. The primary appeal of Scott's seemingly endless array of *Waverley* novels, set in the medieval or early modern past, lay in their rich historical pageantry and sweeping adventure. Sometimes consciously, sometimes not, southerners managed to incorporate Scott's values of chivalry, bravery, honor, and a sense of noblesse oblige into their own nexus of cultural values and to compare them invidiously with what they considered the crass materialistic culture of northern society. Inspired by Scott's depictions, southerners held pseudo-medieval jousts before the Civil War and at least one among convalescing soldiers shortly after the Confederacy's disastrous defeat at Gettysburg. This was the conflict, in historian William Taylor's terms, between Cavalier and Yankee.

Disturbed by the vast economic changes and restless mobility of the population, many Americans—and by no means only southerners— "longed for a class of men immune to acquisitiveness, indifferent to social ambition and hostile to commercial life, cities, and secular progress." To what extent this stark clash of cultures and admiration for the "cavalier" planter class influenced the mass of southern whites remains a matter of conjecture, but for some of the South's most prominent polemicists it was crucially real. Distortions notwithstanding, the romantic image of the Old South, with its pleasant plantation life, benevolent paternalism, and warm personal relationships, was not only to survive the nation's bloodiest war but also to reemerge with renewed force in the following century.

Different historical eras, as noted, nurtured southern romantic nationalism. The example of the ancient world seemingly justified not only slavery itself, but also the existence of a leisured aristocratic class that slavery had made possible. The Middle Ages, in turn, as depicted by Sir Walter Scott and the contemporary Gothic Revival in Europe, fostered romantic images of a feudal society characterized by social equilibrium, stable social values, and a sense of noblesse oblige on the part of an honorable nobility toward its inferiors. Contemporary nineteenth-century developments also abetted the flowering of conservative values and attitudes in the Old South. The Young England movement of the 1840s, spearheaded by Benjamin Disraeli, was a reaction against the hardships imposed upon workers by the rigors of the industrial revolution and the insensitivity of large numbers of profit-driven factory owners. These Young Englanders, a number of whom were aristocrats or members of the landed gentry, generally upheld their nation's agrarian economy and traditions against the rising power and wealth of urban industrialists. Their efforts were paralleled across the Atlantic and south of the Mason-Dixon line.

What had generated a distinct southern culture, according to some proponents, had been the gradual development of an organic society in which masters and slaves, as well as the various classes of nonslaveholding white southerners, had formed interdependent, fruitful relationships. More concerned with a tranquil, beneficent society than with what Thomas Carlyle, a vitriolic foe of industrialism in England, had scornfully called "the cash nexus," they took the offensive against what they considered the misguided and hypocritical denigrations leveled by northern critics.

Given the paucity of conservatives (with some very noteworthy exceptions) who have become academic sociologists in post–World War II America, it is both interesting and ironic that three of the most pronounced defenders of the South and detractors of the North were influenced by the methods of "sociology," a neologism introduced by the Frenchman Auguste Comte. Purporting to be a science of society, sociology, which appealed to liberals and radicals in Europe, became a tool for conservatives in the South.

Henry Hughes published his *Treatise on Sociology* in 1854. In it he defended the South's system of labor as being superior to that of the North. He anticipated additionally that interventionist state governments in time could transform slavery, a private relationship between the owner and his chattel, into "warranteeism," in which the warrantor owned not the person but the person's obligation to perform services. Like Comte, Hughes believed that a "scientific" approach to society would result in progress. The Mississippian's view of slavery, however, while conceptually innovative, was so complex and couched in such an abstruse manner that he guaranteed himself a limited readership.

A more celebrated and read intellectual figure was George Frederick Holmes, who held the chair of History and Literature at the University of Virginia for forty years and who in 1883 published the first college textbook on sociology. In the antebellum years Holmes gained popularity for a vitriolic review of Harriet Beecher Stowe's *Uncle Tom's Cabin*. In it he denounced Stowe as a "foul-mouthed hag"—so much for chivalrous speech—and her book as full of "poisonous vermin" and "putresence." Concluding his intemperate peroration, Holmes dismissed the novel "with the conviction and declaration that every holier purpose of our nature is misguided, every charitable sympathy betrayed, every loftier sentiment polluted, every moral purpose wrenched to wrong, and every patriotic feeling outraged, by its criminal prostitution of the high functions of the imagination to the pernicious intrigues of sectional animosity, and to the petty calumnies of willful slander." Holmes continued, principally in reviews and essay form, to defend slavery as a necessary and beneficent institution. One such review led the book's author to write to Holmes: "You and [Henry] Hughes and I in the last year, it seems to me, have revolutionized public opinion in the South on the subject of slavery." The book was *Sociology for the South*; its author was George Fitzhugh, who would achieve fame second only to John C. Calhoun for his defense of the antebellum South.

Largely self-educated, George Fitzhugh became a lawyer but was able to devote himself to reading and writing, thanks to having married a wealthy woman. A life-long resident of Virginia, this "sage of Port Royal" was known and is best remembered for two works written during the 1850s: *Sociology for the South, or, The Failure of Free Society* (1854) and *Cannibals All!, or, Slaves without Masters* (1857). Some of the ideas he developed in these two books were quite unorthodox compared with those of some of his contemporary southern polemicists. For example, he vigorously and in Burkean fashion rejected the ideas of Thomas Jefferson. By subverting established religion and the practice of entail and primogeniture in Virginia, Jefferson had destroyed a perfectly sensible order in the name of some allegedly higher but totally abstract good. Fitzhugh further denounced Jefferson for the ideal abstraction he posited in the Declaration of Independence, to wit, the equality of humanity. Human experience and plain common sense told otherwise, Fitzhugh asserted. Rights are not inherent; they are earned. Having a dim view of human nature and a high respect for human frailty, he judged that fully nineteen of twenty people deserved to be slaves.

Given the inability of most men to govern themselves, Fitzhugh scorned Jefferson's belief that a government which governs least is best. More government, not less, was Fitzhugh's credo, and such a government was not to be based on the false idol of democratic suffrage to which nineteenth-century Americans had paid their homage. Like Burke and American conservatives, particularly from the Federalist era, he believed in "virtual representation," whereby an elite would rule on behalf of and for the good of the masses. Finally, and unlike most defenders of the Old South, Fitzhugh rejected the notion of an agrarian order. Only an economic nationalism that was promoted at the state level and that fostered improvements in commerce, banking, and transportation could, he warned, keep the South from becoming a satellite of the North.

His animus against the ideas of Thomas Jefferson was not George Fitzhugh's most noteworthy contribution to antebellum southern conservatism. Nor was his impatience with the constitutional defense of southern rights that Calhoun put forth but which he, Fitzhugh, deemed feckless. Rather, it was the conditions of labor in the North and the South that he invidiously compared. (*See Document No. 7.*) The South's slaves, he claimed, were far better off than "slaves without masters," the northern workers. Under the benevolent paternalism of their masters, slaves "are the happiest, and in some sense, the freest people in the world. The children and the aged and infirm work not at all, and yet have all the comforts and necessaries of life provided for them." (Fitzhugh privately admitted to George Frederick Holmes that he had in fact painted an overly rosy portrait: "I see great evils in Slavery, but in a controversial work I ought not to admit them.")

Agreeing with both the American and foreign critics of laissez-faire capitalism, Fitzhugh regarded the conditions of northern workers as loathsome. Workers suffered from low wages and long hours, could not form unions, were constantly threatened with unemployment, and if injured or sick, were thrown upon their own resources, meager as they usually were. Women and children were subject to particular abuses. The agitation of contemporary socialists against the system was further proof of the failure of laissez-faire capitalism, although their agitation for utopian communities was misguided. Ultimately neither laissez-faire capitalists nor socialists could cure the problems of an increasingly industrialized America, concluded Fitzhugh. Meanwhile Fitzhugh extended his concept of feudal paternalism to include poorer, nonslaveholding white southerners. They should be educated, he argued, and brought into an alliance with the planter class, whose property they in effect protected. With slaves accepting their fortunate lot, with poorer whites appreciating both their improved situation and the wise guidance of the aristocracy, southern society would continue to flourish.

Despite their best efforts, southern intellectuals proved unable to conserve the Old South. The war of nerves between two clashing cultures turned to real war when General P. G. T. Beauregard ordered the artillery attack on Fort Sumter. Whether or not the Civil War was an "irrepressible conflict," southern conservatives and reactionaries had helped to ignite the conflagration, one which few of them really desired. And yet for all their destructiveness, questionable ideas, and defense of a heinous institution, they had made genuine contributions to the ongoing conservative tradition. Calhoun's defense of minority rights in a majoritarian democracy remains as important today as it was then. Similarly, the attacks by Fitzhugh and others on unrestrained economic competition and the corresponding vulnerability of the weak under such a system were part of a serious concern that needed articulation. Their call for a benevolent paternalism echoed that of earlier conservatives and was to resonate with later ones. The appreciation of southern apologists for an organic community rather than a rootless individualism was also part of the conservative tradition, as was their insistence upon leadership by an elite.

Northern Conservatives During the Civil War. By concentrating on the contributions of antebellum southerners to conservatism, one tends to forget that conservatism remained a powerful force in the North both during the years preceding the war and in the midst of the war itself. After all, the early principles of nationalism and constitutionalism, vigorously stressed and pursued especially by Federalists, became part of the determination to hold the Union together. In his Cooper Union Address of February 27, 1860, which he called "The Old Policy of the Fathers," Abraham Lincoln spoke out against the expansion of slavery into the territories. Alluding to the prohibition of slavery by the Northwest Ordinance of 1787, he chided those who would now extend slavery, not those who opposed its extension, for being radicals. "What is conservatism?" he asked. "Is it not adherence to the old and tried, against the new and untried?" Lincoln's broad and deep sense of nationalism that he had developed as a Webster Whig continued during the war as he placed the preservation of the union above all other considerations. And while he ultimately endorsed and made possible the end of slavery, as late as February 1865 he manifested the conservative's respect for property when he suggested to his aghast cabinent that slaveholders might be compensated for their losses.

Other northern conservatives rallied to the Union cause but from a different perspective from the radical abolitionists, who saw the destruction of slavery as the chief goal of the war. Conservatives like George Templeton Strong, a New York lawyer, and Henry W. Bellows, a New York Unitarian minister, deplored the democratic passions, which, they believed, had unsettled the nation and had led to conflict. The strong government that was necessary to defeat secession, they hoped, would also restore badly needed order and discipline. Relatedly, Orestes Brownson argued that the war was not one for democracy but for nationalism and constitutionalism. He believed that slavery should be ended but that the North should become more like the South, with its natural aristocracy, social graces, and emphasis upon community. On the slavery issue most northern conservatives during the war probably differed little from most other white northerners, abolitionists excepted: emancipation but not political or social equality for the freedmen. Northern conservatives were generally united in their hopes that with the end of hostilities stability and harmony would return. It is doubtful if they foresaw the intense disorders of the postbellum era.

CHAPTER 4

THE RISE OF LAISSEZ-FAIRE CONSERVATISM

Rapid economic growth effected enormous changes in post–Civil War America. Railroads, whose track mileage increased more than sixfold between 1860 and 1900, served as the primary catalyst for these changes by creating a national market, aiding westward expansion, and stimulating industry. Steel was the principal beneficiary of the railroad boom. By 1890 the United States had overtaken Great Britain as the world's leading producer of steel and pig iron, the yardstick for measuring industrial prowess. Responsible for fully thirty percent of the world's manufacturing with capital investments of ten billion dollars by 1900, its position as the globe's foremost industrial power was undeniable. Other new and basic industries, notably oil and electricity, also helped to galvanize the American economy and to reconfigure the nation's life. Commercial crops, especially wheat, expanded rapidly, further stimulated the growth of railroads and steel, and helped to direct the nation's search for overseas markets.

Hand in hand with the explosive growth of the economy went a major transformation of economic institutions. In place of the small, frequently family-owned businesses that characterized the antebellum era arose large, impersonal corporations. Intense competition among these large capitalized firms led in some instances to consolidation that resulted in monopoly or, more likely, oligopoly, and the destruction of businesses that proved unable to compete. Just as some corporations became richer and more powerful, so, too, did some individuals. A magazine article appearing in 1892 reported the existence of 4,000 millionaires, who owned fully twenty percent of the nation's wealth while a mere one percent of the population owned fifty-four percent of that wealth. These figures convinced many that United States had become, as Benjamin Disraeli said of England, two nations: the rich and the poor. Persistent agitation by industrial workers and farmers throughout the last three decades of the century lent additional weight to this conviction.

Traditional and Laissez-Faire Conservatism Compared. Given these enormous economic and social changes, it was inconceivable that ideas and attitudes would or could remain static. The shock of the new produced too many dislocations to be ignored. Change was the order of the day, and change had to be accepted, opposed, or channeled. Conservatives, no less impervious than others to their surrounding upheavals, responded to change, but not necessarily in predictable, time-worn fashion.

The twentieth-century political scientist Clinton Rossiter tartly noted that the perception of conservatism after Appomattox constituted "the Great Train Robbery of American Intellectual History." From this period emerged laissez-faire conservatism, a term that earlier would have evoked charges of self-contradiction. Considered by Europeans as a defining characteristic of liberalism, the laissez-faire economic theories of Adam Smith and his successors, as well as those of the French physiocrats, were to become, *mutatis mutandis* (the necessary changes having been made), a pillar of conservatism in the Gilded Age. So also was the belief in limited government, a tenet clung to by European political liberals and, more important for American conservatism, by Jeffersonians. The idea of economic freedom had now become closely linked with that of political freedom. American conservatives since the Federalist era had fought for a strong, active national government but now, for the most part, reversed their position. Ironically, this new brand of conservatism in crucial ways failed to conserve. By traditional definition, conservatism protects inherited customs and practices and resists strong, swift change. Contrarily, the new conservatism—which Rossiter and others basically refuse to consider as conservatism at all—impatient with tradition, abetted and perpetuated rapid unsettling changes that fed upon themselves to produce even more change. This metamorphosis evolved during the post–Civil War generation and then generally dominated American economic and political life from the late nineteenth century through the Great Depression. After its fall from grace during the latter economic debacle, it slowly regained strength until today it stands once again as a potent if still highly controversial strand of the conservative movement.

Laissez-faire conservatism differed sharply but not absolutely from traditional conservatism in significant ways. Some differences were more of degree than of kind, although the degree sometimes verged on kind. For instance, both laissez-faire and traditional conservatism believed strongly in the rights and privileges of the individual, but the former exalted "rugged individualism" while subordinating, often flagrantly, those of the community. A sense of *sauve qui peut* (panic) overshadowed the older conservative principle of noblesse oblige. Laissez-faire conservatives also stressed the Social Darwinist corollary that struggle rather than harmony provided the steppingstone to a higher and and more wholesome society. And indeed, a fair number—but certainly not all—of these newer conservatives parted company with their older counterparts over the question of progress. While traditional conservatives remained skeptical as to the possibility or extent of genuine human progress, newer ones such as Andrew Carnegie were more sanguine about its prospects.

Comparisons are murkier in other areas. Christianity or at least a strong belief in a transcendent moral order was a tenet for virtually all pre–Civil War conservatives who articulated their credos. Darwinism and science, or, more properly speaking, scientism, made serious inroads into these religious and moral underpinnings during the nineteenth century. Some laissez-faire conservatives, notably William Graham Sumner, turned from Christianity and a belief in a given moral order to a materialistic framework that encoded ethics, or the lack thereof, in the laws of nature. Other laissez-faire conservatives paid homage to these traditional beliefs or remained discreetly silent on the matter. The clergy divided. While some denounced laissez-faire beliefs and rampant materialism as un-Christian and immoral, others accepted and sometimes stoutly championed them as being compatible with religion and morality.

Significant differences notwithstanding, the conservatism of the age of enterprise continued to share fundamental beliefs and attitudes with the more familiar conservatism that had been an integral part of the nation's history from independence to the Civil War. Like traditional conservatism, the newer one accepted natural inequalities, feared majority rule, and called for leadership and guidance by an elite. Like its older counterpart, laissez-faire conservatism held firmly to the sanctity of property and contracts, and looked to the judiciary to protect these against the leveling demands of reformers. While duly recognizing the striking changes that conservatism underwent in postbellum America, it is imperative to keep in mind the continuities as well.

William Graham Sumner. No one better exemplifies the new laissez-faire American conservatism than William Graham Sumner. Born in 1840 to English immigrant parents of modest circumstances, Sumner graduated from Yale University in 1863, purchased an exemption from being drafted into the Union army, and went to Germany to study biblical scholarship. Ordained an Episcopalian priest in 1869, he left the church to accept a newly created chair of political economy at his alma mater. As for his religion, he noted that "it was as if I had put my beliefs into a drawer, and when I opened it there was nothing at all." Sumner exaggerated since he never abandoned his religious interests, both personal and public, but the statement does correctly imply the secularization of his ideas and values. As a Yale professor until his retirement in 1909, he propounded these ideas and values, stressing their pertinence to current public affairs. By various accounts he became one of the most esteemed professors in the university's history. Filled with pungent observations and sharp arguments, his books and his numerous widely read articles also brought him acclaim as one of the nation's most prominent publicists and intellectual figures, one who had done much to mold the new laissez-faire conservatism.

Various influences shaped Sumner's thinking, none more so than Darwinism. Sumner read the scientific works of Charles Darwin and his "bull dog" supporter, Thomas Huxley. The ideas of the English social scientist Herbert Spencer also proved compelling. Spencer, who coined the term "survival of the fittest" nearly a decade before the appearance of Darwin's *The Origin of Species* and who anticipated important aspects of Darwinian thought, applied the concept of evolution to human societies, and in the process became a lionized intellectual figure both in England and in the United States. Despite the vigorous objections of Yale president Noah Porter, who threatened to dismiss him, Sumner, in what was probably the first real sociology course taught in an American college, assigned Spencer's controversial *Study of Sociology*, a work whose methodology and profuse details he admired. Sumner himself blossomed into a celebrated sociologist whose *Folkways* (1906) became a classic in the field.

While there is some question as to precisely how influential were the ideas of Spencer on Sumner, there is little doubt that the latter became the leading American celebrant of Social Darwinism in the late nineteenth century. For Sumner, as for other Social Darwinists, the law of nature took precedence over man-made law in the scheme of things. Sumner, who rarely minced words, scoffed at the notion that such "natural rights" as life, liberty, and happiness were God-given or nature-given. Rather, these rights were won, if they were won at all, through constant struggle, and with winners and losers. And for the Yale professor, that was exactly how it should be if civilization were to continue to progress:

> If we do not like it, and if we try to amend it, there is only one way in which we can do it. We can take from the better and give to the worse. We can deflect the penalties of those who have done ill and throw them on those who have done better. We can take the rewards from those who have done better and give them to those who have done worse. We shall thus lessen inequalities. We shall favor the survival of the unfittest, and we shall accomplish this by destroying liberty. Let it be understood that we cannot get outside this alternative: liberty, inequality, survival of the fittest; non-liberty, equality, survival of the unfittest. The former carries society forward and favors all its best members; the latter carries society downwards and favors all its worst members.

The title of one of Sumner's most popular essays nicely underscores his point of view: "The Absurd Effort to Make the World Over." "A drunkard in the gutter," he advised, "is just where he ought to be. Nature is working away at him to get him out of the way . . . " Meanwhile: "Every man and woman in society has one big duty. That is, to take care of his or her own self."

The harshness of Sumner's views needs some important qualifications, which few of his detractors have bothered to make. First, his advocacy of a laissez-faire, save-yourself, philosophy was far from total. The working conditions of women and children had to be improved, he insisted, and if owners would not effect such change, the public must. Similarly, he urged that government promote public education. (To the horror of some alumni he urged Yale to admit women and racial minorities.) Somewhat relatedly, he also urged a compassionate policy on immigration at a time when many were calling for the drastic reduction or exclusion of immigrants. As for human suffering, particularly when that suffering was unavoidable, Sumner called for private charity, not the bureaucracy of a welfare state, to care for the needy. The fortunate must care for the unfortunate, he stressed, and while "society can do without patricians . . . it cannot do without patrician virtues."

Qualifications notwithstanding, William Graham Sumner resolutely championed economic laissez-faire as the best means of increasing the aggregate wealth of society, which in turn would make possible material progress. Drawing upon the Protestant work ethic that had influenced his own character development since childhood, he looked to the free workings of the marketplace to augment society's wealth. Competition among businesses and between capital and labor would leave behind the unfit but would advance the overall well-being of society. Hoping to level the playing field, Sumner opposed artificial advantages, most notably the protective tariff, which he denounced as a "legalized robbery" that encouraged plutocracy. Yet he also anathematized currency inflation, whether it was the Greenback agitation of the immediate post–Civil War era or the free coinage of silver campaign of the 1890s, as demands by debtors to defraud their creditors. He accepted the right of labor to organize and to bargain collectively—but grudgingly.

The Gilded Age witnessed no level playing field. Indeed, it became more uneven, a fact that Sumner recognized but for which he could offer no cure or meaningful corrective. The strife between capital and labor worsened and produced increased costs to the consumer; unrestricted business competition paradoxically led to monopoly or oligopoly, the very opposite of what he wished. Sumner pointedly rejected the notion that the government could improve matters. Having personally witnessed the fraudulent vote count in Louisiana during the disputed presidential election of 1876, he became convinced that the government and politics in general provided an endless source for corruption. Politicians during this age controlled the government for personal gain, not for the benefit of the public, while special interest groups, notably the plutocrats, or "jobbers" as he scornfully called them, and the proletarians, sought to capture political dominance to enhance their own narrow and selfish concerns. Sumner did admire some men of wealth, especially, it should be noted, William C. Whitney, his affluent Yale classmate who helped to underwrite his trip to Germany and who periodically gave him funds to supplement his meager professorial income. Sumner also praised thrifty and resourceful workers, whom he regarded as future capitalists rather than lifelong proletarians.

But for Sumner the truly heroic person was "the Forgotten Man" as well as "the Forgotten Woman." (*See Document No. 8.*) Sumner's father, a hard-working, self-educated mechanic, epitomized the Forgotten Man: thrifty, sober, self-reliant, persevering. A model family man, a model citizen, the Forgotten Man asked for no special favors but only to be allowed to pursue his life quietly and with dignity. Viewed in this manner, laissez-faire becomes more than an economic doctrine, or rather, it conjoins the economic with the moral since the virtues that Sumner attributed to the Forgotten Man, if allowed to flourish, abetted the aggregation of capital and the overall well-being of society. To reward the undeserving poor, in contrast, impeded economic progress and at the same time affronted the Victorian moral convictions of the Gilded Age. A society populated with Forgotten Men and Forgotten Women was a *summum bonum* (supreme good) for Sumner, but he lamented that the "forgotten man is never thought of."

Never an optimist, Sumner as he aged became increasingly pessimistic for his country's future. Democracy was viable, he stressed, only if sufficient wealth existed, and that in turn was ultimately dependent upon the availability of unused land. (Sumner anticipated by more than a decade the vital relationship between the people-to-land ratio and democracy that Frederick Jackson Turner posited in 1893 in his frontier thesis of American history.) So far the availability of such land had promoted democracy, but at some future point land hunger would undermine democratic prospects. Further, he complained in an unpublished essay written a year before his death that the increasing concentration of wealth was destroying free competition and that the government had to protect the public from the power of the trusts. Laissez-faire economics had fallen short of its promise. Sumner also rued the imperialism and militarism that burst forth in the late nineteenth and early twentieth centuries. Imperialism and war, he reasoned, curtailed liberties, misdirected capital, and bore unjustly and onerously on the middle classes. At century's end he took a largely unpopular stand with his powerful but futile denunciation of the Spanish-American War in his "The Conquest of the United States by Spain." Just a few months before his death in 1910 he presciently noted that "the next generations are going to see war and social calamities."

Sumner's disappointments and overall pessimism should not obscure his special contributions to the growth of the American conservative tradition. A staunch believer in the primacy of the individual and in old-fashioned virtues, he attempted to steer the narrows between the Scylla of a growing plutocracy and the Charybdis of a looming mass society. While he shortchanged the communitarian aspect of traditional conservatism, he defended its complementary opposite, the rights of the individual. Unwilling in Burkean fashion to venerate the authority of the past, he shaped his views with an eye more to the present and future. He was a moralist who constantly preached against moralizing, an intellectual who forsook the normative for the descriptive, one who hoped to find some small order in science and human reason. Denounced by both twentieth-century liberals and some traditional conservatives, he became a hero to twentieth-century libertarians and free market conservatives. To the laissez-faire conservatives of his own era he was a giant.

The Supreme Court and Laissez-Faire. As Sumner and other publicists helped to frame the laissez-faire conservatism of the Gilded Age and after, the courts, especially the federal courts and more especially the Supreme Court, turned it into constitutional doctrine. Not at once, but gradually. Concerned mainly in the pre–Civil War years with the relationship between the states and the national government, the Supreme Court in the postbellum era turned chiefly to issues related to the government regulation of business. At first the most important judicial decisions seemed to go against business, but by the 1880s the courts had moved in a counter direction and had afforded business—primarily corporate business—a powerful protection it had never enjoyed. Revisionist historians over the past several decades have offered important nuances to this change, pointing out that pro-business decisions were not nearly so one-sided as previous scholars had perceived. Nonetheless, it remains incontrovertible that the courts, especially through their reading of the Fourteenth Amendment and through the commerce clause of the Constitution, contributed powerfully to the rise of laissez-faire conservatism.

Much as William Graham Sumner loomed foremost among Gilded Age intellectuals advocating laissez-faire conservatism, so Stephen J. Field did among its jurists. The son of a New England Congregational minister, Field, after graduating from Williams College in 1838 joined the law firm of his older brother, David Dudley Field, who was also to become a nationally prominent lawyer. (A third, younger brother in this family of high achievers was Cyrus Field, who promoted and financed the first transatlantic cable.) Lured by the excitement of the Gold Rush, Field in 1849 rushed to California, where he never made a fortune but did become chief justice of the state supreme court. The experience of the mining camps and the frontier atmosphere that promoted vigilantism convinced him more than ever of the importance of individual liberty and the rule of law, both of which permeated his future judicial decisions. Appointed associate justice of the U.S. Supreme Court by President Lincoln in the midst of the Civil War, he was to serve the longest term—1863 to 1897—of any justice in Court history other than William O. Douglas.

While clearly intended to protect the civil rights of former slaves, the Fourteenth Amendment was considerably less clear with respect to the legal meaning of its "due process of law" and "equal protection of the laws" clauses. The *Slaughter-House Cases* of 1873 brought this lack of clarity into high relief and occasioned a portentous dissent from Justice Field. In this case a group of Louisiana butchers unsuccessfully brought suit against a state law of 1869 that had granted a monopoly to one corporation to slaughter livestock. The majority of the Court opined that the Fourteenth Amendment was meant primarily to protect the newly emancipated slaves. It also distinguished between rights that derived from United States citizenship and those from state citizenship. The privileges and immunities clause of the amendment, the Court decreed, did not protect the butchers since civil rights emanated solely from state citizenship. Field, however, along with three other justices dissented, viewing the statute as a deprivation of both the clause in question and due process of law. Field argued the the privileges and immunities clause had now given constitutional rights to the natural rights of life, liberty, and property.

Field also strongly dissented in another prominent case of the 1870s, *Munn* v. *Illinois* (1877), a Granger case in which the state set rates for the storage of grain. When the Supreme Court upheld the law, conservatives feared that it had sanctioned class legislation, a thought made more frightening by the bloody example of the recent Paris Commune. Denying that the police power of the state applied to rate-fixing, Field broadened his protective view of business. "I deny the power of any legislature under our government," he asserted, "to fix the price one shall receive for his property of any kind."

A minority opinion at this time, this dissent, along with that in the *Slaughter-House Cases*, soon became a fulcrum of majority opinion for protecting business enterprises against state regulation. In *Santa Clara County* v. *Southern Pacific R.R.* (1886), the Court declared that a corporation was a person and as such received the right of due process as guaranteed under the Fourteenth Amendment. In *U.S.* v. *E. C. Knight* (1895), the first judicial decision involving the Sherman Antitrust Act of 1890, Chief Justice Melville W. Fuller spoke for the majority and ruled that the act did not apply to intrastate manufacturing combinations, however much they might restrain trade. This decision seriously impeded the ability of the federal government to enforce antitrust cases. Federal courts, moreover, increasingly issued injunctions against labor unions that undertook boycotts that impinged upon interstate commerce. When Eugene V. Debs flaunted one such injunction during the convulsive Pullman Strike of 1895, the Supreme Court upheld his incarceration. The 1890s, mired in the worst depression in the nation's history and experiencing formidable labor and agrarian agitation, exacerbated fears for property rights. Conservatives applauded renowned lawyer Rufus Choate when he argued before the Court that the income tax represented "the onward march of communism." They cheered more lustily when the Court, by a 5–4 decision, struck down the tax in *Pollock* v. *Farmers' Loan and Trust Company*. Concurring with the majority opinion, the aged Justice Field denounced the tax as the onset of "a war of poor against the rich." Judicial laissez-faire conservatism reached its apogee in 1905 with the *Lochner* v. *New York* decision. A state law had limited the bakers' workday to ten hours, but the Supreme Court, in a 5–4 decision, ruled that the purpose of the law was not primarily to protect the health of workers, but to regulate their hours per se. If allowed to stand, they reasoned, the statute would set a dangerous precedent for future government regulatory legislation that would deprive an individual of his liberty to make a contract. The closeness of the vote in *Lochner* symbolically speaks to the lack of unanimity on the question of laissez-faire constitutionalism in the Gilded Age and into the early twentieth century. Still, it was a triumph for the kind of interpretation of the Constitution to which such Supreme Court justices as Morrison R. Waite, Melville W. Fuller, Joseph P. Bradley, Rufus Peckham, David J. Brewer, and above all, Stephen J. Field, had given voice.

Andrew Carnegie. William Graham Sumner and Stephen J. Field, as well as other exponents of laissez-faire conservatism, closely linked political and economic freedom. So, too, did the most articulate business spokesperson for the age of enterprise, Andrew Carnegie. Born in Scotland to poor but industrious Scottish parents who embraced the democratic Chartist movement, Carnegie emigrated with them in 1848 to the United States, where they settled in Pittsburgh. The "rags-to-riches" myth, as expounded during the age of enterprise in the Horatio Alger tales and in such other hortatory "success literature" as Elbert Hubbard's *A Message to Garcia* (1899), was largely (but by no means entirely) just that: a myth. But not in the case of Andrew Carnegie. Beginning as a bobbin boy earning $1.20 per week, he moved on to become a telegraph operator, an assistant to the head of the Pennsylvania Railroad, vice-president of the railroad, and an entrepeneur in oil, iron, and other businesses. In 1873 he began to concentrate on his steel interests, and by 1900 his Carnegie Steel Company dominated the industry. The following year he accepted the offer of J. P. Morgan and sold his company, which became the centerpiece of U.S. Steel, the first billion dollar corporation in the nation. His personal fortune amounted to roughly $400 million.

If astounding wealth were the sole measure of the man, Andrew Carnegie would find very little if any place in the history of conservatism. But light-years more than any other "captain of industry" or "robber baron"—the nomenclature largely dependent upon one's bias—he expressed his philosophy whose component parts give added dimension to late nineteenth-century conservative thought.

In 1868, when he was thirty-three years old, Carnegie wrote an instructive note to himself: "Thirty-three and an income of $50,000 per annum! . . . To continue much longer overwhelmed by business cares and with most of my thoughts wholly upon the way to make more money in the shortest time, must degrade me beyond hope of permanent recovery. I will resign business at thirty-five . . . " Carnegie, of course, neither resigned nor ceased to make more money, but the uneasiness conveyed in his memorandum carried over and helped to shape what he later called "the gospel of wealth," a blend of high idealism and rampant materialism.

For Carnegie, as for William Graham Sumner, it was imperative to create wealth, for without it there could be neither progress nor civilization itself. Although he was not traditionally religious, the steelmaker, like the Yale sociologist, persistently preached to his audiences the Protestant virtues of hard work, thrift, and sobriety, which he assured them made capital accumulation possible. He also reminded them in his series of essays collected as *Triumphant Democracy* (1887) that the American political system, buoyed by economic prosperity, had given individuals not only political and civil rights but also the liberty to advance themselves and their society materially. In other words, democracy and materialism thrived symbiotically.

A third positive factor in the creation of wealth was evolution. Like Sumner, Carnegie was a true believer in evolution but unlike the professor, the Croesus of steel was convinced that it necessitated a progress that could neither be halted nor reversed. A hero-worshipper of

Herbert Spencer, whom he addressed in correspondence as "Master," Carnegie saw the evolutionary social process working benevolently as a historically restricted system of economics gave way to the higher one of laissez-faire. Like other Social Darwinists, he stressed the slow as opposed to forced pace of change, which is to say, he cautioned against state interference with the natural market laws of supply and demand. Individualism propelled economic and social progress, and "the exceptional man in every department must be permitted and encouraged to develop his unusual powers, taste, and ambitions . . . " Applied to the world of humans, the Darwinian world, "red in tooth and claw" and harshly competitive, was good for the race, although, as Carnegie readily admitted, not for every individual.

Unlike some businessmen of the era, Carnegie had a social conscience, and a very big one at that. The individual, as far as he was concerned, possessed the right to personal wealth. But that individual also had the duty to return that wealth to society from which it derived. Yet Carnegie, like Sumner and like many other businessmen of the era, distinguished between charity and philanthropy, arguing that financial assistance should go to those who were willing but circumstantially unable to help themselves. This was the doctrine of stewardship, and Carnegie, who preached concern for his workers but, as illustrated by his role in the Homestead strike of 1892 practiced otherwise, in this instance vigorously practiced what he preached. Calling it a disgrace to die rich without having contributed to the well-being of others, he donated an estimated $350 million of his personal fortune to libraries, higher education, an international endowment for peace, and even church organs (though not churches themselves). While his credentials as a conservative have been questioned, his concept of stewardship dovetailed with the beliefs of other conservatives in their concern to protect private property and for rule by an elite and a corresponding practice of noblesse oblige. So, too, did his belief in controlling the pace of change, despite his having been a leading actor in the frenzied rush of post–Civil War industrialization.

Carnegie's term "gospel of wealth" consciously or not implies a union of religion and riches. American clergy reacted sharply to this fusion. Some became Social Gospelers who denounced laissez-faire economics, preached cooperation rather than competition, and reviled the rich while taking up the cause for the working class and the impoverished. Others, however, defended the status quo and admired wealthy entrepeneurs. At least one equated the acquisition of wealth with morality. The Reverend William Lawrence, Episcopal Bishop of Massachusetts, declared in 1900 that "in the long run, it is only to the man of morality that wealth comes. . . . Godliness is in league with riches. . . . Material prosperity is helping to make the national character sweeter, more joyous, more unselfish, more Christlike." Earlier, the Reverend Henry Ward Beecher, the most famous Protestant divine of his time, pontificated that "God has intended the great to be great and the little to be little." As for those who decried poverty, Beecher challenged: "I do not say that a dollar a day is enough to support a working man. But it is enough to support a man!" He haughtily concluded in Social Darwinian tones that "the man who cannot live on bread and water is not fit to live." Another Protestant clergyman, the Baptist minister Russell Conwell, saw no reason why anyone had to subsist on bread and water. This founder of Temple University reputedly delivered a lecture, "Acres of Diamonds," on six thousand separate occasions during which he cheerfully pointed out to audiences that wealth lay all about them, and that it was not only their right but their God-given duty to acquire it. Whether or not Lawrence, Beecher, Conwell, and their ilk were true conservatives remains debatable, but it is clear that they added to and helped, as it were, to sanctify the emergent hands-off variety of conservatism.

The Politics of Laissez-Faire. Political conservatism at the onset of the Gilded Age was best represented by liberals, that is to say, by Liberal Republicans. These were Republican reformers who balked at the pandemic corruption of the Grant administration and of the nation at large. Their political successes on the national level were virtually nonexistent—their attempt to defeat Grant in the 1872 election resulted in fiasco. A sufficent number did bolt their party to help to swing the extremely closely contested 1884 presidential election in favor of the Democratic candidate, Grover Cleveland, but many were disappointed that Cleveland did not inaugurate sweeping reforms. A significant number of these Liberal Republicans—Mugwumps as they generally were called during the election and afterwards—subsequently became Democrats and were somewhat more effective in obtaining political reforms at the municipal level.

Beyond their disgust with Grantism, the Liberal Republicans/Mugwumps shared a number of common principles and attitudes with other laissez-faire conservatives of the era. Like their transatlantic cousins, the nineteenth-century English liberals, they accepted the premise that free trade or at least lower tariffs would promote general prosperity, as would hard money as opposed to a devalued currency. Like Sumner and other laissez-faire advocates, they opposed monopoly both in business and labor. They usually supported businessmen during labor strikes, and while deploring the nation's unabashed buccaneering entrepeneurs, they admired others, such as the high-minded New York iron and steel magnate, Abram Hewitt.

As enthusiasts of economic laissez-faire policies, the Liberal Republicans/Mugwumps could be expected to oppose active government in the nation's economy, although they did call for regulation of the freewheeling railroads. But their opposition to government went beyond economic ideology. Like their earlier counterparts who had opposed the spoils system of Andrew Jackson and his followers, these Gilded Age figures deplored the debasement of government service, indeed, of democracy itself. Party patronage and cronyism, not merit and moral character, provided the criteria for government appointments and brought inferior men to Washington. These officeholders then proceeded to initiate ill-conceived or downright harmful policies, that is, when they concerned themselves with matters of state at all since, charged their critics, they were more interested in advancing their self-interests or the sectarian interests of their party. These were the worst men, and they had taken the rightful place of "the best men," as the historian John G. Sproat sarcastically called them. (Sproat denounced their pro-business bias and limited sympathy for labor; their anti-immigrant position; and their ultimate opposition to Reconstruction state governments for their disenfranchisement of white southerners and prolonged use of federal troops to protect the rights of former slaves.)

As intellectuals and journalists, and aided by certain business leaders like Abram Hewitt, the Liberal Republicans\Mugwumps represented an elite group. A profile of these reformers in New York and Boston at the time of the 1884 election showed that they were highly educated (thirty-seven percent attended college); that half were lawyers or businessmen; and that three-quarters of them belonged to three "elite" Protestant sects: Episcopalianism, Unitarianism, Congregationalism. These "best men" strove to raise the level of politics and to some extent did. The Pendleton Act of 1883, passed with bipartisan support, formally introduced civil service with its competitive examinations into the

federal government. Initially covering only fifteen percent of government workers, civil service embraced more than forty percent of government positions by the turn of the century. Not all reformers were
convinced that the introduction of civil service would or could reverse
the downward trajectory of democracy, however. Confessed one of them,
E. L. Godkin: "This experiment in Democratic Government is practically sure to fail. The trouble is I'm afraid I shan't be here to see it fail."

Born in Ireland in 1831, the son of an Anglo-Irish clergyman,
Edward Lawrewnce Godkin came to the United States in 1856. A firm
Unionist and gifted polemicist, he became the first editor of the *Nation*
magazine when it was founded in 1865. As the long-time editor of this
periodical and for a shorter period the *New York Evening Post*, he proved
a dynamo in the shaping of public opinion among educated readers. The
journalist and reformer Oswald Garrison Villard wrote of the recently
deceased Edward Lawrence Godkin in 1903 that "in all the field of
American daily journalism, there is not one today to measure up to him
as critic, writer, as scientific student of politics nor one person so bril-
liant . . . "

Influenced by his early reading of the English liberals John Stuart
Mill and Jeremy Bentham, Godkin experienced no difficulty in adapting his laissez-faire convictions to American developments. A certain
flexibility characterized these convictions. In "Who Will Pay the Bills
of Socialism?" an essay written in 1894, he proved himself, like Sumner, willing to invoke useful state intervention, as, for example, in the
education of children. Yet it was a fantasy, he warned, to believe that the
government or the very rich had sufficient money to bring happiness to
all, or that even if there existed such wealth, there similarly existed anyone who could wisely distribute it.

Flexibility notwithstanding, Godkin remained an advocate of laissez-
faire conservatism and a committed foe of contemporary democracy.
(*See Document No. 9.*) The Grangers turned "from one form of swindle
to another," while advocates of free silver were infecting the nation with
socialist and communist ideas. "Trade unions," he fumed, were "hostile
to civilization and drags on the heels of both moral and material progress," and he urged their prosecution under terms of the Sherman
Antitrust Act. Minorities fared no better. He urged a restricted suffrage
in order to foster good government. Prospective immigrant and African
American voters should be required to pass a literacy test, which ultimately would be required of all voters. As for women voting, Godkin

called Susan B. Anthony and her followers "wild visionaries." In 1900, two years before his death, the embittered journalist permanently re-crossed the Atlantic to settle in England.

Had Godkin lived through the ensuing Progressive era it is likely that his alienation from American democracy would have grown. Granted that the progressives' attack on municipal corruption paralleled his own, he probably would have been dismayed by the growing pace of regula-tory intervention at all levels of government. Nor can there be much doubt that dismay would have turned to disgust at various progressive reforms to democratize politics, notably, but not solely, the direct elec-tion of senators and women's suffrage. Although diversely and contro-versially interpreted—one radical historian of the 1960s termed the Pro-gressive era "the triumph of conservatism"—progressivism represented a major attack on some basic premises of laissez-faire conservatism.

CHAPTER 5

CONSERVATIVE CUSTODIANS OF CULTURE

The Genteel Tradition. The winds of change buffeted traditional cultural values during the age of enterprise no less than they did to the nation's economic, legal, and political institutions and mores. These perplexing challenges intensified the customary impulse of conservatives by ensconcing them as custodians of culture, in some instances more so than they desired. Always a term of some ambiguity, "culture" for Americans living at any time from the end of the Civil War until the outbreak of World War I denoted a respect verging on veneration for European but especially English literary, artistic, and scholarly accomplishments. American defenders of this high culture generally contended that it was a complement to and not an enemy of progress and democracy. Their critics thought otherwise. Even the Spanish-born Harvard philosopher George Santayana, himself a conservative, took exception to what he famously termed this "genteel tradition," which he believed inhibited intellectual and artistic development. "America," he informed an audience in 1911, "is a country with two mentalities, one a survival of the beliefs and standards of the fathers, the other an expression of the instincts, practice, and discoveries of the younger generations. In all the higher things of the mind—in religion, in literature, in the moral emotions—it is the hereditary spirit that still prevails . . . " While the extent to which the genteel tradition may have obstructed intellectual and artistic innovations remains a matter of conjecture, that it was both powerful and dedicated is well established. Its expression and influence were manifest in most of the nation's elite eastern universities; in its leading intellectual journals, such as Godkin's *Nation*, the *Atlantic Monthly*, the *North American Review*, and *Harper's*; in its major publishing houses; and in the words and works of notable individual writers, clergymen, and artists. Writers—novelists, poets, essayists, literary critics, philosophers—gave particular expression to the genteel tradition. To varying degrees, some remain known (although not necessarily read) a century later: Godkin, Charles Eliot Norton, James Russell Lowell, George William Curtis, Richard Watson Gilder, Thomas Bailey Aldrich, and Santayana's colleague in the Harvard Department of Philosophy, Josiah Royce, to name several. Others, acknowledged and applauded in their time, remain as footnotes to the past.

Most of these genteel men of letters came of age before the Civil War and as young men were sanguine about the prospects for a democratic culture as well as for democracy itself. Far from acting as stolid custodians of conservative culture, they welcomed progressive change and rode the currents of fashionable literary innovations such as romanticism. The postwar era, however, dampened their enthusiasm for change. The ticking of the biological clock doubtlessly accounted for some—but only some—hardening of the cultural arteries. Disillusioned by the pervasive materialism of American life and the degradation of democratic politics, faced with the loss of traditional religious authority through the attacks of Darwinism and the "higher criticism," which was imported from Europe and which questioned the authenticity of the Scriptures, they turned increasingly to culture for an escape or as a substitute for religion. They also turned to culture to elevate the manners and morals of the public and to educate their tastes for the esthetic. This frequently involved condemning literary works that openly and realistically dealt with sex, violence, or radical ideas. They were wary of the symbolist and outrightly hostile to the decadent movements, but understood that these reached a limited readership.

In contrast, the much more widely consumed works of realism and naturalism—the critic Irving Babbitt referred to the latter as "realism on all fours"—especially those of such writers as Henrik Ibsen and Émile Zola, were their particular *bêtes noires*. Even a sometimes skeptic of the genteel tradition, William Dean Howells, a fine literary realist and one who wrote with sympathy and discernment on such controversial issues as socialism and divorce, pledged that he would never write anything that he would not wish his daughter to read. Frequently derided for their highbrow efforts, the genteel writers reached only a limited audience as they preached, so to speak, to those already sitting in the amen corner. One historian of this group noted that they "did not lead or innovate; but they did not intend to. They merely controlled, for a time. They were significant because they were the architects of a culture that embodied conservatism in a threatening age."

Charles Eliot Norton in many ways typified the plight of the genteel custodian of American culture. The sole surviving son of Andrews Norton, the "Unitarian pope" and scholar at the Harvard Divinity School, Norton was born to an old and respected New England family, inherited wealth, and cultural privilege. He graduated from Harvard and in the mid 1850s toured Europe, where he became besotted with early Italian art and architecture and where, in England, he met and befriended several of the intellectual and cultural elite. Like his friend James Russell Lowell, he invidiously compared European with American culture to the detriment of the latter. Still, he believed that with time his native land could and would realize noteworthy cultural achievements. Having lost his religious faith, moreover, Norton, influenced greatly by the English art critic and theorist John Ruskin, perceived a new basis for morality in art, which then and henceforth served as his secular religion.

Like his fellow New Englanders Lowell and Henry Wadsworth Longfellow, Norton was an adept translator of Dante. Appointed in 1873 as Professor of the History of Art at Harvard, where his cousin Charles W. Eliot was serving as president, he taught courses until nearly the end of the century on the Italian poet and also on the fine arts, particularly those that related to the High Middle Ages. Published in 1880, his highly regarded study of Italian church building in the Trecento solidified his position as a major art scholar and critic, and gave form to his artistic preferences. Through his published writings but even more through his classroom and voluminous correspondence, the Unitarian pope's son labored both to elevate esthetic tastes and also to use his personal esthetic canons to critique contemporary political and socioeconomic developments. Pleased for the nation's general economic prosperity, as the century waned he increasingly complained of its lack of culture, manners, and political highmindedness. (*See Document No. 10.*) Noted one of his students: "The dear old man looks so mildly happy and benignant while he regrets everything in the age and the country— so contented, while he gently tells us it were better for us had we never been born in this degenerate and unlovely age. . . . "

Henry Adams shared Norton's distaste for the Gilded Age. The scion of two presidents and the son of a prominent Liberal Republican who nearly was nominated for president in 1872, Adams turned his back in disgust at Grantism and forsook active politics. His novel *Democracy* (1908) dissected Gilded Age politics, laying bare its corruption and allegiance to party at all costs. Adams and his brother Brooks were shaken by the events of the nineties. Their finances imperiled by the 1893 depression, the brothers, like others of the economic middle class, felt trapped between plutocrats and proletarians. Fearing socialists more, the brothers reluctantly sided with the well-to-do, but not without privately exchanging anti-Semitic diatribes against capitalistic financiers, both foreign and domestic. It was at this time that Henry Adams described himself as a "conservative Christian anarchist."

The Lure of Medievalism: Henry Adams and Others.

Religion traditionally has been a fundamental tenet for conservatives in general. The Adams family, however, experienced a precipitous decline in religious feeling, deteriorating from the firm convictions of John Adams to the doubts of John Quincy Adams, to the largely secularized religion of Charles Francis Adams, to the passionate but ultimately unsuccessful search for belief in a world of change on the part of the "conservative Christian anarchist." Henry Adams confessed to Brooks that he had "a weakness for science mixed with metaphysics," and that he was "a dilution of a mixture of Lord Kelvin and St. Thomas Aquinas." His interest in the scientific world of the nineteenth century led him first to accepting Darwinism. (He noted wryly in his *Education* (1918) that the spectacle of the American presidency descending from Washington to Grant was sufficient to upset the whole idea of evolution.) Later he moved beyond Darwinism to physics and made Kelvin's Second Law of Thermodynamics, along with Sir Isaac Newton's law of inverse squares, Josiah Willard Gibbs's law of phase and James Clerk Maxwell's theory of gases, the basis for his prediction that human energy, like that of the universe, was dissipating. As a result, he grimly prophesied, the world would destroy itself sometime during the first half of the twentieth century.

While Adams the anarchist erroneously applied scientific principles to human affairs to paint a bleak picture of the future, Adams the conservative Christian turned to an idealized past: the Middle Ages. He taught medieval history at Harvard during the 1870s, despite professing ignorance of the subject. While his brother Brooks stressed the beneficent workings of medieval economics in *The Law of Civilization and Decay* (1895), Adams emphasized its art and thought in his *Mont-Saint-Michel and Chartres* (privately printed, 1904; published, 1913). The twelfth century, one whose cultural, religious, and social unity contrasted favorably with the "multiplicity" of his own century, represented a golden age for Adams. In the *Education* he elaborated on this comparison, juxtaposing the Virgin of Chartres, his special icon and idol, with the Dynamo, the symbol of an all-powerful technology that he first saw with awe at the Paris Exposition of 1900. Whatever his sentimental predilections, Adams acknowledged that the Virgin, "who had acted as the greatest force the Western world ever felt," had become subordinate to her mechanical rival. The age of faith had yielded to the age of the machine, and unity was no more.

The Middle Ages served as a lodestar for other critics who suffered from the malaise of late nineteenth and early twentieth-century American life. Like their European and especially English counterparts, American medievalists, rather few in number that they were, found in the example of the Middle Ages not only wholesome culture but also a regard for the commonweal that seemed sorely lacking in their own contemporary world. Charles Eliot Norton had praised fourteenth-century Italy for having "less caste and rank division" and "more human class relations" and "republican spirit," which permitted both art and a healthy individualism to thrive. American arts-and-crafts groups and individuals like the Roycrofters and Elbert Hubbard hailed the highly influential work of William Morris and his English disciples, who were in revolt against the dehumanizing effects of the machine and industrial capitalism. Only a revival of medieval craftsmanship, they claimed, could restore dignity and a sense of meaning to human labor. They agreed with Karl Marx's description of the Middle Ages as the golden age for the workingman, but declined his prescription of violent revolution in favor of education and publicity.

Medievalism had no more fervent American exponent than the architect Ralph Adams Cram. Winning prestigious college and church commissions that included the United States Military Academy at West Point, the Princeton University Graduate School, and New York's Cathedral of St. John the Divine, Cram had become one of the nation's most prestigious builders by the time of World War I. In the process he had also become the high priest of Gothic architecture, a style that had enjoyed renewed favor at the turn of the century. (An admirer of medieval art and literature, he had also managed to convince a reluctant Henry Adams to permit a public edition of *Mont-Saint-Michel and Chartres*.) Architectural achievements notwithstanding, Cram steadfastly refused to think of himself solely as a builder. He believed that architecture constituted a touchstone for civilization to which it both gave and reflected values. In the long run, art could be no better or worse than the milieu from which it sprang. Consequently, he was fully as concerned for the quality of religious, socioeconomic, and political values as for artistic ones. A Gothicist in architecture (although he did sometimes build in other styles), he looked admiringly to the organic communitarian spirit of the Middle Ages, with its unified Christendom, its high democracy led by a responsible and responsive elite, its craft guilds and artistic creativity, and its reasonable scale of living. (*See Document No. 11.*) A prolific writer, he invidiously compared the excellence of medieval life and institutions to modern Western civilization. In the latter he found the dysfunctions of a "low" democracy: the greed and amorality of industrial and financial capitalism with its attendant class strife, selfish individualism and dessicated communal spirit, a growing rootlessness and anomie of the people, and a Christian religion that had fractured badly since the onset of the Protestant Reformation. To restructure modern life in accordance with medievalism became a lifelong concern for Cram. His roseate, almost Edenic, vision was just that. The historical Middle Ages differed in marked respects from the one he—and, for that matter, Henry Adams—depicted. Still, as John Ruskin had earlier noted, medievalism should be considered for its helpful mythic qualities: "The things that acutally happened were of small consequence—the thoughts that were developed are of infinite consequence." Mythic or not, the features of medievalism succored Christian conservatives like Cram, who saw in the Middle Ages "the nearest approach to the Christian commonwealth man has thus far achieved."

Tradition Versus Modernism in the Arts. The advent of modernism in the arts involved other artists besides Cram in the battle to conserve traditional culture. The neoclassicism of Paris's Ecole des Beaux-Arts profoundly affected such major American architects as Richard Morris Hunt and Charles F. McKim. Through their own work and through the influence they exerted on others, these men figuratively shaped the nation's taste and literally shaped its physical being with public buildings and palatial private mansions fashioned from ancient Greek and Roman, as well as Renaissance, designs. The enormously gifted Louis H. Sullivan and Frank Lloyd Wright preached and practiced an innovative modernism. Their work was appreciated, but the triumph of the classical-styled buildings at the "White City," the Columbian Exposition held in Chicago in 1893, insured the dominance of the soundly imitative over the seductively innovative until after World War I.

The battle over painting raged more fiercely between the custodians of culture and the modernists. Much as the upholders of the genteel tradition in literature condemned the frank depiction of social problems in realism and naturalism, genteel art critics deplored the representation of urban lower class life and mores by the so-called Ash Can school of painting. At the very least, however, these eight artists, headed by Robert Henri, could be understood. That was considerably more than could be said for the work of other modernists, particularly European ones.

For centuries representational painting, whatever its particular genre or the individual genius of the artist, had been de rigueur in the Western tradition. A series of shocks repeatedly assaulted that tradition from the late nineteenth century onwards: impressionism, expressionism, fauvism, primitivism, cubism. Some American collectors admired and purchased the new art, but other connoisseurs, museums, and the general public demurred. So, too, did several important art critics, who remained loyal to various traditional styles, including the academic painting against which modernism had revolted. In 1911 Kenyon Cox, who was also a respected painter, defended the high-minded and harmonious classical tradition: "It does not deny originality and individuality—they are as welcome as inevitable. It does not consider a tradition as immutable or set rigid bounds to invention. But it desires that each new presentation of truth and beauty shall show us the old truth and the new beauty, seen only from a different angle and colored by a different medium. It wishes to add link by link to the chain of tradition, but it does not wish to break the chain." Cox, like other conservative custodians of culture, condemned the modern artist who senselessly alienated himself from conventional society and felt it necessary to abhor the bourgeoisie and their values.

Two years later New York hosted the Armory Show, the most famous exhibition of art in the nation's history. Bringing together some sixteen hundred European and American paintings and sculptures, the show, which then traveled to several other large cities, exposed numerous Americans for the first time to the avant-garde. Cox fumed at the art, denouncing modernism and direly predicting that if artists and the public did not return to a reenergized traditionalism art "will cease to exist." Theodore Roosevelt had mixed feelings, as befitted a complex man of both liberal and conservative persuasion. Noting that his Navajo rug was finer than Marcel Duchamp's much discussed cubist work, *Nude Descending a Staircase*, he advised his countrymen that the show had much merit. And they listened. The Armory Show helped pave the way for the acceptance of modern art in the United States and its ultimate critical if not popular acceptance.

The Alienation of George Santayana. The year of the Armory Show also witnessed the permanent departure from American shores of George Santayana, who had been teaching philosophy at Harvard since 1891. Perhaps his mixed parentage—an American mother, a Spanish father—had made it too difficult to belong wholly either to the United States or to Europe. In any case, he seems to have found life in America increasingly untenable. Looking back from his European vantage point, he reflected in *Character and Opinion in the United States* (1920) that "the luckless American who is born a conservative, or who is drawn to poetic subtlety, pious retreats, or gay passions, nevertheless has the categorical excellence of work, growth, enterprise, reform, and prosperity dinned into his ears . . . so that he either folds up his heart and withers in a corner . . . or else he flies to Oxford or Florence or Montmartre to save his soul—or perhaps not to save it." He added: "American life is a powerful solvent. It seems to neutralize every intellectual element, however tough and alien it may be, and fuse it in the native good will, complacency, thoughtlessness, and optimism." It was the liberal optimism and "moral materialism" that most bothered the conservative Santayana. Americans of all stripes—idealist philosophers like his Harvard colleague Josiah Royce, genteel critics and reformers, Protestant clergymen, businessmen—simply lacked the conservative's sense of life's tragedy, approached art as philistines, and suffered from a democratic "singular preoccupation with quantity." The artistic manifestations of Roman Catholicism brought esthetic comfort to the wandering Spanish-born philosopher, as did its emphasis on hierarchy and order, but not its theology. An anomaly among conservatives, Santayana was an avowed atheist, who once wittily remarked that there was no God and that Mary was His mother. Surviving both World War I and World War II, Santayana died in Rome in 1952 after years of nursing home care by nuns.

In his essay "The Genteel Tradition in American Philosophy" (1911), Santayana claimed that the American intellect was the sphere of women. He disdained this "feminization of American culture." So, too, did others, who, whatever their viewpoint concerning the American intellect, were deeply distressed by what they perceived as a softening of the nation's masculine and moral fiber. For most of these critics, however, the enthronement of materialism and commercial success much more than feminism per se had occasioned this decline. As a result some became exponents of the warrior tradition, a culture with distinct although not exclusive conservative overtones.

The Martial Spirit. Between the 1890s and World War I the United States embarked upon a policy of overseas expansion that brought it a war, an overseas empire, an interoceanic canal, a two-ocean navy, repeated interventions in Latin American affairs, and heightened tensions in Asia and the Pacific. Expansionism cut across party lines and permitted no neat distinctions between liberals and conservatives. Notable Progressive reformers championed this activist foreign policy; individuals of varying conservative persuasions—William Graham Sumner, Charles Eliot Norton, and George Santayana, for example— opposed the Spanish-American War and its imperialist aftermath. Economic and geopolitical factors as well as domestic concerns helped to reverse the nation's traditional isolationist policy, but so also to an extent did the polemics of important individuals, such as Senator Henry Cabot Lodge with his "Large Policy" of hemispheric expansion, and Captain (later Admiral) Alfred Thayer Mahan with his persuasive *The Influence of Seapower upon History* (1890). Theodore Roosevelt, before, during, and after his presidency, brandished the "big stick" of force, although he practiced a more cautious diplomacy. In 1896 he complained to Lodge that the moneyed classes were "producing a flabby, timid type of character which eats away the great fighting qualities of our race." As assistant secretary of the navy he informed his audience at the Naval War College that "there are higher things in life than the soft and easy enjoyment of material comfort. It is through strife, or the readiness for strife, that a nation must win greatness." Sneering that "a timid lack of patriotism is found in a few doctrinaires and educated men," he leveled the brunt of his criticism at businessmen who put their selfish financial interests before "the self-sacrifice necessary in upholding the honor of the nation and the glory of their flag." "No triumph of peace," he concluded, "is quite so great as the supreme triumph of war."

While Roosevelt put into practice his martial spirit and became a hero of the Spanish-American War, Brooks Adams praised the warrior culture and, like his brother Henry, excoriated that of *homo economicus*. "The most martial and energetic people the world had ever seen" populated the Roman Empire, claimed Adams, but "a pure plutocracy" brought ruin to both. *The Law of Civilization and Decay* (1895) traces the historic ascendancy of the business classes over others, culminating in their modern dominion. Adams was persuaded, moreover, that this plutocratic dominance sooner or later would result in the destruction of cvilization.

Little known then or now, Homer Lea exemplified the glorification of the martial spirit and the warrior critique of commerce. Physical deformities precluded service in the Spanish-American War for the disappointed, Stanford University-educated Lea, but an acquaintance with emigrant Chinese revolutionaries living in San Francisco opened other possibilities. Crossing the Pacific, this Sinophile helped the unsuccessful Boxers and other Chinese patriots to unseat the Dowager Empress. In Europe at the time the Chinese revolution of 1911 erupted, Lea met with Sun Yat-sen, accompanied him to China as his chief of staff, but died the following year at age thirty-six.

Two works, *The Valor of Ignorance* (1909) and *The Day of the Saxon* (1912), convey Lea's admiration for the military, his contempt for the world of finance and commerce, and his prognosis for international politics. Unlike the commercial spirit, which he loathed, he did not oppose industrialism if it abetted military prowess, but "when a country makes industrialism the end it becomes a glutton among nations, vulgar, swinish, arrogant, whose kingdom lasts proportionally no longer than life remains to the swine among men. . . . It is this commercialism that, having seized hold of the American people, overshadows and tends to destroy not only the aspirations and world-wide career open to the nation, but the Republic." Lea both admired and feared the rapid rise to power of Japan since the Meiji restoration. In *The Valor of Ignorance* he praised the rejuvenation of the Japanese warrior society that had made possible military victory over both China and Russia during the Sino-Japanese and Russo-Japanese wars respectively. Warning his countrymen of this "yellow peril," he cited their racial prejudice against the Japanese, including San Francisco's humiliating segregation of Japanese students in 1906. War was sure to come with Japan and with it, he predicted, the invasion of the Philippines, Hawaii, and the American West coast. So much for the "valor of ignorance" that turned its back on a noble martial spirit in favor of a decadent commercialism.

In the half century that followed the Civil War various individuals and groups of individuals served as custodians of a culture laden with traditional values and assumptions. At the time they were variously apprehensive that the forces of a debased democracy, a corrosive materialism, a degeneration in national character and morals, and the advent of modernism in the several arts would seriously weaken that culture. When the guns of August 1914 opened fire, many of those custodians who were still alive feared for the very existence of that culture and for civilization itself.

CHAPTER 6

CONSERVATISM BETWEEN THE WARS

Woodrow Wilson declared that the United States was entering World War I to make the world safe for democracy. In the immediate aftermath of the war, Ralph Adams Cram, who had vigorously supported the Allied cause, tartly queried who was going to make the world safe from democracy. Not all conservatives shared the architect's extreme anti-democratic bias, but some did chafe at the tenor of events and attitudes that gave the postwar decade its distinctive flavor. Still, the decade was pleasing to those who equated commerce with conservatism and who agreed with President Calvin Coolidge that "the chief business of the American people is business." Sinclair Lewis might lampoon the businessman in his novel *Babbitt* (1922) and advertising executive Bruce Barton might verge on the sacrilegious when he extolled Jesus as a smooth business operator in his popular *The Man Nobody Knows* (1925), but the fact remains that this "prosperity decade," as it has been called, was prosperous for many Americans. The Progressive impulse and ability to curb some excesses of capitalist enterprise remained but in diluted form. Meanwhile probusiness legislators convened in congress; three probusiness presidents (Harding, Coolidge, and Hoover) resided in the White House; and the majority of justices sitting on the High Court continued to render decisions generally favorable to business interests. But there remained dissenting conservatives who refused to equate the good society with material success and who viewed other considerations as more important. Foremost among these during the Jazz Age were the New Humanists and the Southern Agrarians.

The New Humanism. The New Humanism, despite the similarity in nomenclature, differed sharply from the humanism of the Renaissance. While the latter advanced secularism at the expense of the otherworldliness of the Middle Ages, its twentieth-century namesake criticized the excessive materialism of modern times. More properly, the New Humanism descended from the genteel tradition, with which it shared a good deal in addition to its castigation of materialism. Both were concerned custodians of traditional culture and learning, believers in leadership by the elite, and opponents of an emergent mass democracy. The two were largely literary movements, and neither exerted significant influence outside higher education and writers' circles. The New Humanism reached its apogee in the 1920s, but its two most important figures, Irving Babbitt and Paul Elmer More, whom T. S. Eliot would later call "the two *wisest* men that I have known," had given it much of its direction in the prewar years.

After graduating from Harvard in 1889 and subsequently holding positions at the University of Montana and Williams College, Irving Babbitt returned in 1894 to teach in the French Department at his alma mater, where he remained until his death in 1933. In the not unbiased opinion of his friend and intellectual comrade-at-arms, Paul Elmer More, whom he had met in 1892, he was possibly the greatest teacher the nation had ever experienced. Reminiscences from dozens of former students, some of whom went on to preach the gospel of the New Humanism, attest to his pedagogical prowess. But it was largely through his books, notably *Literature and the American College* (1908), *Masters of French Criticism* (1912), *Rousseau and Romanticism* (1919), and *Democracy and Leadership* (1924), that Babbitt helped to give substance to the movement.

From his earliest writings Babbitt offered a crucial distinction between humanism and humanitarianism. The humanist, he noted, was concerned about perfecting the individual; the humanitarian searched for ways to elevate humanity as a whole. For Babbitt, the former was the realist, the latter the quixotic adventurer who generally did more harm than good. Evoking ancient Greek philosphy and Eastern religions, Babbitt stressed the need for moderation and restraint. This "inner check" was necessary to combat the pernicious human tendency to excess, which had manifested itself historically and currently in Western thought and practice. For this he particularly blamed the scientific humanitarianism of Francis Bacon and, even more, the sentimental humanitarianism of Jean-Jacques Rousseau. (Few writers have ever denounced Rousseau as vehemently as Babbitt.) Bacon had promoted science in the hope that it would benefit humanity. Regrettably, according to Babbitt, science during the intervening centuries had been pressed into service by despotic rulers and expansionist nations. (Bacon did say that "knowledge is power.") Exacerbating this scientism was romanticism, which Babbitt loathed and for which he blamed Rousseau. This wide-ranging nineteenth-century movement inspired the "never ending quest after the ever fleeting object of desire." This, along with the

Rousseauian belief in the natural goodness of people, promoted unrealistic expectations for progress. The substitution of mass democracy for constitutional democracy had ensued as had the exaltation of humanitarianism, which encouraged individuals to avoid taking responsibility for their actions and instead to blame misfortunes on the shortcomings of society. He suggested that society "substitute the doctrine of the right man for the rights of man." To an extent his concerns mirrored those of Herbert Hoover, who was concerned, particularly during his depression-ridden presidency, that too much aid would destroy an individual's character and self-reliance.

Only a proper humanism, argued Babbitt, could spawn those who could deal intelligently and forcefully with contemporary problems. Colleges could educate superior individuals through a curriculum weighted toward the classics rather than through a series of elective courses, which Babbitt detested. The classics would appeal to both the reason and imagination of students and would train future leaders for wisdom and character. This "saving remnant" would then guide others: "Let man first show that he can act on himself, there will then be time enough for him to act on other men and the world."

The question of religion divided numerous New Humanists from Babbitt, who tried to steer a middle course between naturalism and a supernaturalism. He accepted the existence of a universal principle of the good and was aware that his ideals of moderation and self-restraint were themselves religious virtues. Yet he insisted on positing his convictions from a human, not theological, point of view. Probably personally an agnostic, this Sanskrit scholar was highly sympathetic to Buddhism. For contemporary Christianity, in contrast, he had strong reservations. He told the religious Paul Elmer More that "what you get in the churches nowadays is religiosity, the religion of feeling, aestheticism, the cult of nature, official optimism, talk about progress, humanitarian sympathy for the poor." Sometime thereafter the once close friendship began to cool.

Like Babbitt, Paul Elmer More was a man of letters. In the decade before World War I he served consecutively as the literary editor of two of E. L. Godkin's former bailiwicks, the New York *Evening Post* and the *Nation*. Both then and now his reputation rests essentially with his multivolumed *Shelburne Essays* (1901–1921), which ranged widely over diverse subjects and in which can be found the gist of his New Humanism. He accepted a position at Princeton University in 1914, teaching philosophy and the classics there for twenty years while continuing his scholarship. No friend of the New Humanism, Henry L. Mencken thought of the Princeton professor as the nearest thing to a true scholar the United States then possessed.

Religious differences did not negate the secular convictions that More and Babbitt mutually shared. Like Babbitt, More stressed the "inner check," moderation, and decorum. He also was a confirmed elitist and critic of democracy, as made manifest in his *Aristocracy and Justice* (1915), the ninth and most politically oriented volume of his *Shelburne Essays*. Like Babbitt and countless other conservatives over time and place, he longed for an aristocracy based on talent and character. Similar to the Harvard professor, he stressed the educative powers of the classics to create this class. (*See Document No. 12.*) Like Babbitt— but even more so—the *Shelburne Essays* author was concerned with questions of property. His views were more complex than generally considered. At the turn of the century he pilloried the pious preachings of Andrew Carnegie and John D. Rockefeller and denounced materialism for having precluded the growth of a healthy national culture. A few years later he referred to "the sordid cruelties of Wall Street." Yet he persistently attacked socialism and exalted property rights, more from a practical than legal standpoint. The complementary evils of socialism and humanitarianism, he inveighed, were committed to redistributing property, resolutely refusing to recognize that property was not an end in itself but a means to a higher end: civilization. Secular happiness, he asserted in *Aristocracy and Justice*, is so closely linked to the possession of property that "to the civilized man the rights of property are more important than the right to life."

Taken both in and out of context, More's seemingly callous remark about the preeminence of property rights has offended people, no more so than at the time of the Great Depression. And as economic prosperity gave way to economic debacle, the New Humanism also withered. Internal disagreements as well as attacks from other literary critics sapped its powers. Mencken, for one, called the New Humanism the "natural and inevitable refuge of all timorous and third-rate men—of all weaklings for whom the struggle with hard facts is unendurable. . . . " Of greater importance, writers and intellectuals turned more directly to the immediate social and political problems that confronted a nation in distress. For all their limited appeal and longevity, however, the New Humanists had raised important questions, offered new insights, and enhanced the conservative tradition. As More noted, the role of critics was to "stand with the great conservative forces of human nature, having their fame certified by the things that endure amid all the betrayals of time and fashion."

In the estimation of Henry Louis Mencken the American farmer was not a member of the human race. Rather, he was "a tedious fraud and ignoramus, a cheap rogue and hypocrite . . . and deserves all that he suffers under our economic system and more." Mencken, with his urban, "wet," antifundamentalist prejudices, especially loathed southern farmers, whom he derided as "Fundamentalists armed with dung forks." Less vitriolic than Mencken, other critics, mainly though not entirely from the North, deplored various developments in the South during the 1920s: the intensified racial, religious, and ethnic bigotry personified by the Ku Klux Klan; religious fundamentalism and anti-intellectualism highlighted by the Scopes Trial; widespread public support for prohibition mixed with widespread evasion of the law. They tended to agree with Mencken that the postwar South was a cultural wasteland. The South, as in the antebellum period, found itself on the defensive, but once again it found vocal and skilled defenders, particularly in the group of twelve writers collectively called the Southern Agrarians.

Agrarians and Decentralists. The immediate forebears of the Southern Agrarians were four poets—John Crowe Ransom, Allen Tate, Donald Davidson, and Robert Penn Warren. Coalesced around Vanderbilt University in the early 1920s, they published a small but highly respected literary magazine, *The Fugitive*. At first they showed little if any interest in regional culture, but stung by the criticism of outsiders that the South offered little of value, they became dedicated, self-conscious southerners intent upon publicizing the virtues of their region. In the process they were joined by eight others—most of whom also were or had been students or teachers at Vanderbilt—as the Fugitives metamorphosed into the Southern Agrarians.

Published in 1930, *I'll Take My Stand* represents the most famous and most representative collective thinking of the Southern Agrarians. The book's very title is redolent of lyrics from the popular song "Dixie" and aptly conveys a preview of the defiant tone of several essays found within the book itself. Southern Agrarianism, as put forth in *I'll Take My Stand* as well as other books and essays by the Agrarians, is at its core an attack on modernism and a defense of humanism. Not the New

Humanism of Irving Babbitt and Paul Elmer More, which struck them as too abstract and linked too closely with the classics, but the humanism of the older South, which they contrasted favorably with the contemporary American way of life experienced outside the South. (*See Document No. 13.*) Industrialization and the worship of material progress, they complained, had eroded that way of life. The Agrarians confessed in the introduction to their essays that they were writing the book because their fellow southerners seemed to want to embrace the "industrial ideal." Thanks to industrialists, whom they deplored as much as they did communists and socialists, humans had lost their sense of vocation. Broadening their indictment, they noted that neither the arts nor the amenities of life could resist the corrosive forces of this industrialism. Nor could religion or the human sense of awe that had always viewed nature "as something mysterious and contingent." In place of overly industrialized society the Agrarians urged an agrarian society "in which agriculture is the leading vocation, whether for wealth, for pleasure, or for prestige—a form of labor that is pursued with intelligence and leisure, and that becomes the model to which the other forms approach as well they may. . . . The theory of agrarianism is that the culture of the soil is the best and most sensitive of vocations, and that therefore it should have the economic preference and enlist the maximum number of workers."

The regional agrarianism of the Twelve Southerners was reminiscent of that of their illustrious ancestor Thomas Jefferson. For all of them, the farm—whether great or small, profitable or subsistent—offered the immeasurable satisfactions of an ambient culture that was firmly rooted in family and community values. As the Great Depression deepened, however, the critique of industrial capitalism broadened, bringing support for a back-to-the-land program from such diverse decentralist individuals and groups as Ralph Adams Cram and the Catholic rural life movement.

Although differing in particular details, the American decentralists agreed that a certain exodus to the countryside and a more widespread ownership of property were needed if economic recovery, greater social justice, and an enhanced quality of life were to become realities. The New Deal initially buoyed their hopes, especially with its attack on rural poverty in the form of a program in 1933 to relocate 25,000 families on subsistence homesteads and the establishment of several greenbelt communities. However, conflicting economic priorities and later the opposition to the homesteads by Rexford Guy Tugwell, who headed the Re-settlement Administration, severely jolted their hopes.

The coup de grace to the back-to-the-land dreams of the Southern Agrarians and the decentralists of the 1930s came after World War II in the form of the flight of Americans not to exurbia but to suburbia. Yet from time to time a call is still heard for a return to rural America and to farming. The gifted Kentucky farmer-writer Wendell Berry, for one, has eloquently rearticulated the close connection between farming and the larger culture, speaking to long-established concerns as well as to modern day problems such as environmentalism. And there has been some return of southerners who had migrated or their offspring or even non-southerners to the South. That return, however, has been largely to the region's cities and suburbs. Given the history of America's demographics, which witnessed the mass of people steadily and inexorably moving away from rural areas, the vision of the Southern Agrarians and decentralists probably was doomed from the outset. Still, these critics posed searching questions regarding the weaknesses of an industrialist-capitalist economy and its materialist culture. In putting forth an alternative model of society that stressed communitarian over individual concerns, moreover, they rekindled that part of the conservative tradition that had been overshadowed by laissez-faire conservatism.

As previously noted, laissez-faire conservatism had much in common with traditional conservatism. But whereas the latter placed the individual within the broader context of communal institutions and values, the former stressed the primacy of the individual above other considerations. Although this crucial distinction between the two groups was frequently blurred, the increasing power of communism, socialism, and democracy in the early twentieth century conjured up fears, both real and exaggerated, of a mass society that could and perhaps would destroy the liberty of the individual. These fears of statism and mass society, reified by the triumph of Bolshevism in the Soviet Union and the spread of socialism elsewhere, impassioned libertarians, the nomenclature frequently used to denote twentieth-century advocates of laissez-faire. Even more did the advent of the Great Depression and the New Deal.

H. L. Mencken. Probably no man did more to popularize libertarianism during the 1920s than the scourge of the South and the American farmer, H. L. Mencken. Although he never developed a rigorous philosophy, the pungent language and devastating wit of his writings made him, with the possible exception of Walter Lippmann, the preeminent journalist of the first half of the twentieth century. Indeed, Lippmann referred to this "Sage of Baltimore" in 1926 as "the most powerful personal influence on this whole generation of educated people." As editor of the widely read *American Mercury*, which he cofounded in 1924 and edited solely for a decade beginning the following year, Mencken lashed out against forces that repressed individual freedom: the Ku Klux Klan, fundamentalism, prohibition, nativism, puritanism. A civil libertarian, he denounced the lack of fairness in the infamous trial of Sacco and Vanzetti, and pilloried those who opposed John Scopes's right to teach Darwinism to his high school students. He also led the fight against literary censorship, notably against bluestockings who wished to ban James Joyce's *Ulysses*, and, despite all sorts of personal racial, religious, and ethnic biases, he opened the pages of the *Mercury* to talented African American writers. The *Mercury*, in fact, published more pieces by George Schuyler, an African American who became a staunch conservative and anticollectivist, than by any other writer. (Schuyler asserted that Mencken was always "favorably disposed toward Negro writers who had anything to say.") During the 1920s Mencken freely mixed political and economic conservatism with libertarianism. Several months before the initial issue of the *Mercury* appeared he confided that he hoped to steer a course between the impractical liberals who "chase butterflies" and the titans of finance who "sob and moan for endangered capital." He added: "Certainly there must be room in the middle for an educated Toryism—the true Disraelian brand. It exists everywhere, but in the United States it has no voice." Mencken's "educated Toryism," however, frequently drifted rightward and became largely indistinguishable from the reactionary, as the traditional conservative's distrust of human nature and democracy deteriorated into disgust. The common people were at various times the "booboisie," "homo boobiens," or "homo neanderthalis" for Mencken, who asserted that "a progressive is one who believes that the common people are both intelligent and honest; a reactionary is one who knows better." Mencken's elitist hero was partly the survivor of the Social Darwinian struggle, partly the cultural superman of Friedrich Nietzsche. (Mencken did his best to popularize Nietzsche and German culture, and nearly fell into difficulties during the anti-German furor that swept the nation once it had become involved in World War I.) His *Notes on Democracy* (1926), while admitting that democracy had a few positive characteristics, underscored his overall contempt. What kind of system, he snorted, permits a person to advance but then makes an inferior person his equal? Suffering from the disease of envy, democracy allows only the liberty of the have-nots to destroy the liberty of the haves. "How can any man be a democrat who is sincerely a democrat?" he asked.

Concerned largely with cultural, social, and political commentary, Mencken devoted little attention to the economic matters of the twenties. He did scoff at businessmen and he did persistently poke fun at President Calvin Coolidge, but the dour Vermonter of famously laconic speech inspired, almost invited, satire. But Mencken's economics were safely capitalistic. In the first issue of the *Mercury* he warned that the wish of radicals to uproot capitalism was "as full of folly as the Liberal proposals to denaturize it by arousing its better nature." In subsequent issues he attacked socialists, labor agitators, and economic reformers, much as had William Graham Sumner, a fellow libertarian whom he admired.

The advent of hard times made it impossible for Mencken to slight economic questions. Like so many of his countrymen, he initially accepted President Hoover's prediction that prosperity was just around the corner. When it was not, Mencken, like others who would rue their choice, voted for Franklin D. Roosevelt in the 1932 presidential election. Convinced that democracy was a failure and that only a strong man could solve the problems of the Depression, Mencken suggested in early 1933 that a constitutional convention be held to provide for kingship in place of the presidency, and that Roosevelt should serve as a de jure rather than as a de facto monarch. (Not surprising for a medievalist, Ralph Adams Cram, some of whose essays Mencken published, also wished to exchange the presidency for a constitutional monarch.) The Roosevelt-Mencken honeymoon did not lead to lasting connubial bliss. In time Mencken reacted strongly against the sweeping New Deal programs, their cost, and the growth of government bureaucracy. He also changed course with respect to Roosevelt himself, denouncing the president for dictatorial ways and for fomenting class antagonisms. The Sage of Baltimore concluded that democracy and capitalism were not compatible, and that the former had caused the nation's economic ills. Roosevelt and the New Deal had intended to restore the nation to economic health, but in Mencken's opinion they had failed and in their quest were destroying individual liberty. If American society crowded the individual in the twenties, the state was threatening to crush him in the thirties.

Opposition to the New Deal Grows. Stunned by the enormity of the Depression, a number of other conservatives, both traditional and libertarian, initially either supported or suspended judgment on Roosevelt and his policies. Soon, however, extensive federal spending, relief programs, bureaucratic controls, and the end of the gold standard sired opposition. What they deemed as a lack of substantial recovery galvanized conservatives into stronger attacks by 1934. Stung by this growing opposition, especially from the business community, the president denounced "economic royalists" and, urged onward by advisers, turned the general direction of the New Deal from recovery to reform. Vindicated by the congressional elections of that year, he oversaw the enactment of several major laws that hugely widened the rift between the New Deal and conservatives: the Wagner Act, which substantially increased the power of organized labor; the Revenue Act, the so-called "soak-the-rich" measure that raised income taxes on the wealthiest, as well as corporate, estate, and gift taxes; the Public Utilities Company Act, which increased the government's regulatory powers; and the Social Security Act, which many conservatives denounced as socialistic.

Both organizations and individuals spearheaded the conservative attack on the New Deal and the expansion of statism, which they were convinced would destroy capitalism and individual freedom. (The libertarians more than traditional conservatives equated the two.) Existing business groups like the National Association of Manufacturers regarded Roosevelt's policies as leading the nation down a slippery road to socialism. So, too, did the newly organized American Liberty League. Founded in August 1934, the League brought together conservative business and political opponents of the New Deal. Support from such wealthy individuals as Alfred P. Sloan, Jr. and John Jacob Raskob, respectively the president and a former executive of General Motors, and various members of the Du Pont family filled its war chest; bipartisan politics added noted Democrats, including two former presidential candidates, John W. Davis and Al Smith, to enhance expected Republican strength. (Four of the League's officers, in fact, were Democrats.) The League supported various anti-New Deal congressional candidates in the 1934 elections. By the following year, with a reputed membership of 150,000, it had become the nucleus of conservative opposition to the president and his policies, seriously likening Roosevelt to the great dictators of the 1930s, Hitler, Mussolini, and Stalin.

Albert Jay Nock. Probably no single individual protested the centralized planning strategies of the Roosevelt administration in particular and statism in general more incisively than Albert Jay Nock, a prominent man of letters who was both the friend and ally of Mencken and Cram, as well as a formative influence on numerous conservatives and libertarians, including George Schuyler, William F. Buckley, Jr., and the economists Frank Chodorov and Murray Rothbard. Born in Scranton, Pennsylvania, in 1870 but raised largely in Brooklyn, New York, Nock nearly decided to pursue a career as a professional baseball player but opted instead to become, like his father, an Episcopal priest. Losing his religion, he left the ministry—like William Graham Sumner, whose ideas he respected—to become a journalist. Politically, he was a Wilsonian progressive until World War I. Opposed to the war and to the greatly expanded wartime powers of the federal government, he became disillusioned with liberalism and turned to philosophical anarchism. At that point he believed in the essential goodness of humans and laid the blame for their corruption on bad or inept government and laws. In numerous essays and in biographies of Jefferson, Rabelais, and the nineteenth-century single taxer, Henry George, he spelled out his libertarian views on the paramountcy of the individual.

Gradually, however, his benign view of human nature curdled into misanthropy. Various American conservatives, including Irving Babbitt, had warned that democracy, by giving rise to "mass man," was imperiling modern civilization. The Spanish intellectual Ortega y Gasset expressed this concern more analytically in *The Revolt of the Masses* (1930): "Democracy in its degenerative form leads to a general lowering of values, since the mass man does not seek excellence but more comfort, and to intolerance of individual differences, since the mass man feels comfortable when everyone behaves as he does." Influenced by Gasset's arguments as well as by those Oswald Spengler had earlier set forth in his gloomily fatalistic *The Decline of the West* (1918–1922), Ralph Adams Cram wrote "Why We Do Not Behave Like Human Beings." Published in the September 1932 issue of the *American Mercury*, the essay profoundly impressed Nock and added weight to his increasingly saturnine views. That same year Nock published *The Theory of Education in the United States*, which was based on a series of lectures that he had delivered in 1931 at the University of Virginia. In his lectures Nock, who had developed a love for the classics as a young man, complained that higher education was turning out technicians but failing in its duty to inculcate the liberal arts. This was the point that Irving Babbitt had made almost a full generation earlier, that University of Chicago president Robert Maynard Hutchins and his allies in education were making in the 1930s, and that Allen Bloom would remake a half century later. Still, Nock concluded, most people were simply not educable.

Convinced that most humans could not be trusted to govern themselves, Nock abandoned his optimistic philosophical anarchism in favor of a libertarianism that acknowledged the need for a strictly minimal limited government, the sort that John Stuart Mill in his *On Liberty*, Herbert Spencer, William Graham Sumner and other nineteenth-century advocates of laissez-faire had accepted. Nock remained vehemently opposed to statism in general and the New Deal in particular, although it is important to note that he also deplored corporations with their power to limit competition and destroy small businesses.

Nock's brief against statism is detailed in *Our Enemy, The State* (1936), a work that has remained a staple of libertarian literature. In this book Nock drew a distinction between social power, that of individuals and private associations, and state power. Although his definitions were never crystal clear, he did indicate that state power was not the same as government, which he, unlike dedicated philosophical anarchists, presumed could act beneficently. Government provides for defense against foreign enemies and maintains justice at home; the state is exploitative. Born out of conquest and confiscation, the latter exists solely to further the economic interests of one class over another, as the New Deal clearly showed. Thus the purpose of the state is antisocial. By maintaining the forms but betraying the substance of republicanism, the Constitution had betrayed the Declaration of Independence, according to Nock. Such subsequent developments as judicial review, fixed political terms in office, and the essentially bipartisan nature of American politics abetted the centralization of state power, which had reached new heights of class exploitation under the aegis of the New Deal. While predicting that industrial and financial dislocations eventually would destroy state power, Nock was extremely pessimistic for the present and immediate future.

All that could be done until the destruction of state power and the rebirth of social power was for "the Remnant," those select few who could appreciate true liberty, to preserve civilized life as best they could.

Continued Opposition to the New Deal. Conservatives and libertarians alike, ranging from the Liberty League to H. L. Mencken and Albert Jay Nock, hoped to thwart President Roosevelt's reelection bid in 1936. Even before the election, however, they were frustrated by the Republican party's nomination of Alfred ("Alf") Landon, the politically moderate governor of Kansas who supported various New Deal measures, over former President Hoover, who bitterly denounced the New Deal for steering the nation down the road to fascism. Humiliation was added to frustration as Roosevelt scored a lopsided victory and Democratic congressional victories ensured huge majorities in both houses of Congress. Still, it is highly improbable that Hoover would have fared better than the unfortunate Landon.

Emboldened by the margin of victory for both himself and his party, Roosevelt in early 1937 pushed for the single most controversial domestic measure of his entire presidency: the reorganization of the Supreme Court. The laissez-faire conservativism that had played such a prominent role in the judicial decisions of the High Court in the years of Justice Stephen J. Field had continued to do so through Roosevelt's first administration. From 1934 to 1936 the Court, to the satisfaction of most conservatives and libertarians, invalidated a dozen New Deal measures. Believing that the severity of the Depression as well as overall changes in public opinion demanded government activism and an end to the Court's power to negate needed programs, the chief executive in early February 1937 sent to Congress his "court packing" plan. If accepted, this would have allowed him to appoint a second judge for each federal judge who was over seventy years of age and still sitting. Practically speaking, this would enable him at the time to name as many as six new justices to the Court. Less than candid in putting forth his plan—he argued that he wished to streamline the federal judiciary and to ease the burdens of work for the judges—he immediately encountered strong opposition not only from traditional conservatives and libertarians as expected, but from many liberals as not expected. Bipartisan opposition to playing politics with the Supreme Court doomed his plan to defeat, but as he cheerfully acknowledged in 1938, he had lost the battle but had won the war. The Court never again invalidated a major New Deal law, and Roosevelt was able to appoint nine justices before his death in 1945.

The Court-packing plan solidified and augmented opposition to the president and the New Deal. And by no means were these opponents committed conservatives. The famed journalist and intellectual Walter Lippmann, who earlier had embraced first socialism and then progressivism but who by the 1930s had become deeply concerned over the growth of the federal government's power, spoke to the fears of antistatists in *The Good Society* (1937). It was illusionary to believe that a planned economy in times of peace could be achieved without creating despotism, he warned. Lippmann, whose growing conservatism was characterized by his insistence on leadership by a responsible elite and not by the tergiversations of a mass democracy, did grant that benevolent despots might be found. Still, no guarantee whatsoever existed that benevolence would accompany despotism.

By 1938 the New Deal had stalled. The Court-packing plan inadvertently had resulted in the creation of a coalition of revitalized Republicans and dissident, mainly southern, Democrats hostile to the president and his policies. James MacGregor Burns, a Roosevelt biographer, shrewdly noted that his subject had actually lost the battle to reform the Court, won the subsequent campaign, but in the long run had lost the war. Although relieved that the New Deal had lost its momentum, conservatives could take scant comfort. The programs and philosophy of the New Deal were in place and already had already achieved substantial changes in the powers of government and in the relationship between the public and private sectors of the economy. Far from resenting this intrusion by the government into what conservatives deemed the legitimate private domain of American life, voters seemed more than willing to accept it. The evidence abounded that statism and mass society, the chief concerns of traditional conservatives and libertarians during the years that intervened between the world wars, had grown appreciably. Nor was the end of that growth in sight. Small wonder that a depressed Albert Jay Nock could entitle his remarkable autobiography *Memoirs of a Superfluous Man* (1943), or that Ralph Adams Cram could gather his essays into a work he called *The End of Democracy* (1937).

CHAPTER 7

THE POSTWAR CONSERVATIVE REVIVAL

Had the New Deal sounded the death knell of conservatism? A few years after World War II the prominent cultural critic Lionel Trilling in *The Liberal Imagination* (1950) described conservatism as basically lacking in ideas and expressing itself "only in action or in irritable mental gestures which seek to resemble ideas." He concluded that liberalism provided the nation's only intellectual tradition. Other liberals concurred. In his *The Liberal Tradition in America* (1955) the political scientist Louis Hartz also noted the conspicuous lack of a conservative tradition in the United States, a lack which he believed had stemmed from having had no feudal, class-ridden past. As a result, Americans, with but scattered exceptions, were Lockean liberals who genuflected before the altar of democratic capitalism. Major liberal historians of the period, including Pulitzer Prize-winner Richard Hofstadter, greatly influenced both their peers and graduate students by reinterpreting the American past as one that featured a basic consensus rather than divisive conflicts. In his widely cited *The Vital Center* (1949), Arthur M. Schlesinger, Jr. argued that liberals and conservatives should not wage internecine war against one another but should stand fast against the destructive forces of both the extreme Left and Right. Daniel Boorstin, historian and future Librarian of Congress, acknowledged that Americans in many respects were conservative but were not Conservative. A practical people, they were nonideological, as he theorized in *The Genius of American Politics* (1953). From a nonconservative perspective, the sociologist Daniel Bell announced that postwar America was bearing witness to *The End to Ideology* (1960).

Despite the denigrations, the questioning of whether the tradition even existed, the blurring of its distinctiveness from the American liberal tradition, and the prediction that as an ideology it no longer served a meaningful purpose in American intellectual life, conservatism enjoyed renewed vigor after World War II. This resurgence was both wide and deep, with new ideas poured into old bottles and old ideas filling new bottles. No monolithic movement emerged, however. Instead, conservatives tended to champion one of three major causes: anticommunism, libertarianism, traditionalism. Sometimes overlapping, sometimes incompatible, these causes engaged the efforts of tyros, converts, and veteran campaigners who strove to adapt conservative ideas and principles to contemporary needs and in the process made conservatism a more intellectually stimulating and broadly appealing movement.

The Anticommunist Crusade. The Cold War powerfully engaged the efforts of conservatives and helped to fuel the conservative movement after 1945. The growth of Soviet power and widening rift between the USSR and the United States focused the attention of numerous conservatives who perceived Soviet intentions as a quest for global dominion. Intensifying their convictions and fears were a host of events that included the establishment of Soviet puppet regimes in Eastern Europe countries, the Berlin blockade of 1948, the Soviet acquisition of nuclear weapons, the fall of China to communism, and the Korean War. The sensational domestic spy trials of Alger Hiss and Julius and Ethel Rosenberg during this same period also helped to turn many conservatives into cold warriors.

True believers who lose their original faith frequently embrace a new faith with equal if not greater fervor. This was certainly the case for a number of former communists who became dedicated anticommunists after the proverbial failing of the light. Not all ex-communists or fellow travelers became conservatives, of course, but many did, and vociferously so. Some of the most notable of these included: James Burnham, Frank Meyer, William S. Schlamm, Suzanne La Follette. Among the prominent individuals who were once on the far but noncommunist Left but who turned to the Right during the Cold War were the literary figures John Dos Passos and Max Eastman. Beyond question, however, the most famous of all the converts was Whittaker Chambers, whose testimony against Alger Hiss led to the latter's conviction of perjury for having lied that he had never belonged to the Communist party. Published in 1952, *Witness* was Chambers's account of how he and Hiss conducted espionage for the Soviet Union during the 1930s. This heavily detailed but engagingly written work became a bible for conservative anticommunists and its author a heroic figure. Not the least reason for this was that it brought a certain discredit upon the New Deal for having trusted and rewarded the well-educated, well-groomed Hiss, who as a State Department official in 1945 had attended the Yalta Conference and helped to organize the first meeting of the United Nations. There was also the consideration that Chambers, after his years as a communist, had become a devout Christian and had come to look upon the Cold War as a struggle between the spiritual forces of light (the West) and the materialistic powers of darkness (communism). Many conservatives, particularly the immediate post–World War II generation, viewed the Cold War in these Manichean terms, frequently and pejoratively appending the epithets "godless" or "atheistic" to the already pejorative "communism."

Although conservatives were strongly anticommunist, they differed as to the means for bringing about the system's destruction. Some argued that the most realistic policy was that of containment, famously outlined by the diplomat and sovietologist George F. Kennan. Published pseudonymously in the July 1947 issue of *Foreign Affairs*, the Kennan article warned of Soviet expansionism and counseled that the West would have to remain vigilant and firm against hostile Soviet probings, but that eventually communism would succomb. History subsequently would record that the United States did successfully pursue this policy of containment, but at its inception the policy, which had not urged strong armaments, seemed too passive and feckless for some. Calling for more direct confrontation, Frank Meyer justified a first-strike use of nuclear weapons should the occasion warrant; William Schlamm thought the United States should persistently confront the Soviet Union with the possibility of war. Anticommunist hardliners applauded the rhetoric of John Foster Dulles, who at times denounced containment, spoke of rolling back communism, and threatened "massive retaliation." President Dwight D. Eisenhower softened his secretary of state's rhetoric, however, and the failure of the United States in 1956 either to intervene in the Hungarian uprising or to aid Great Britain, France, and Israel against Egypt in the Suez Canal dispute gave the lie to Dulles's aggressive posturing.

Some conservatives were firm anticommunists but more reluctant cold warriors. Isolationism had found favor with large numbers of conservatives during the 1930s, especially those in the Midwest. Conservatives played a large role in both the leadership and rank-and-file membership of the America First Committe, which bitterly opposed the nation's involvement in World War II until the attack on Pearl Harbor. (Both pacifists and radicals, like the socialist Norman Thomas, also were America Firsters but supported noninvolvement for quite different reasons.) While most conservative isolationists rallied around the wartime flag, many afterwards initially wanted no part of a confrontation with the Soviet Union. Foremost among these in terms of visibility and the respect he commanded was the senior Republican senator from Ohio, Robert A. Taft.

Robert A. Taft. For Taft, national self-interest was the paramount factor in foreign policy. The purpose of that policy, he argued, "is not to reform the entire world or spread sweetness and light and economic prosperity to the people who have lived and worked out their own salvation for centuries, according to their customs and to the best of their ability." He added: "We do have an interest, of course, in the economic welfare of other nations and in the military strength of other nations, but only to the extent to which our assistance may reduce the probability of an attack on the freedom of our own people." Taft never had any illusions as to the nature of communism, which at the time of World War II he regarded as a greater ideological, although not military, threat than Germany to the United States. But as the "iron curtain" fell across Europe and the friction between the United States and the Soviet Union heated into hostility, he urged caution. Believing that the Soviets did not want war, or at least not for the foreseeable future, in 1947 he opposed the Marshall Plan, which he considered too costly and needlessly provocative, and proposed cutting the defense budget in half. That same year he gave grudging support to the Truman Doctrine to combat communism in Greece and Turkey but insisted that the policy should not be construed as a similar commitment to oppose communism elsewhere. Opposed to entangling alliances, he voted against the establishment of the North Atlantic Treaty Organization in 1948, as well as against the Truman administration's proposal to enact universal military training. (*See Document No. 14.*)

Taft, like a number of other critics of President Truman's foreign policy, was less cautious with regard to communism in Asia. When China fell to the Communists in 1949, he urged that the United States provide defense for the Nationalists on Formosa (Taiwan). But even here he believed that any American military support should come only through the Navy and Air Force. Taft generally deplored the committal of American ground forces anywhere, but particularly so on the Asian land mass. He did initially support the president's decision to deploy forces against the North Korean invasion of South Korea in 1950, but soon denounced Truman for not having sought congressional approval for his action and became a sharp critic of the conduct of the war.

Taft narrowly lost his party's presidential nomination to the hugely popular Dwight D. Eisenhower in 1952 and died the following year. His failure to become president and his subsequent demise dealt a powerful blow to those anticommunists who were not committed to the liberation of communist-dominated peoples on a global scale through the threat or actual use of military action. Serving as a global policeman, no matter how benevolent the intention, the United States could easily win enemies and lose friends, warned Taft. The Ohioan opposed both Henry Luce's concept of an "American Century" and the European-oriented foreign policy tenets of eastern internationalists, and warned that an arms race would create staggering budget deficits and inflation that in turn would threaten both national and individual well-being.

Though an important spokesperson for foreign policy, Taft was best known for his thoughtful and not always predictable conservative leadership on domestic issues. Although he opposed most New Deal measures as well as the Fair Deal measures of President Truman, he approved of federal government support for public education and public housing. As coauthor of the Taft-Hartley Act (1947), he sought to limit the powers of organized labor, but he also denounced President Truman's threat in 1946 to draft striking coal miners into the Army. Although an unswerving believer in capitalism, he was never an enthusiastic supporter of corporate interests, especially monopolistic ones. No more did he favor unnecessary or what he considered unconstitutional government intervention into the private sphere. A stalwart individualist, he instead trusted the small businessman and the average citizen to pursue their self-interest without the "corrupting idea that we can legislate prosperity, legislate equality, legislate opportunity."

Taft's preference for a limited government, one that deferred to private interests whenever possible, to local rule, and to fiscal restraint, dovetailed with that of traditional mainstream conservatives. Some conservatives, however, went beyond the senator in their distrust of government and in their adherence to the principles and practices of laissez-faire. These libertarians constituted a second major component of the postwar conservative revival.

Libertarianism. A major stimulus to libertarianism during the postwar era came from abroad, namely from the so-called Austrian School of economics whose critique of Marxism and other forms of socialism dated back to the latter nineteenth century. The rise of fascism and World War II resulted in the diaspora of numerous European intellectuals from their homelands. Among those émigrés who eventually settled in the United States was Ludwig von Mises. Resolutely opposed to any form of statism, this scholarly economist denounced government planning and intervention as wholly incompatible with capitalism. Less willing to define the matter in such black-and-white terms was his younger Austrian colleague, Friedrich A. Hayek, who initially migrated to Great Britain and became a British subject before he left for the United States, where he subsequently taught economics at the University of Chicago.

Concerned by the socialist beliefs of many British intellectuals, including its economists, Hayek in 1944 published a nontechnical, unusually well-written book on economics that was to achieve international reknown, *The Road to Serfdom*. Dedicated "to the socialists of all parties," the work argued that the totalitarianism of the 1920s and 1930s developed from earlier socialist trends, and that "the guiding principle that a policy of freedom for the individual is the only truly progressive policy remains as true today as it was in the nineteenth century." In his introduction to the paperback edition of the book published a dozen years later, Hayek, who by this time was in the United States, noted that the welfare state had largely replaced socialism and that some of its aims were both "laudable" and "practicable." Yet he cautioned against rushing to embrace them since some might not be compatible with individual liberty. Quoting the skeptical British philosopher David Hume, he reminded readers that "it is seldom that liberty of any kind is lost all at once." Once the state controls a certain portion of the nation's economic resources, its effects on the remaining portion balloon so that in an indirect manner its control is nearly total. At that point it is not difficult to discern the ruinous consequences for both individual freedom and democracy.

Others besides Hayek and Mises contributed to the growth of libertarianism during the 1940s and 1950s. Notable among them was Frank Chodorov, a friend and disciple of Albert Jay Nock since the 1930s. Like Nock, Chodorov, an opponent of American participation in World War II, was unabashedly antistatist and antimilitarist. During the fifties he published two fittingly titled libertarian books that won for him an increasing audience: *One Is a Crowd* (1952) and *The Income Tax: Root of All Evil* (1954). Especially concerned with the inroads socialism and New Deal liberalism had made in the nation's colleges and universities, he founded the Intercollegiate Society of Individualists (ISI) in 1953 to disseminate gratis libertarian and other pertinent publications. In later years ISI became the more broadly based Intercollegiate Studies Institute, which served to coordinate the efforts of various conservative groups and to make available conservative literature. To this day ISI also publishes *Campus*, the only national conservative newspaper written and edited by students.

The revival in 1950 of *The Freeman*, Albert Jay Nock's highly praised journal of the early 1920s, also contributed to the intellectual resurgence of libertarianism. Henry Hazlitt and John Chamberlain, along with Suzanne La Follette, Nock's esteemed associate with the original *Freeman*, opened the pages of their journal to various writers, including Hayek and Mises, who were well known for their antistatist stances. Meanwhile the Foundation for Economic Education (FEE), founded in 1946, opened its pocketbook to assorted anticollectivist individuals and became a prototype for later think-tanks. The defense of classical economics became a trademark also of the Department of Economics of the University of Chicago. Preceding the arrival of Hayek in 1952, Henry C. Simons and Frank H. Knight were the department's leading economic liberals immediately after the war. The two served as mentors to a young student who later would also teach economics at the university and win a Nobel Prize: Milton Friedman.

While economists and assorted polemicists did much to advance the cause of libertarianism and free market enterprise, none reached as wide an audience as did Alice Rosenbaum, who with Rose Wilder Lane and Isabel Patterson represented a formidable triad of antistatist women writers. Escaping from the Soviet Union after the Bolshevik Revolution and subsequent civil war, she migrated to Chicago and then to Hollywood, where she pursued a career as a screenwriter but largely failed because, she believed, she was not a communist at a time when the latter were prominent as screenwriters. Disappointed, the former Alice Rosenbaum, who by this time had changed her name to Ayn Rand, turned to fiction. Her second novel, *The Fountainhead* (1943) attained spectacular popularity, as did her later *Atlas Shrugged* (1957). Both works embodied the principles and spirit of her extreme libertarianism, which she called objectivism. She defined her philosophy with a simplicity that beguiled millions of mostly younger readers. Its essence was pure selfishness: "the concept of man as a heroic being, with his own happiness as the moral purpose of his life, with productive achievement as his noblest activity, and reason as his only absolute." Liberty and capitalism were inextricably linked, she stressed, and so as to reify the connection she sometimes gave public lectures while wearing a dress decorated with dollar signs. Her acolytes absorbed the message that capitalism served liberty and vice versa, and the most famous of them, Alan Greenspan, went on to a distinguished public career that has included service as chairman of the Federal Reserve. Rand and her ideas have also influenced the Libertarian party.

Many conservatives agreed with her passionate anticommunism, defense of private property, and exaltation of individual liberty. Rand, for her part, delineated her objectivism from conservatism and increasingly viewed conservatives with contempt. The point deserves further explanation in order to show how the uneasy relationship between libertarians and conservatives could degenerate into outright antipathy. Rand broke with William F. Buckley, Jr. and the *National Review* during the late 1950s, at least partly because Whittaker Chambers savagely reviewed *Atlas Shrugged* but also because her militant atheism was ultimately incompatible with the expressed theism of Buckley and several of his associates. She denounced conservatives for their inability to embrace capitalism wholeheartedly since it conflicted with their sense of altruism, which, in her opinion, was incompatible with capitalism. "If the 'conservatives' do not stand for capitalism," she exploded, "they stand for and are nothing." Conservatives who embraced tradition—as most did—also experienced her scorn. She wrote in "Conservatism: An Obituary" (1962):

> The plea to preserve "*tradition*" as such, can appeal only to those who have given up or to those who never intended to achieve anything in life. It is a plea that appeals to the worst elements in men and rejects the best: it appeals to fear, sloth, cowardice, conformity, self-doubt—and rejects creativeness, originality, courage, independence, self-reliance. It is an outrageous plea to address to human beings anywhere, but particularly here, in America . . .

New and Traditional Conservatism. The fulminations of Ayn Rand notwithstandung, tradition, along with anticommunism and libertarianism, played a major role in the postwar conservative revival. During the late 1940s and early 1950s the "new conservatism," to use the term earlier coined by the poet and historian Peter Viereck, emerged. This professor at Mount Holyoke College praised such traditional European conservatives as Disraeli and Churchill for their wisdom and high-minded principles. Indeed, it was the return to Christianity and ethical values that Viereck claimed for the new conservatives, as opposed to the existing conservatives, who, he lamented, seemed more inclined to libertarianism, laissez-faire economics, or political allegiance to the Republican party. As George H. Nash, a prominent historian of conservatism in the United States, has pointed out, the new conservatives were more concerned with what the individual should be like rather than what particular freedoms he should enjoy. Viereck believed that the individual should be ethical, rational, and willing to utilize that self-restraint which the New Humanists had exalted.

Viereck also believed that the individual should be an adamant foe of totalitarianism of all kinds. (George Sylvester Viereck, his father, was a Nazi sympathizer who was incarcerated during World War II; Peter served in the U.S. Army during the conflict as did his brother, who was killed.) During the early years of the Cold War Viereck called for the destruction of communism rather than its containment and "peaceful coexistence," but was revolted by McCarthyism and those conservatives who accepted the actions of the Wisconsin senator. Animadversions against McCarthy notwithstanding, he lashed out in *The Shame and Glory of the Intellectuals* (1953) against those who had unswervingly opposed Naziism and fascism but who had muted their criticism of communists. Liberals in particular, he protested, were not sufficiently anti-communist.

Paradoxically for a "conservative," Viereck with regard to domestic matters was a political liberal who accepted the premises of the welfare state inaugurated by President Roosevelt. The New Deal, he argued, had become an integral part of the nation's existence and therefore conservatives should commit themselves to preserving it. To uproot it, as many traditional or "old" conservatives were trying to do, was to act the radical. Although philosophically conservative, Viereck admired Adlai Stevenson and supported his two bids for the presidency in the fifties. Like other new conservatives in general, he was part of the "vital center," the liberal-conservative nexus of the arch-liberal Arthur M. Schlesinger, Jr.

Neither the New Deal, Adlai Stevenson, nor Arthur Schlesinger, Jr. won the applause of traditional conservatives like Russell Kirk. A sometime college professor—many of the major postwar conservative intellectuals were professors—Kirk exercised a profound influence on the resurgence of conservatism. Growing out of his doctoral dissertation,

The Conservative Mind (1953) was a detailed interpretation of conservatism since the late eighteenth century both here and in Great Britain. The book influenced traditional conservatives during the postwar era much as Friedrich A. Hayek's *The Road to Serfdom* galvanized libertarians and classical economic liberals, and Whittaker Chambers's *Witness* inspired anticommunist conservatives. Brought out by Henry Regnery, who subsequently became and remained for decades the leading publisher of conservative books, it positioned Edmund Burke as the chief figure in the making of the modern conservative intellectual tradition. Kirk, a convert to Roman Catholicism and admirer of both Albert Jay Nock and the New Humanists, offered defining characteristics of true conservatives: a belief in a transcendent moral order, prescription, prudence, and social continuity. He also claimed for them a belief in elitism and fear of the masses, and in equality before God and the law but not in other matters. His journal *Modern Age*, founded in 1957, helped to disseminate the ideas and values in which he so strongly believed.

Kirk's traditionalism extended to education. An adamant defender of the liberal arts and high academic standards, in 1953 he resigned his professorship from Michigan State College (later Michigan State University) in protest against what he deemed its misguided decisions to admit unqualified students and to include in its curriculum such decidedly nonliberal arts courses as canoeing and fishing. Until his death in 1994 he continued to excoriate the lowering of standards and the radicalization of the academy that resulted in the introduction of multicultural and "politically correct" courses. He aired his views in *Academic Freedom: An Essay in Definition* (1955), *The Intemperate Professor* (1965), and *Decadence and Renewal in the Higher Learning* (1978), as well as in numerous articles, essays, and reviews in his journal *The University Bookman* and in a regular column he wrote for *National Review*.

Southern conservatives also made important contributions to the postwar conservative revival. Some of the original Agrarians, especially Allen Tate and Donald Davidson, continued to uphold southern traditions and to lash out against the rampant commercialism and secularism that they believed were bringing an accelerated social malaise and spiritual decline to the United States and to the West at large. Joining them were younger scholars, notably Richard Weaver and M. E. Bradford.

Shedding his youthful socialism, the North Carolina-born Weaver began to make common cause with the Agrarians sometime during World War II. At that time he also began to teach English and rhetoric at the University of Chicago, where he remained until his death in 1963. While he wrote books on language and the South, his principal contribution to conservatism was probably *Ideas Have Consequences* (1948). A closely argued work, *Ideas* shows, as did the writings of Ralph Adams Cram, a marked respect for medievalism—its Christian religion and formal philosophy, its communitarian values, even its theory and practice of chivalry. Modern man, protested Weaver, had abandoned his spiritual and environmental values to worship "the gods of mass and speed." To use one of his favorite terms, modern man lacked piety. Weaver also extolled the hierarchical structure of medieval society as a cure or at least a palliative for the modern maladies wrought by mass democracy.

With the death of Weaver in the early 1960s, M. E. Bradford, a former student of Donald Davidson at Vanderbilt University, became, arguably, the preeminent luminary of the southern conservative tradition. His numerous books and articles, written during a thirty-year span of teaching English and politics at the conservative-oriented University of Dallas, were scholarly paeans to both antebellum and postbellum southern traditions and institutions. Willing to take strongly unpopular stands—he savagely impugned the character as well as the policies of Abraham Lincoln—his fearless but politically imprudent views in all likelihood during the 1980s cost him first the directorship of the National Endowment for the Humanities and then the position of National Archivist. Family and communal values, religion, environmentalism, and limited government were his special values. So, too, was inequality. For Bradford, equality, which had become the current opiate of the masses, was illusory since individuals started the race of life unequally; equality of opportunity was also chimerical since a struggle for it was bound to lead to augmented state powers that would induce leveling and mediocrity. Appalled by what he saw, he announced that he had become a reactionary, which was "a necessary term in the intellectual context we inhabit late in the twentieth century because merely to conserve is sometimes to perpetuate what is outrageous."

The sociologist Robert Nisbet was another influential traditional conservative to emerge during the postwar years. After receiving his doctorate from the University of California at Berkeley, he went on to enjoy a distinguished academic career elsewhere, mainly at the University of California at Riverside, where he taught for nearly two decades (1953–1972). In 1953, the same year as Russell Kirk's *The Conservative Mind*,

Nisbet published his first major work, *The Quest for Community*, in which he delineated a theme that was to appear persistently througout his later writings. Nisbet argued that the "single most decisive influence upon Western social organization has been the rise and development of the centralized territorial State." Like Henry Adams and Ralph Adams Cram, the sociologist greatly admired the Middle Ages, but less so for its culture and religion than for its institutions and functionalism. Avoiding the extremes of anarchy and tyranny, the medieval world balanced liberty and order, thus permitting the individual to pursue a wholesome self-development while partaking of and contributing to communal values. The modern world changed all that. Various political philosophers, notably Hobbes and Rousseau, laid the groundwork for the powerful state that the French Revolution brought into existence. Nationalism and democracy furthered statism in the nineteenth century; totalitarianism created the omnipotent, omnipresent state in the twentieth century. Anarchism theoretically promised liberty as a counterpoise to statism, but in actuality could provide no antidote since humans were gregarious by nature and desired some sort of bonding, which resulted in an all-encompassing state. Was there a middle ground?

For Nisbet, voluntary associations—churches, universities, unions, clubs and fraternal organizations, to name some—provided the middle ground that acted as a buffer between the extremes of an atomistic, isolating individualism and the encroaching dictates of state power. Nisbet was not the first commentator to note the importance of these associations, and he freely acknowledged his debt along these lines to Alexis de Tocqueville. Like the Frenchman, he hoped that this voluntarism, in addition to keeping statism at bay, would foster tradition and maintain hierarchical structures to militate against the excesses of a leveling mass democracy. Unlike their nineteenth-century British and Continental counterparts, twentieth-century American liberals increasingly had accepted the notion of the superiority of public power to achieve positive benefits. For the traditional conservative Robert Nisbet, however, freely chosen, intermediate bodies of associations pointed the way to the good society.

William F. Buckley, Jr. A public opinion poll that asked who was the most noteworthy American conservative of the past half century might well find one name atop the list: William F. Buckley, Jr. Certainly no one did more during the 1950s to engage the interest of the public at large in the conservative revival than did this gifted writer and media personality. Born in 1925 to a large and wealthy Catholic family—his father first made and lost a fortune in Mexican business and real estate before amassing a second fortune in Venezuelan oil—Buckley soon after World War II followed in the footsteps of his older brother, James, who later became a United States senator for New York, and enrolled in Yale University. The years at Yale reinforced the already strong conservative beliefs that had derived from family influences and from his acquaintance with his father's friend Albert Jay Nock. The contentious political science professor Willmoore Kendall served as an unofficial guru to Buckley during these years. A former left-winger who had become an unrelenting foe of communists and only somewhat less so of liberals, Kendall propounded a kind of populist majoritarianism that ran counter to the free expressions of a pluralist open society. Indeed, he seemed at times to have espoused the sort of "tyranny of the majority" that Tocqueville had warned against a century earlier. (Kendall so aggravated the liberal establishment at Yale that it bought out his tenure.) Other professors and whole departments bolstered Buckley's conservatism through their miseducation, which he described in his first book, *God and Man at Yale* (1951). Written with the acknowledged help of both Kendall and Frank Chodorov, this highly controversial work invoked radical means to achieve conservative ends. Yale, according to Buckley, had neglected its mission to foster both Christianity and capitalism. Clinging to the sacred shibboleth of academic freedom, moreover, it had permitted its faculty to express views that contested or even contravened overarching and widely accepted religious and economic values. Evidencing the influence of Kendall's majoritarianism, Buckley called upon the trustees of the university to exert their prerogatives and to turn Yale away from educating through the marketplace of contending ideas and into a bastion that conserved and transmitted orthodox ideals that were especially needed in the age of the Cold War.

Buckley's second book, *McCarthy and His Enemies*, proved hardly less controversial than his first one. Coauthored with his brother-in-law, L. Brent Bozell, and published in 1954, it was by no means a whitewashing of the Wisconsin senator's behavior. The latter's excesses disturbed other concerned conservatives, such as Whittaker Chambers, Robert Nisbet, Russell Kirk, and Peter Viereck. But the book, in essence, did defend McCarthyism itself. Communist penetration of the government had occurred, and the State Department in particular had failed to ferret out subversions. Thus, according to Buckley and Bozell, a strong response such as McCarthyism had been necessary to safeguard the ultimate security of the nation, even if it meant suppressing certain freedoms of expression.

Aside from *Human Events*, which had been founded in 1944 but which had only a limited circulation, no important conservative journal existed by the mid-fifties. That all changed in November 1955 with the initial appearance of what would become the most widely subscribed conservative journal for the rest of the century. As editor of *National Review*, William F. Buckley, Jr. brought together the disparate elements of postwar American conservatism. Libertarian contributors and associates included Frank Chodorov, Max Eastman, Frank Meyer, and John Chamberlain; Russell Kirk, Richard Weaver, and Donald Davidson were among those from the ranks of traditional conservatives. Most prominent among the early cohorts, however, were the fiercely anticommunist former radicals, who included, besides Eastman, Meyer, Chamberlain, and Weaver, James Burnham and William Schlamm. Buckley himself encompassed through his strong adherence to capitalism, Christianity, and anticommunism the assorted strands of conservatism that came together in the pages of *National Review* and his book, *Up from Liberalism* (1959). (*See Document No. 15.*) Not surprisingly, the merger of disparate conservatives frayed in time, gave way to new and shifting emphases, and witnessed defections, such as those of the libertarian Ayn Rand and the discomfited atheist Max Eastman. But meanwhile the journal thrived, its circulation surging from 30,000 in 1960 to 95,000 five years later.

Conservatives could look back at the end of the fifties with genuine satisfaction at the gains they had made since the end of World War II. While conservates as individuals were frequently at odds with one another and were held together—when they were held together at all—largely by their general allegiance to the ship-of-state *National Review*, conservatism itself could legitimately deny that it was only a series of "irritable mental gestures which seek to resemble ideas." Indeed, the most compelling achievement of conservatism in the postwar era was its increased intellectual vitality and respectability.

Unfortunately, renewed intellectual vigor and acceptability did not translate into political power. In fact, there seemed to have existed an inverse correlation between intellectual growth and political strength.

The elections of 1946 brought renewed hopes to conservatives as Republicans gained control of the 80th Congress, their first domination of both houses since 1928. Hopes for rolling back the New Deal were quickly dashed, however. New York Governor Thomas E. Dewey, a moderate, won the Republican party's presidential nomination over his conservative rivals. He then preceded to lose a seemingly unlosable election in one of the greatest political upsets in the nation's history to incumbent President Harry S. Truman, who had ridiculed the "do nothing" 80th Congress. The next presidential election proved even more galling to a number of conservatives. The Republican party's decision to nominate Eisenhower rather than Taft bitterly disappointed them; the subsequent eight years of the Eisenhower presidency did little to console them. Eisenhower considered himself a moderate, and while he verbally opposed statism, he left the heritage of both the New and Fair Deals intact. Conservatives of various stripes attacked him for failing to cut taxes and government spending at home, for the lack of a coherent policy based on conservative principles, and for the failure to do more against communism abroad. It was symptomatic of the conservatives' disappointment with Eisenhower that the *National Review* endorsed him tepidly as the lesser of two evils, the greater evil being the deeply liberal Adlai Stevenson, in the 1956 election. Nor did the journal endorse a presidential candidate in 1960. Conservatives would have to wait for a genuinely conservative aspirant to appear. That wait would not be long.

CHAPTER 8

CONSERVATISM IN AN AGE OF TURMOIL

Few decades if any in American life have presented as much turmoil as did the 1960s, which in retrospect appears to have been a watershed in the nation's history. The Vietnam War, the struggle for civil rights, rioting in cities and on college campuses, the adversarial counterculture, and the assassination of three major leaders badly divided the American people and called into question long-held values and beliefs. As radicalism moved from the coffee houses to the streets, many invoked almost unto triteness the lament of William Butler Yeats that the center could not hold together. "Coming Apart," the title of historian William L. O'Neill's detailed study of the decade, tersely but aptly caught the sense of the times. Like others, conservatives experienced the confusion with grave concern and with varying responses. As also with others, their world would never be the same even after the flood of events crested and began to subside.

The sixties opened on at least one positive note for conservatism with the founding of the Young Americans For Freedom (YAF). The infusion of young people into its ranks added new ideas and vigor to the conservative movement and gave the lie to the widespread popular stereotype of the conservative as an aged curmudgeon. Angered by Richard Nixon's capitulation to New York Governor Nelson Rockefeller's demand to include a liberal civil rights plank in the Republican party's platform, a small number of young conservatives met in September 1960 at the home of their intellectual hero and mentor, William F. Buckley, Jr., in Sharon, Connecticut, to reaffirm their convictions and to devise strategey. The "Sharon Statement" underscored their commitment to individualism, free enterprise, and unswerving anticommunism, and sowed the seeds for further political action. (*See Document No. 16.*)

The Goldwater Crusade. It did not take long for YAF to find a political hero to complement its intellectual idol in the person of the junior Republican senator from Arizona, Barry Goldwater. A descendant of nineteenth-century Jewish immigrants, Goldwater, who was reared an Episcopalian, first entered politics as a Phoenix city councilman in 1949. Two years later he won a seat for the United States Senate. A confirmed capitalist with a pronounced anti-union bias (although he treated workers in his family's department store with benevolent paternalism), he criticized President Eisenhower for not balancing the budget, lowering taxes, or taking stronger measures to win the Cold War. He also opposed Eisenhower's support for federal aid to education, but, it should be noted, he gladly supported federal largesse for the Central Arizona Project, a large-scale irrigation undertaking that his state needed. An outspoken critic of liberalism, Goldwater reached the hearts and minds of YAF and numerous conservatives with the publication in 1960 of *The Conscience of a Conservative*, ghostwritten for him by L. Brent Bozell. Patrick (Pat) Buchanan, the noted contemporary journalist, television host, and sometime presidential candidate who then belonged to YAF, called the book "our testament." He added: "For those of us wandering in the arid desert of Eisenhower Republicanism, it hit like a rifle shot." *Conscience*, with its sales ultimately in the millions, significantly boosted Goldwater's presidential aspirations for 1964, although he privately acknowledged that he had lost much of his desire to run after the assassination of President Kennedy.

Conservatives may have found a true believer in the senator, but the beliefs were not acceptable to the majority of the electorate, especially since the outspoken Goldwater rarely trimmed his verbal sails. Nelson Rockefeller most likely would have won his party's nomination had the birth of a child to his second wife not rekindled voter resentment of his earlier messy divorce and cost him the California primary. After Rockefeller's decline, moderate Republicans, fearful that Goldwater's immoderate views boded ill for the election, turned to first one candidate then another in a desperate but unsuccessful effort to stop the Goldwater bandwagon. Having won the party's nomination, Goldwater refused to hold out the olive branch to moderates. "I would remind you," he informed them, "that extremism in the defense of liberty is no vice. And let me remind you also that moderation in the pursuit of justice is no virtue."

The Goldwater campaign to win the presidency was a disaster. Although he toned down his rhetoric, his position on several issues alienated moderate independent voters as well as those from his own party. Criticizing the legacy of big government bequeathed by the New Deal, he impiously raised the possibility of privatizing two sacred cows, the Tennessee Valley Authority (TVA) and Social Security. (He never proposed ending Social Security, as critics charged, but suggested that participation in it might be optional.) He did soften his oppositional stance on the enforcement of civil rights, but too much damage had already occurred: Goldwater had voted against the Civil Rights Act of 1964. (*See Document No. 17.*) Remarked the Reverend Martin Luther King, Jr.: "We see dangerous signs of Hitlerism in the Goldwater campaign." (Goldwater personally believed in the integration of public schools but believed that the decision for integration or segregation should devolve upon individual states. Furthermore, he had supported the Civil Rights Acts of 1957 and 1960.) It was his suggestion for dealing with the increasingly explosive situation in Vietnam that probably most worried voters and allowed opponents to portray him as a dangerously reckless, possibly unstable, and certainly unsuitable potential chief executive. The use of tactical nuclear weapons to defoliate trees and thereby deprive the enemy of refuge would save South Vietnam from communism, he suggested. Maybe so. But the suggestion helped to send Goldwater to one of the worst defeats in presidential election history, one in which only his native Arizona and five states from the Deep South gave him their electoral votes. Elected along with President Lyndon B. Johnson, moreover, were commanding Democratic majorities in both houses of Congress. To the consternation of conservatives, this permitted Johnson to push through his Great Society programs, with their promise of welfarism and increased government bureaucracy, huge budget deficits, and higher taxation.

The Goldwater debacle produced more than the strewn flotsam and jetsam of crushing defeat. Viewed in perspective, the senator's candidacy allowed conservatives to play a much more significant role in the Republican party, culminating in the election of Ronald Reagan as president in 1980. His candidacy also further reshaped the party's constituency in dramatic fashion by converting it from a party that enjoyed biracial support to one whose supporters were overwhelmingly white. The transformation did not begin with Goldwater but with the Depression politics of the 1930s, when for the first time since Reconstruction a majority of African American voters cast their ballots for a Democratic presidential nominee. Relatedly, white southern Democrats joined with Republicans in Congress to form a conservative coalition that blocked the forward motion of the New Deal after 1938 and dominated Congress for the next twenty years. Eisenhower shattered the myth of the "Solid South" by winning several southern states in both of his election bids, as did Richard M. Nixon in 1960. Nixon nonetheless polled nearly one-third of the black vote; Goldwater four years later won a mere six percent of that vote. The latter's stance on civil rights doubtlessly repelled large numbers of black voters while simultaneously attracting large numbers of white voters, especially from the South. It was uncertain at the time whether this striking alteration in the constituency of the Republican party was a one-time occurrence or whether it represented something more permanent. In hindsight it is clear that the latter has become the case, and that the white South has become a bastion of Republican strength.

Thanks largely to growing dissatisfaction with the quagmire in Vietnam, Richard M. Nixon was able win the 1968 presidential election despite garnering only forty-three percent of the popular vote. He was victorious in all southern states except for the five from the Deep South, which went for third-party candidate Governor George Wallace of Alabama, and Texas, which gave its votes to the liberal Democratic candidate, Vice President Hubert H. Humphrey. Nixon also won the electoral votes of every western state with the exception of Washington. This newly found Republican strength as well as the populist strength of the American Independent Party candidate George Wallace, whose popularity extended northward beyond the Mason-Dixon line, suggested a fresh strategy to Kevin Phillips, an active young conservative. Published the year after Nixon's election, Phillips's *The Emerging Republican Majority* called upon the GOP and conservatives to fashion a Sunbelt strategy to woo voters in the South and West by focusing on their discontent with the welfare liberalism of the federal government. He also suggested that the party try to win over Catholic ethnics in the northeastern cities. Racial tensions, he declared, had created a rift within the ranks of Democrats. Many who had supported the liberalism of the New Deal with its philosophical bent of taxing the few for the benefit of the many now resented the liberalism of the Great Society with its reverse policy of taxing the many for the advantage of the few. After three decades the Republican party continues successfully to employ Phillips's Sunbelt strategy. (Less successful have been those attempts to lure northeastern ethnics who have remained in large cities rather than taking flight to the suburbs.)

By decade's end a name had been given to the rank-and-file conservative voters Phillips and others were describing and pursuing during the 1960s: the "silent majority." More akin to the "forgotten man" of William Graham Sumner than of Franklin D. Roosevelt, the so-called silent majority held traditional middle-class values and beliefs that ran counter to both the radicalism and much of the liberalism of the sixties. Strongly patriotic, they supported the military effort in Vietnam while questioning why more was not done to achieve victory. They strongly opposed the eruptions of violence that marred the struggle for civil rights. They generally if less than wholeheartedly approved of the non-violence strategy of the Reverend Martin Luther King, Jr., but deplored the violent rhetoric and sometimes violent activities of more radical black militant individuals and groups like the Black Panthers. No more did they countenance the seemingly endless demonstrations by large numbers of students and their sympathetic professors against the war and for civil rights that disrupted the nation's college campuses. This rebellion against collegiate authority and authority in general began with the Free Speech movement at Berkeley in 1964 and served as the model for subsequent disruptions, which escalated, *pari passu* (side by side), with the fighting in Vietnam. William F. Buckley's quip in 1967 that he would rather be governed by the first 2,000 names in the Boston telephone directory than by the faculty of Harvard seemed appropriate to many in light of what was happening in and to higher education. Middle America searched for answers as to what had caused so many of their economically advantaged and cossetted sons and daughters to reject their values and to turn to these collegiate disruptions and to the counterculture of drugs, hippiedom, rock music played at eardrum-splitting decibels, and promiscuous sexuality that seemed as overt as it was widepread. Not all college students (or their professors) were radicals by any means. In 1970 the membership of YAF stood at roughly 70,000. Still, it was the much numerically smaller radical Students for a Democratic Society (SDS) and the still smaller but more violent Weathermen who, abetted by media coverage, reified the typical student in the public mind.

The Warren Court. The Warren Court was no part of the counterculture, but its judicial pronouncements were similarly upsetting to conservative intellectuals and members of the silent majority alike. Not known as a liberal Republican in California politics before his appointment as Chief Justice by President Eisenhower—an appointment the latter later bitterly rued—Earl Warren quickly became persona non grata to conservatives. Initially some resented his marshaling of the other justices of the Supreme Court to render a unanimous decision in

Brown v. *Board of Education of Topeka*, the landmark 1954 desegregation case. They further resented him and other justices for the decisions that safeguarded the individual rights of communists. Warren wrote the majority opinion in *Pennsylvania* v. *Nelson* (1956), which ruled that only federal laws could make it a criminal offense to advocate the overthrow of the federal government. The following year the Court overturned the conviction of fourteen communists under the Smith Act in *Yates* v. *United States*.

Upon the retirement of Justice Felix Frankfurter in 1962 and the subsequent appointment of Arthur Goldberg, liberals enjoyed a majority on the Warren Court. They then proceeded in the years before the Chief Justice's retirement in 1968 to render a number of decisions that further galled conservatives, who deplored the Court's lack of judicial restraint. Judicial activism, conservatives argued, was against the original intent of the framers of the Constitution. Further, the results of this activism, particular coming on the part of unelected officials, went against the grain of public opinion. (This latter argument represented a reversal of early conservative beliefs that the Court could and should protect against majoritarian democracy; it also underscores the changing priorities of conservatism over time.) Those opposed to Vietnam War dissenters were displeased by *Bond* v. *Floyd* (1966), which ruled that the Georgia House of Representatives could not refuse to seat a duly elected representative who had spoken respectfully of those who opposed being drafted for the war. Many conservatives with strong family and religious values took offense when the Court in *Jacobellis* v. *Ohio* (1963) ruled that sexually explicit material could be published and distributed. Some, particularly Roman Catholics, were chagrined by the Court's decision in *Griswold* v. *Connecticut* (1965) to overturn a nineteenth-century state law that forbade the use of contraceptives and made the offering of advice on birth control a criminal offense. Even more controversial was *Engel* v. *Vitale* (1962), which ruled that prayers in public school were unconstitutional. This decision infuriated conservatives as no other decision by the Warren Court did during the 1960s, and attempts to reverse the ruling persist to this day. Given the widespread rioting and looting throughout the nation's cities and the precipitous decline in respect for traditional authority, law and order ranked high on the list of priorities for the silent majority of middle America. Once again the Warren Court disappointed them. *Mapp* v. *Ohio* (1961) narrowed the permissability of evidence garnered in searches; *Gideon* v. *Wainwright*

(1963) ruled that a defendant had the right to legal counsel even if the state had to provide one. More controversial was the *Miranda* v. *Arizona* decision in 1966 that ruled against self-incrimination and demanded that individuals be informed of their rights by the police. This so-called Miranda warning capped off the Warren Court's seeming concern for individual rights at the expense of public safety. Few conservatives mourned when the Chief Justice stepped down.

Libertarians and Traditionalists Battle. If few conservatives found anything to cheer in the decisions of the Warren Court, many more were pleased by the remarkable revival of classical economics in the nation's colleges and universities and also by its influence on public policy. Although a number of free-market economists at other institutions of higher learning joined the revolt against Keynesian hegemony, those at the University of Chicago continued preeminent. With the publication of *Capitalism and Freedom* in 1962, Milton Friedman rose to the forefront of the Chicago School. Friedman insisted in his book, which by the 1990s had sold more than 400,000 copies, that capitalism and freedom were inextricably linked and that both flourished when a minimalist state was present. He challenged the assumptions of those economists who believed that depressions, recessions, and assorted other economic problems were the result of the shortcomings of capitalism. Denying that capitalism was responsible for the Great Depression of the 1930s, he blamed the calamity on mismanagement by the government. He wrote in *A Monetary History of the United States, 1867–1960* (1963) that the Federal Reserve System had overseen the nation's monetary supply "so ineptly as to convert what otherwise would have been a moderate contraction into a major catastrophe. . . . "

Friedman warned against the destabilizing effects of government intervention in modern times as well, citing that its use or misuse of monetary policy to reduce unemployment in the 1970s eventuated in inflation and a stagnant economy, better known at the time as "stagflation." A market economy without favors for interest groups, abetted by a more or less fixed rate in the nation's money supply, he argued, would induce steady but noninflationary growth. Elected president of the American Economic Association in 1967 and awarded the Nobel Prize in Economics in 1976, Friedman was widely acclaimed by his peers, including some who strongly disagreed with him, not only for his scholarly writings but for the innovative ideas and concrete proposals that he either formulated or championed. At least two of these became reality during the presidency of Richard Nixon. The latter accepted Friedman's monetarist argument that the nation would best be served by abandoning the practice of having the government set the price of gold and instead allowing floating rates of exchange. Vigorously debated by the economic pundits, that innovation was too arcane for the general public. Friedman's argument that the draft should be abolished was not. The Nixon administration, beset by draft-burning, draft-dodging anti-Vietnam protesters, ultimately opted for a volunteer Army in place of conscription. Friedman's ideas did not please all conservatives. A number of them opposed the formation of a volunteer Army. Even more opposed as too radical his proposal for a negative income tax that would help the poor with the added advantage of dismembering the welfare state.

Other recommendations that Friedman has espoused remain lively topics of public discourse. His calls for a balanced budget amendment and for a flat income tax have received widespread support from conservatives but as yet no adoption. In light of the widespread violence and general decline in educational standards that have afflicted the nation's public schools, Friedman urged an alternative system of vouchers for parents who wished to send their children to religious or other private schools. Many conservatives have backed this proposal, but so far only a few communities such as Milwaukee are engaged in this experiment. Proponents of educational vouchers took heart in late 1998 when the Supreme Court refused to review a challenge to the Milwaukee program. Except for William F. Buckley and a small number of others, few traditional conservatives have supported what probably has been the distinguished economist's most radical proposal: the legalization of drugs.

The strong disagreement between traditional conservatives and libertarians over the question of the legalization of drugs was but one issue that divided the two groups during the late 1960s and early 1970s. They had forged an unofficial alliance during the postwar era as they made common cause against statism and the New Deal heritage that their common opponents, the liberals, were defending. Yet that alliance was a fragile one since, both philosophically and historically speaking, much set the groups apart. Given its inherent brittleness, it failed to withstand the the pressures of the Cold War.

Murray Rothbard, an economist and a major spokesperson for libertarianism until his death in 1995, figured importantly in the internecine struggle on the Right. An admirer of such past venerable antistatists as Sumner, Mencken, Nock, and Taft, he generallly accepted the oversize umbrella that William Buckley and *National Review* had held out to the diverse constituents of the Right, including the libertarians, in the fifties and early sixties. But a central tenet of Rothbard's libertarianism was his isolationism and refusal to countenance a worldwide campaign against communism, which was one of the chief concerns of Buckley and his journal. Not a pacifist, Rothbard opposed war because it promoted statism and deprived the individual of liberty and possibly life itself. As for communism, it would eventually collapse from its inherent economic weaknesses.

Vietnam and the turmoil of the sixties widened the differences between Rothbard and the libertarians on one side and Buckley and the more centrist conservatives on the other to gulflike proportions. Rothbard, who had broken with *National Review* shortly after it had opposed Soviet leader Nikita Krushchev's visit to the United States in 1959, vigorously opposed involvement in Vietnam as well as costly Great Society programs at home, both of which were part of the "welfare/warfare state." So, too, did some other prominent libertarians, including the former conservative Karl Hess, who had served as speechwriter for Barry Goldwater but who had deserted mainstream conservatism once he had decided that the commitment to laissez-faire economics by the business community was merely empty rhetoric. Hess, who traversed the political Right, now condemned the draft and compared the FBI to the Soviet secret police.

More striking was the dissension that seethed within YAF. During the organization's biannual meeting held in the summer of 1969, a determined minority denounced not only the draft but also William Buckley, heretofore the groups most respected ideologue and paladin. While insisting that they still belonged to the political Right and that they rejected Marxism, some of the these protesters issued a call for an alliance with SDS. An admirer of how SDS supposedly had been able to synthesize individual freedom and communal life, Karl Hess also advocated that the Old Right and New Left should join forces in refusing to pay taxes or to be drafted, and in aiding draft resisters. The former Goldwaterite reproved: "Vietnam should remind all conservatives that whenever you put your faith in big government for *any* reason, sooner or later you wind up as an apologist for mass murder." With their additional beliefs that such controversial issues as drugs, abortion, and alternative life styles were solely personal matters and not to be determined by law or social mores, many radical libertarians were bound to clash with the majority mainstream conservatives.

Fusionist conservatives like Frank Meyer tried to mend the rift by claiming that both traditionalists and libertarians met on the common ground of defending past and present freedoms. But by the early 1970s the rift had become irreparable. Two angry Columbia College students observed that libertarians had "finally accepted the fact that they had been abandoned by the liberals, used and misled by other radicals and sold out by the conservatives." Meanwhile more senior libertarians like Rothbard denounced Buckley and the *National Review* conservatives as apologists for the welfare state, citing not only their support for the war and armaments, but also for their acceptance of such large-scale federal projects as the space program and for the Nixon administration's restrictions on imports. Buckley rejoined by distinguishing between what he considered the sensible antistatist economics of such men as Ludwig von Mises, Friedrich A. Hayek, John Chamberlain, Henry Hazlitt, and Wilhelm Röpke and the extremism of libertarians like Rothbard, who had argued that even lighthouses should be privately owned and operated. "The American conservative believes that the state is as often as not an instrument of mischief as of good," he noted, but added that "one does not therefore argue against the existence of the state." Interestingly, *Happy Days Were Here Again*, a book of essays by Buckley that was published in 1993, bore the subtitle: *Reflections of a Libertarian Journalist*.

Despite the attacks of libertarians and the extreme Right, some of whom bitterly resented his condemnation of the fiercely anticommunist John Birch Society for its misguided zeal, Buckley remained the single most visible and articulate exponent of popular conservatism during the 1960s. As host of the television talk show *Firing Line* and through the pages of *National Review* and his syndicated column "On the Right," he reached millions of Americans. He also ran for mayor of New York City on the New York Conservative party ticket in 1965, winning thirteen percent of the vote in this stronghold of liberalism and engaging even those who did not vote for him with his thoughtful proposals, erudition and wit. (Asked what he would do if he won the race, he replied that he would demand a recount.) Moreover, by distancing himself from the John Birch Society and its founder, Robert Welch, Buckley had made conservatism more acceptable to many middle-of-the-roaders. By the end of the decade, in fact, conservatism was becoming increasingly welcome to a small but noteworthy group of dissident liberals, who collectively were to become known as neoconservatives, a term initially used in 1976 by the democratic socialist Michael Harrington to describe right-wing socialists but almost invariably used by others to describe liberals who had moved to the right.

The Rise of Neoconservatism. Often referred to as its "godfather," Irving Kristol as late as 1979 expressed doubts as to whether "there really is such a thing as neoconservatism." Lacking an official organization, meetings, or specific programs and conflicted with internal differences, it was not a "movement," he clarified, but an "impulse" or "persuasion." Further, such prominent so-called neoconservatives as Norman Podhoretz, Daniel Bell, Seymour Martin Lipset, Daniel Patrick Moynihan, Nathan Glazer, Samuel Huntington, and James Q. Wilson, to name several, were also loath to use the term; two others, Robert Nisbet and Edward Banfield, referred to themselves simply as "conservatives." Kristol whimsically added that he might be "the only living and self-confessed neoconservative, at large or in captivity." Among neoconservatives, moreover, he was the sole prominent Republican until the Reagan presidency. Its resistance to a facile definition or to a membership that resisted its nomenclature notwithstanding, neoconservatism by the end of the seventies had become a dynamic component of contemporary American conservatism.

As might be surmised, the roots of neoconservatism lay with the increasing discontent of certain liberals with the upheavals of the 1960s. As Kristol famously quipped, a neoconservative was a "liberal who has been mugged by reality." At some point during the sixties some liberals began to doubt the efficacy of various Great Society programs. While they were by no means opposed to all programs that helped to ameliorate poverty, they sensed that the programs were too costly and too ambitious to reform society and its institutions, and instead were inducing inflation, racial tensions, and assorted other problems. They also concluded that government entitlements by themselves could not solve the problems.

Assistant Secretary of Labor Daniel Patrick Moynihan, a former Harvard professor and future four-term senator from New York, in 1965 authored the Moynihan Report (officially called *The Negro Family: The Case for National Action*), in which he cited the breakdown of the family structure as an important component of the impoverishment of many blacks. Meant to aid the Johnson administration in its quest to fund antipoverty programs, the report elicited charges of white racism. Major urban race riots over the next few years further dismayed liberals. Similarly shocking were the widespread outbursts of anti-Semitism by blacks, especially since Jewish liberals historically had been in the vanguard of the struggle for civil rights. In New York City, for example, the Ocean Hill-Brownsville teachers' strike of 1967 seemed less a struggle between educators and the local community than one between Jews and blacks. When a memo that Moynihan wrote to President Nixon in 1970 in which he called for a period of "benign neglect" toward blacks was leaked to the press, race relations took yet another turn for the worse. Liberal dreams of civility and brotherhood seemed just that: dreams. Without a doubt, black anti-Semitism would help to account for the diaspora of disillusioned Jews from liberalism to neoconservatism.

Vietnam also played a pivotal role in the alienation of hitherto dedicated liberals. By and large liberals had stood as true-believing cold warriors in the post-World War II era. Convinced that communism presented a global menace, they accepted military preparedness and vigilance as the price of freedom. Most also accepted intervention in Vietnam as part of that steep price and continued, however uneasily, to support the military effort in hopes that a communist triumph could be averted.

One major initial dissenter from this scenario was the future neoconservative Norman Podhoretz, who in 1960 became the editor of *Commentary*, the single most influential liberal intellectual journal until the appearance of *The New York Review of Books* a few years later. At first Podhoretz moved the journal from its traditional anticommunist position to one that was sympathetic to the New Left and the counterculture. By the late 1960s, however, he gradually began dissociating from the excesses of the Left. With the crucial capture of the Democratic presidential nomination by Senator George McGovern in 1972 the breach between radicalized Democrats and a number of traditional liberal Democrats like Podhoretz, Moynihan, Jeane Kirkpatrick, Ben Wattenberg, and Podhoretz's wife, the writer and editor Midge Decter, widened. Opposed to McGovern's overt sympathy for antiwar protesters and for various demands of the counterculture, they formed the Democrats for a Committee for a Democratic Majority. Richard M. Nixon, a principal villain for liberals since the early Cold War years, had become preferable to the deeply liberal senator from South Dakota, who seemingly had become hostage to the New Left.

By the early 1970s neoconservatism may not have had a strictly defined program but it did possess certain recognizable principles and beliefs. For one, it was strongly anticommunist and nationalistic. A number of the future neoconservatives had begun on the Left as democratic socialists or Trotskyites before turning to Cold War liberalism. First as liberals and then as neoconservatives, they construed communism as a worldwide menace that must be contained and ultimately defeated. To achieve this they counseled that the United States, as the leader and most influential member of the free world, remain actively engaged in global politics. The precise strategy of anticommunist strategy differed among individual neoconservatives, some adopting a militantly hawkish stance, others less so. For some, moreover, anticommunism and foreign policy in general occupied a lower rung on their agenda than domestic concerns.

Related to the determined anticommunism of neoconservatives was their growing defense of capitalism. Irving Kristol paraphrased the British novelist E. M. Forster and gave "two cheers for capitalism." At various times a professor at New York University's School of Business Administration, a senior fellow at the American Enterprise Institute, and a regular contributor to *The Wall Stree Journal*, he has stoutly justified capitalism as necessary for a free society and for economic growth that underpins material well-being. Writing in 1976, he predicted that "in the end, all of the inequalities of bourgeois society must yield to the great dissolvent, money, which knows nothing of race or religion or ideology." Yet over the years he has not lauded capitalism uncritically. (*See Document No. 18.*) Rather, what he, as well as some other neoconservatives, has urged is the acceptance of the welfare state without the crushing effects of big government, that is, the maintenance of a market economy complete with the proverbial safety net to catch those who for diverse reasons need basic support. Once again differences arose within the group as to whether to emphasize the free market or the safety net, but most sought to strike a balance between the two. In defending capitalism, Kristol and others took pains to distance themselves from the libertarian conservatives and their quest for a pure free market system. In turn, libertarians denounced the welfarism and assorted compromises that the neoconservatives embraced.

In addition to its anticommunism, nationalism, and defense of capitalism, neoconservatism concerned itself with values and morals, or, more properly speaking, the attack on traditional values by the New Left and the counterculture. Although coming from the opposite ends of the political spectrum, the New Left and certain right-wing libertarians, including Milton Friedman, during the 1960s and the 1970s had adopted what Kristol termed nihilism in their laissez-faire approach to questions that had a strong moral content such as those affecting the family. He noted that "neoconservatives look upon the family and religion as indispensable pillars of a decent society." Thus, the emphasis on individual liberty and secularism was eroding the structure of bourgeois society and was a graver threat to liberal capitalism than was socialism itself. If government had to intervene to protect these values, so be it.

There was a distinct populist flavor to the neoconservative defense of both the values and interests of middle-class Americans. Neoconservatives disparaged what they considered the snobbish elitism of those who scorned such values and interests, which is to say, the liberal establishment. Yet they were themselves an elite group, consisting largely of journalists and professors who hoped to restore the good morals and good manners of a virtuous civic polity. The broad cultural concerns of neoconservatism could best be discerned in the editorials and articles of *The Public Interest*, the journal established by Kristol and Daniel Bell in 1965 and that did for the visiblility and popularity of neoconservatism what *National Review* achieved for the conservative movement in the 1950s. *Commentary*, *American Scholar*, *Encounter*, *Foreign Policy*, and *Atlantic Monthly*, among others, also expounded assorted neoconservative concerns during the 1970s.

This is not to say, of course, that only neoconservative journals and journalists made significant contributions at the time to the broader conservative movement. *National Review* remained a major force, as did *The American Spectator*, whose editor, R. Emmett Tyrrell, Jr., delivered his encomiums for captialism and his attacks on socialism and liberalism with gleeful Menckenian irreverence. Tyrrell possessed a strong strand of libertarianism like the Sage of Baltimore, whom he much admired, but unlike Mencken, he was not antidemocratic. Neither was George Will, who has referred to himself as a "Tory" conservative and who has been one of the most influential conservative journalists for more than twenty years. Wary of the affinity of neoconservatives for nineteenth-century liberalism, he praised Robert Nisbet and his preference for autonomous social groups. Yet unlike most traditional conservatives and more like the new conservatives of the 1950s, Will did not distrust an active goverment. When the private sector failed to satisfy public needs it was the duty of the government to fill the breach. This, for Will, represented "statecraft as soulcraft," which also is entrusted with safeguarding and balancing the people's social and cultural values. He noted that "we need a public philosophy that can rectify the current imbalance between the political order's meticulous concern for material well-being and its fastidious withdrawal from concern for the inner lives and moral character of citizens."

One such consuming cultural concern for neoconservatives as for both traditional conservatives and many nonconservatives was the turmoil and assorted academic policies that confronted national higher education. Student disruption of the normal educational process vexed them most, but the policy of affirmative action ran a close second. While lauding efforts to permit greater numbers of suitable minority students to colleges and universities, they balked at federal government mandated affirmative action policies to achieve this goal. For critics of affirmative action—and they were largely but not entirely conservatives— this was a misguided policy that established a system of quotas that allowed lesser qualified minority students to enter colleges and universities to the exclusion of more qualified non-minority students. This "affirmative discrimination," to use the title of Nathan Glazer's polemical book, had the further adverse effect of casting into doubt the genuine ability of minority students who could have competed without the imposition of artificial advantage, a point convincingly argued by the conservative African American scholar and journalist Thomas Sowell. During the 1970s James Bakke, a young Californian who had been denied admission to medical school at the University of California at Davis, claimed that the University had accepted lesser qualified black students and that he had been the victim of reverse discrimination. The Supreme Court in *Regents of the University of California* v. *Bakke* (1978) upheld his plea, outlawed any quota system per se, but permitted continued use of race and gender as factors to be considered in admissions. This case, decided by a 5–4 vote, failed to resolve the question of affirmative action, which, along with multiculturalism, continued to bestir conservatives during the 1980s and the 1990s.

Certain other positions advanced by individual neoconservatives during this time encountered hostile receptions ranging from frostiness to rage. Edward C. Banfield, dissenting from the accepted views of the consensus of liberal urban planners, argued in *The Heavenly City* (1970) that many well-meaning programs, such as school busing and assorted programs for the urban poor, caused more problems than they solved. Attacked for his views, he gave up an endowed chair at the University of Pennsylvania to return to Harvard. The criminologist James Q. Wilson, according to some, may have failed to have become Dean of Arts and Sciences at Harvard because of certain views enunciated in *Thinking about Crime* (1975) and elsewhere. Prominent among these was a dispassionate defense of the death penalty that ruffled the feathers of liberal academics. The future Nobel Prize-winning Edward O. Wilson, the father of sociobiology who stressed the importance of the genetic component of human behavior, was verbally attacked as a "racist" and "Nazi" and physically assaulted. Even more verbal abuse came to Richard Herrnstein, Arthur Jensen, and the Nobel Prize winner and inventor of the semiconductor, William Shockley, for their much publicized and controversial views on the subject of intelligence.

However contentious their views, neoconservatives had become a powerful intellectual force to be reckoned with by the end of the 1970s. From the pages of their widely respected journals and from the professorial pulpits of prestigious universities, they helped to shape discourse on public issues and to offer new insights into the nature of American conservatism. One astute critic of neoconservatism estimated that as early as the beginning of the decade perhaps a quarter of the nation's most eminent intellectuals could be classified as neoconservatives. Not that all traditional conservatives accepted their views. While most applauded their appeal for a regeneration of ethics and morals and their strong opposition to communism (though not always their strategy), some felt uncomfortable with the emphasis on capitalism that some neoconservatives placed. As they and assorted nonconservative critics pointed out, capitalism, whatever other virtues it possessed, historically had served as a solvent and not a conserver of institutions, traditions and customs. From a different angle of vision, some traditional conservatives deplored the accommodation neoconservatives had made with the welfare state. Right-wing libertarians also lashed out against what they considered the betrayal of marketplace economics and by the activist anticommunist and nationalistic foreign policy advocated by neoconservatists.

As much if not more than ever, it was evident that conservatism was a tradition of diverse strands. But thanks to the growth of neoconservatism—as a persuasion, impulse, or, *pace* Irving Kristol, movement—conservatism, broadly speaking, had more than regained the vigor it had lost at the time of the Goldwater debacle in 1964. Had they been able to read into the future, conservatives would have discerned that even greater vitality lay just ahead.

CHAPTER 9

CONSERVATISM ASCENDANT:
THE REAGAN YEARS AND AFTER

The popular adage that movie actors and actresses constitute America's royalty may not be true, but one of them did become the president of the United States, and a conservative one at that. Gradually abandoning the New Deal liberalism that had characterized his career in Hollywood, Ronald Reagan moved to the right, initially as a corporate spokesman and then as a two-term governor of California. An extremely effective speaker—he was called the "Great Communicator" during his presidency—he won acclaim from conservatives for a nationally televised speech on behalf of Barry Goldwater's presidential bid in 1964. Impressed further by his gubernatiorial policies, conservatives supported his presidential aspirations in 1968, 1972, and 1976. Finally nominated by the Republican party in 1980, Reagan swept to victory over incumbent Jimmy Carter, who labored under the onus of the nation's high inflation and unemployment rates and its pain over the holding of more than fifty American hostages by Iran.

Reaganomics. Arguably the first conservative president since Calvin Coolidge, Ronald Reagan pledged to restore economic vitality by lowering taxes and by diminishinging the regulatory role of the federal government. Supply-side economics informed his fiscal policies. The so-called Laffer Curve, named after economist Arthur Laffer by the neoconservative Jude Wanniski of *The Wall Street Journal* during the 1970s, promised to produce sufficient government funding by lowering taxes. According to this theory, lower taxes would induce greater private investment, which would in turn generate tax revenues. Budget Director David Stockman, who subsequently recanted his faith in supply-side economics, helped to fashion the Economic Recovery Tax Act of 1981, which substantially lowered income and business taxes. All classes, but especially the upper class, benefited from these cuts. At the same time, Congress heeded the president's call to reduce government spending and enacted significant cuts for the regulation of business, environmental programs, and for various social welfare programs. A few years later Charles Murray lent credence to these cuts in his controversial study, *Losing Ground: American Social Policy 1950–1980* (1984), in which he argued that social programs enacted since World War II had actually worsened the condition of people they were supposed to assist. This book, along with George Gilder's *Wealth and Poverty* (1981) and Michael Novak's *The Spirit of Democratic Capitalism* (1982), were central to the intellectual defense of supply-side economics during the 1980s.

By late 1981 a severe two-year recession set in, thanks in large part to an increase in interest rates by the Federal Reserve to combat inflation. Refusing to resort to Keynesian deficit spending to stimulate the economy, Reagan held firm to his beliefs, and by the time the recession ended, inflation had dropped substantially, unemployment had eased, and interest rates, though still very high, had abated considerably. Whether this was more the result of the president's supply-side policies or other factors, most notably the global reduction in oil prices and the administration's decision to augment defense spending, is unclear. But what is certain is that the remainder of the Reagan presidency administration were years of general if uneven prosperity marked by considerable economic growth and manageable rates of inflation and unemployment.

A major component of so-called Reaganomics was the effort to diminish the government regulation of private enterprise. This was particularly evident with regard to environmental matters. To the consternation of environmentalists, the Environmental Protection Agency (EPA) diluted the guidelines for removing toxic wastes and diminishing pollution, while the Department of the Interior attempted to permit private enterprise the use of certain public lands. Denying that it was hostile to environmentalism, the administration argued that overregulation had been counterproductive and that businesses could police themselves. Budgets were trimmed for various other federal agencies as well. This was in line with the president's Inaugural Address contention that "government is not the solution to our problem: government is the problem." Reaganomics, it was argued, was a success, having served simultaneously to diminish big government (although the number of federal employees actually increased by one percent during the Reagan presidency) and its spending in certain areas. But if Reaganomics was a success, it was a qualified one. Foreign trade deficits grew dramatically, as did annual budget deficits. Despite his professed belief in fiscal conservatism, the president never submitted a balanced budget to Congress, and by the end of his presidency the national debt had trebled to an astronomical sum of nearly $3 trillion, although the debt as a share of the gross domestic product (GDP) did show a marked decrease during his second administration. Tax cuts accounted for some of the increase in the nation's indebtedness, but even more came from huge increases in defense spending.

The Supreme Court Turns Right. While numerous critics both then and now have questioned the overall effects of Reaganomics, none have doubted that Reagan succeeded in refashioning the federal judiciary. A two-term president, he was able to appoint nearly half of the nation's federal district and appeals judges. Most of these appointments were of high quality, as were his appointments to the Supreme Court. The latter, however, proved more controversial.

Conservatives had denounced the judicial activism of the Warren Court that had resulted in sanctioning liberal values, had been disappointed by the basically middle-of-the-road decisions handed down by the Court under Earl Warren's successor, Warren E. Burger, and had been appalled by the legalization of abortion in *Roe* v. *Wade* (1973). Determined to retint the Court's philosophical complexion from moderate to conservative, Reagan proceeded to make a series of unmistakably conservative appointments. The first one, in 1981, was that of Sandra Day O'Connor, who became the Court's first female justice and who, despite her liberal views on abortion, had solid conservative credentials. Five years later he named Justice William Rehnquist to succeed retiring Chief Justice Burger. A conservative Arizona Republican who had been active as a Goldwaterite, Rehnquist first came to the Court in 1971 and made his mark as a conservative and as a dissenter. (As an associate justice he held the record for the most dissents in Court history.) Antonin Scalia succeeded to Rehnquist's chair, thereby becoming the Court's first Italian-American justice. As a professor of law and as a judge sitting on the D.C. Circuit Court of Appeals, Scalia was noted for both his formidable intellect and deep-seated conservative convictions. The nomination of Robert Bork, who had served as United States Solicitor General and was currently a circuit court judge, provided both the president and conservatives with a stunning defeat in 1987. An outspoken foe of judicial activism and proponent of an "original intent" reading of the Constitution (*See Document No. 19.*), Bork was pictured by his foes during Senate hearings as inimicable to women and minorities. The African

American conservative Thomas Sowell defended Bork from these accusations, as did other female and minority conservatives, but to no avail. Having lost his fight for Bork, the president appointed and won confirmation for a less controversial conservative, Anthony M. Kennedy, a circuit judge, in his stead.

The bare majority that the conservatives (Rehnquist, O'Connor, Scalia, Kennedy, and Byron R. White, who had been sitting since 1962) held on the Court increased during the presidency of Reagan's Republican successor, George Bush, with the addition of David Souter in 1991 and Clarence Thomas in 1992. The former was a noncontroversial appointment, who has proven considerably less conservative than anticipated; the latter was highly contentious and has not disappointed conservatives. At age forty-three the youngest appointee to the Court, Thomas was a federal appeals court judge of limited experience whose views on abortion, school prayer, and the death penalty pleased conservatives. Accused during his confirmation hearings of sexual harassment by a former subordinate when he chaired the Equal Employment Opportunity Commission (EEOC), Thomas denied the charges and lashed out at his Senate critics for alleged racism. Despite the huge controversy, he won confirmation.

As a result of the appointments by both Reagan and Bush, the Supreme Court moved to the right during the 1980s and the 1990s, although not as much as some conseratives would have preferred. While not making abortion illegal, the Court has narrowed its parameters. It has also upheld the death penalty, broadened the powers of the police, contained the rights of defendants, and made strong inroads into affirmative action programs, beginning with *City of Richmond* v. *J. A. Croson Company* (1989) in which it struck down a fixed percentage of contracts for minorities. Recently it also reasserted the doctrine of states' rights in *Alden et al.* v. *Maine* (1999), ruling that "sovereign immunity" protected states from private lawsuits brought to enforce federal laws that regulated the workplace (overtime pay, in this instance). Handed down the same day, the *College Savings Bank* v. *Florida Prepaid Postsecondary Education Expense Board* and *Florida Prepaid Post-secondary Education Expense Board* v. *College Savings Bank* decisions similarly protected the states against patent and copyright infringement suits on the same grounds. This reassertion of states' rights represents a decided and possibly decisive reversal of the supremacy of federal regulatory powers in matters ranging widely from environmentalism to civil rights.

Not all conservatives have wished to diminish the regulatory powers of the federal government, however. Some have vigorously urged Washington to apply such powers to specific and highly controversial issues involving social and moral concerns. From the 1970s onward many of these conservatives were part of the New Right and/or the Religious Right.

The New Right and the Religious Right. Disappointed Republicans formed the core of what the media called the "New Right," much as dissident Democrats were more or less simultaneously giving substance to neoconservatism. The New Right generally shared common views with traditional conservatives on economic matters and foreign policy. But as George H. Nash has pointed out, "whereas the traditionalist conservatives of the 1940s and 1950s were academics in revolt *against* rootless, mass society, the New Right is a revolt *by* the 'masses' against powerful liberal elites." Unlike traditional conservatives and neoconservatives alike, the New Right was a populist revolt of average citizens against what they considered the social and moral decline of the nation. More specifically, they objected to forced school busing, the denial of prayer in public schools, inferior education, pornography, abortion, crime, affirmative action, radical feminism and gay rights. The failure of Republican presidents Nixon and Ford and Republican congressional leaders to redress their grievances led to popular insurrection. Thanks to skillful organizational talents, particularly those of former YAF member Richard Viguerie, the New Right blossomed during the 1970s from a coterie of grassroot efforts and single-issue groups into a more complete national phenomenon.

Like reformers of all persuasions, the New Rightists were more than likely to espouse more than one cause. But many stressed a particular cause above others. Antischool-busing activists supported like-minded political candidates; right-to-lifers pushed for a constitutional amendment prohibiting abortion; opponents of gay-rights protective legislation defeated referenda in four states. The most dramatic victory of the New Right coalition, however, came with the defeat of the Equal Rights Amendment (ERA). Passed by Congress in 1972 and sent to the states, the ERA seemed certain of ratification. By 1974 thirty-three of the thirty-eight states needed to ratify the amendment had done so. Phyllis Schlafly, who earlier had helped to energize the presidential candidacy of Barry Goldwater through her book, *A Choice, Not an Echo* (1963), believed that the amendment would undermine the family by destroying the traditional role of women in the family. Additionally, older and divorced women would suffer, and the amendment would have a deleterious effect on the rights of husbands, police work, the military, and education. Urging women to look at their strengths rather than at the inequalities they have experienced, she stressed that "the Positive Woman looks upon her femaleness and her fertility as part of her purpose, her potential, and her power. She rejoices that she has a capability for creativity that men can never have." Along with other conservatives, she led an unexpectedly successful STOP-ERA movement. Congress allowed an extension of the period for passage from 1978 to 1982, but the amendment still fell two states short of ratification. Meanwhile Schlafly and her organization, the Eagle Forum, have continued to the present to play an active role in espousing profamily causes.

Pro-family causes also highlighted the agenda of the Religious Right, whose membership overlapped with the New Right. Composed largely of Protestant fundamentalists and evangelicals, but with socially conservative Catholics, Jews, and Mormons as well, the Religious Right did not become a noteworthy force in national politics until the late 1970s. At that point various ministers and secular figures, concerned that American society was becoming a moral cesspool, came together to form the Moral Majority. Led by the Reverend Jerry Falwell, a Baptist minister with a congregation in Lynchburg, Virginia, the Moral Majority espoused basically the same moral and social causes as the New Right. (*See Document No. 20.*) Falwell and the Reverend Pat Robertson proved to be especially adept televangelists as they reached out to a large audience that frequently viewed religious programming. The Religious Right strongly supported the 1980 presidential candidacy of Ronald Reagan, who appeared as a champion of moral and cultural conservatism despite the fact that he would become the nation's first divorced chief executive. While Reagan consistently lauded the goals of the Religious Right during both his terms in office, his failure to work more assiduously to outlaw abortion and to bring back prayers to the public school proved disappointing. The failure to achieve such concrete goals, along with the financial malfeasance of one prominent televangelist and a sexual scandal involving another, had weakened the image and the political effectiveness of the Religious Right by the end of the 1980s.

Cultural concerns, particularly as they pertained to higher education and to the arts, also highlighted the agenda of conservatives during the

Reagan presidency and after. Bitterly contested, they have been fittingly termed "the culture wars."

The Culture Wars. The curricula and purposes of higher education, as well as who should or should not attend colleges and universities, historically have divided partisans but never more than in the past thirty years or so. The politicization of these already controversial and substantial matters has intensified the division many times over. At the heart of the battle looms the perception of Western civilization. Some educators, especially but not solely those who were radicalized by the events of the 1960s, see the West as the oppressor of non-Westerners. Frequently written and/or taught from a Marxist or otherwise radical perspective, this scenario casts white males—predominantly the capitalist ones in the modern centuries—as the exploiters of women and racial minorities. Conservatives read Western history more benignly. Without denying the crimes and misdeeds of the West, they point to its positive accomplishments: the expansion of diverse liberties and the rule of law over time; the improvement of material standards of living for countless humans; the cultural achievements that have illuminated human existence.

Since the 1970s college curricula have changed dramatically, particularly as they encompass nontraditional courses on race and gender. By the early 1990s more than 300 programs in African American studies and more than 500 such programs in women's studies existed. Although few thoughtful educators of any political persuasion would deny that certain liberal arts courses such as history and literature had not paid sufficient attention to the role of women and minorities, many felt that the pendulum had reversed too far the other way. Women and minorities, they pointed out, could receive greater inclusion in traditional courses rather than in the narrower programs of gender and race, which frequently seemed more interested in generating "political correctness" and self-esteem rather than pursuing as much dispassionate analysis as possible. Sharing the concerns of conservatives, Arthur M. Schlesinger, Jr. warned that multiculturalism raises legitimate fears for the social fragmentation of society. By threatening the delicate balance between political unity and ethnic diversity, it invites "the disuniting of America." The neoconservative scholar Diane Ravitch further noted that multiculturalism, while pluralistic by definition, sometimes has become, especially among some Afrocentrists, a particularistic multiculturism that distorts historical facts and preaches and practices precisely what it so loudly condemns, namely ethnocentrism.

Critics also objected to the fierce attacks on Western literature by multiculturalists, who dismissed the canon as nothing more than a prejudiced list of the works of "dead white males." More than sixty years ago, Robert Maynard Hutchins, a devoted apostle of courses on the Great Books, noted that "a classic is a book that is contemporary in every age. That is why it is a classic." Defenders of the classics have stressed, moreover, that the canon has not been a fixed entity. Still, some have deplored the inclusion of multicultural works into canonical courses at various colleges as political and ephemeral.

One might reasonably suppose that the cultural wars over the canon were limited to the prolixities of academics. Yet the general public's response to Allan Bloom's *The Closing of the American Mind* (1987) indicated otherwise. Despite its wide-ranging erudition and the occasional denseness of its prose, the book, to the astonishment of critics and the author alike, became and remained a nonfiction bestseller for many months. Quite simply, Bloom, who was then a professor of philosophy at the University of Chicago, his alma mater at which he had studied the Great Books and inherited an abiding reverence for the Western classical tradition from the philosopher Leo Strauss, had struck a sympathetic chord with others holding conservative views on education.

The events of the 1960s made Bloom pessimistic for the future of American higher education. As a philosophy professor at Cornell in 1969, he witnessed and was horrified by the violence of the Black Power movement and the countenancing of it by the administration and a significant number among the faculty. He likened this "unmitigated disaster" to the Nazi violence and browbeating of German educators of the 1930s. Radical students, he observed, were elitists who despised middle-class Americans and their values. Nearly two decades later in his bestselling book he elaborated on what he considered the failures of contemporary education. By trying to avoid conflict and by assuming, *parti pris* (position taken in advance), the relativity of truth and morals, colleges had been derelict in their duty to educate. By embracing relativism, they led students along the path of irresponsiby for their actions. At the same time multiculturalism and too much specialization were eviscerating a traditional liberal arts education, which Bloom commended for its role in self-development. Straying from education per se, Bloom, to the huzzahs of other conservatives, decried divorce

("America's most urgent social problem") and illegitmate births for having weakened the vital institution of marriage. He also denounced rock music for its harmful effects on the majority of the young, who could no longer differentiate "the sublime from trash."

Whether or not they enjoyed rock music, a number of young students agreed with Bloom's gloomy assessment of an enfeebled modern higher education. As the conservative national student newspaper *Campus* lamented, nearly 80 percent of the nation's colleges and universities in the 1980s no longer required a course in Western civilization for graduation; 45 percent failed to require a course in English or American literature; 77 percent asked for no foreign language; 41 percent required no mathematics; 33 percent required no natural or physical science. The paper further agreed with the judgment of Gertrude Himmelfarb, an internationally prominent historian and wife of Irving Kristol, that students, "bored with trivia, with a specious relevance, with a smorgasbord of courses, with the politicization of all subjects and the fragmentation of all disciplines . . . might welcome a return to a serious, structured curriculum and to a university that is an intellectual and educational, not a political or therapeutic community." Many students as well as their professors, liberals as well as conservatives, were also opposed to the imposition of "politically correct" speech codes by colleges and universities. By the end of the 1980s no less than 60 percent of the latter had incorporated such codes in a well-intentioned effort to protect the sensibilities of women and minorities but with a resulting diminution of freedom of expression.

Affirmative action also heated the cultural wars. Critics of the policy won important victories in the 1990s. The first triumph came in 1996 when a federal Court of Appeals struck down a race-based admission policy adopted in 1992 by the University of Texas School of Law. The ruling in this *Hopwood* case, so-called for one of the four plaintiffs, extended to the states of Louisiana and Mississippi as well. A second major victory came that same year when California voters approved Proposition 209, a referendum that called for an end to the affirmative action admissions policy employed by the University of California. Leading the campaign to approve Proposition 209 was the racially mixed Ward Connerly, who had risen from childhood indigence to become a successful businessman. Sounding very much like Thomas Sowell, who had been denouncing affirmative action since the 1970s for its racist implications that minorities could not succeed on their own merits, Connerly observed: "We have used racial preferences to prop up a system of artificial diversity instead of doing the heavy lifting that leads to real equality." Not surprisingly, Connery and African American opponents of affirmative action received considerable verbal abuse, particularly from African American proponents of that policy.

Despite their relative paucity in numbers and the heated opposition they generated, prominent black conservatives continued to speak out on important issues during the 1980s and 1990s. Their number included such productive scholars besides Sowell as the economist Walter Williams, the political economist Glen Loury (who later retracted his conservatism) and the professor of literature Shelby Steele, whose *The Content of Our Character* (1990) discerned a decline in racism and urged African Americans to forego feelings of victimization and concentrate on personal development and self-help policies. William Raspberry and Cal Thomas, as well as Sowell, were widely read syndicated columnists. In the political arena, J. C. Watts of Oklahoma became a leading Republican figure in the U.S. House of Representatives in the late 1990s. Alan Keyes, a former state department official and ambassador to the United Nations Economic and Social Council with a Harvard Ph.D., campaigned for the Republican presidential nomination in 1996 and 2000. A dedicated and highly vocal conservative, the strongly religious Roman Catholic Keyes supported school prayer, school vouchers, and two-parented families while attacking abortion and affirmative action. Other prominent African American conservatives during the last two decades have included Robert Woodson, a former officer of the National Urban League, and J. A. (Jay) Parker, a former national board member of YAF. A supporter of the Goldwater presidential candidacy in 1964, Jay has been called "the founding father of the contemporary black conservative movement in America."

The culture wars also raged outside academe. Between 1988 and 1990 the National Endowment for the Arts (NEA) evoked the wrath of conservatives and others for having funded two highly controversial events: a photographic exhibition of explicit homoeroticism by Robert Mapplethorpe and a depiction of a crucifix by Andres Serrano that many found blasphemous. As a result the besieged director of the NEA ultimately resigned, and Congress threatened to cut appropriations for the organization. In 1995 the venerable Smithsonian Institution's Air and Space Museum also became embroiled in controversy when it mounted an exhibition that focused on the atomic bombs that were dropped on Japan to hasten the end of World War II. Veterans' groups and congressmen protested that the text that accompanied the photographs contained inaccuracies and was overly sympathetic to the Japanese. The Smithsonian reluctantly revised the text, and the exhibit's director quit.

Unresolved complex questions resurfaced with the disputes involving the NEA and the Smithsonian. Does freedom of expression have limits? Should taxpayer dollars support that which most taxpayers find highly objectionable? Should the federal government support the arts and if so, to what extent? Beyond these questions, with their critical legal, moral, and economic implications, was the further question of the state of the arts themselves in the late twentieth century.

Hilton Kramer, a distinguished critic and editor of *The New Criterion*, has been commenting on the arts in the United States for more than four decades. As the historian J. David Hoeveler has pointed out, Kramer's aesthetic taste represents the modernist wing of American conservatism unlike the antimodernist tastes of the traditional Right. Unlike typical critics of both the Left and the Right, this former art editor for the *New York Times* has minimized the supposedly irreducible historical hostility between the avant-garde and the bourgeoisie. Instead, he has perceived a symbiotic relationship. (*See Document No. 21.*) Art expanded the horizons and enriched the pleasures of the bourgeoisie. In return, far from being stereotypical philistines, the bourgeoisie ultimately accepted the various effusions of new art and indeed succored its acceptance by not only buying its works but by creating the means of its exhibitions through museums, galleries, artistic publications, and so forth. The general tolerance engendered by the liberal democracy that the middle classes espoused and sometimes went to the barricades for further abetted the avant-garde.

The radicalism of the 1960s threatened wholesome modern art as well as liberal democracy, according to Kramer. Marxists and other radicals politicized modern art by denouncing the abstract expressionism of the internationally renowned New York School of Artists both as an adjunct of American Cold War imperialism and for its elitism. The Left further politicized and trivialized art by exalting works that supported the radical agenda, regardless of the inherent quality of those works. Kramer, a *soi-disant* (self-styled) neoconservative who likened the choice of art displays by some museums and curators to affirmative action, did not share the views of those traditional conservatives who, like the custodians of culture of the late nineteeth century, saw art as a buttress for morality or substitute for religion. But he did share their concern and ardent dislike for what they considered the debasement and radicalization of art that informed postmodernism and for the disparagement of Middle America. So, too, did the long-time managing editor of *The New Criterion*, Roger Kimball, who singled out academics for degrading learning and culture in *Tenured Radicals: How Politics Has Corrupted Our Higher Education* (1990)

End of the Cold War. The culture wars were heating up during the 1980s just as the Cold War was winding down. Indeed, the end of the Cold War became the most heralded event of the decade and of the presidency of Ronald Reagan.

Reagan owed his election in 1980 in good part to his ability to exploit the unpopularity of his opponent's foreign policy problems, notably President Carter's inability to resolve the hostage situation in Iran, his vacillation with regard to the Soviet Union's invasion of Afghanistan, and the treaties that ceded control of the Panama Canal to Panama. (Interestingly, both William F. Buckley, Jr. and Barry Goldwater, again serving as a United States senator, supported the treaties.) Due to the Vietnam tragedy, the subsequent debate as to what should constitute a proper foreign policy and willingness to undertake intervention, and the worrisome buildup of Soviet military capabilities, the United States stood as an uncertain giant at the time of the election. First as a candidate and then as president, Reagan promised to restore the United States to its preeminent position as the world's foremost superpower. Toward this end he persuaded Congress to allocate enormous spending to strengthen the military. Initially denouncing the Soviet Union as the "evil empire," he ultimately softened his stance.

Following Soviet leader Mikhail Gorbachev's introduction of the reform policies of glasnost and perestroika, the United States and the Soviet Union in 1987 signed the Intermediate Nuclear Force Treaty, which eliminated intermediate-range nuclear weapons from Europe. The Soviets withdrew from Afghanistan the following year, and in 1989, *annus mirabilis* (wonderful year), the Berlin Wall came down and Soviet forces withdrew from their satellite states. The Cold War had ended. Whether the fifty-year conflict between the United States and the Soviet Union had terminated primarily because the Soviet Union could not compete with the United States in military spending or because of internal Soviet economic weaknesses and a program of reform and openness that had the unintended effect of unbottling the proverbial genie was the subject of much debate. Some, including Soviets as well as Americans, claimed that the prospective development and deployment of the Strategic Defense Initiative (SDS), a project encouraged by Reagan, left the Soviet Union with no real choice but to end the Cold War. Whether or not the president foresaw that massive American military spending would have such a pronounced effect, he emerged as a hero to many Americans, certainly not least of all to conservatives.

Although the end of the Cold War and the defeat of communism gratified conservatives of all hues, neoconservatives had special reasons to feel pleased. For one thing, President Reagan's foreign policy vindicated cherished beliefs. The intellectual origins of neoconservative foreign policy had derived from the strong "vital center" anticommunism of the early Cold War liberals Arthur M. Schlesinger, Jr. and Reinhold Niebuhr, who claimed that communism had become the most dangerous enemy of a liberal democratic society. That consensus foundered on the shoals of Vietnam, but a new one gradually emerged in the 1970s for neoconservatives. First, they stressed that force, even in the wake of the Vietnam trauma, must remain a viable component to safeguard national interests. Second, they pointed to a related failure of nerve by the nation's leadership and a failure to combat attacks on American foreign policy with similar attacks on American democracy at home by left-wing critics.

The Carter administration fueled the angst of neoconservatives. For these disillusioned Democrats, Carter's seeming weakness in the face of an ever more ominous Soviet Union, his ultimately abortive Strategic Arms Limitation Treaty II (Salt II), his Central America policy (particularly his unwillingness to aid the Somoza regime in Nicaragua against the Sandinistas), his failure to aid the Shah, his coddling Third World sensitivities, and not least of all, his more even-handed approach to the Middle East, possibly to the detriment of Israel, provided the proverbial straw that broke their backs. In the 1980 election they deserted Carter and turned to Reagan.

While at times differing with respect to tactics rather than overall strategy, neoconservatives generally lauded the Reagan administration's foreign policy. There were exceptions, and strong ones at that. Senator Daniel P. Moynihan, whose brief stint as United States ambassador to the United Nations during the Ford presidency had greatly pleased many neoconservatives (and conservatives in general) by his vigorous defense of American policies and his refusal to countenance the often hypocritical carpings of Third World countries, broke with neoconservatives and other Reaganites over the president's aid to the contras in Nicaragua and to the government in El Salvador. Another dissenter, coming from an opposite direction, was Norman Podhoretz. The most hawkish of the prominent neoconservatives, he called for total victory over the Soviet Union, distrusted Gorbachev's program of glasnost and perestroika, and fulminated against Reagan's warming attitude toward the Soviets. But the senator and the editor of *Commentary* were the exceptions, albeit major ones, to the rule.

Beyond their roles as approving intellectuals, the neoconservatives took an active part in the formulation and enactment of the administration's foreign policy. Foremost among them was Jeane Kirkpatrick, whose writings on foreign policy issues came to the attention of Reagan during his campaign for the presidency. Once elected, Reagan persuaded her to lay aside her professorship in political science at George Washington University and to become United States ambassador to the United Nations. Kirkpatrick, who had briefly served in the state department in 1957, became the first women to hold this UN position. Early on she opposed Reagan's decision to lift the grain embargo that President Carter had imposed as a result of the Soviet intrusion into Afghanistan. Otherwise her views generally coincided with his, and in fact sometimes exercised a defining force.

In her four years at the UN Kirkpatrick articulated the policies of the administration and, as Moynihan earlier had done, acidly chastised both communist and Third World nations who opposed them. The distinction she drew between authoritative and totalitarian regimes, while not wholly novel, helped to give intellectual ballast to a vulnerable position. If democracy is so important, charged both foreign and domestic critics, why does the United States support a variety of known dictators? Advocates of realpolitik responded that in an imperfect world one needs the support of all sorts of friends against one's enemies, or as Franklin D. Roosevelt noted of one Latin American dictator, he might be a son of a bitch but at least he's our son of a bitch. Kirkpatrick refused to offer this standard reply of the realists. Instead, in what came to be called the Kirkpatrick Doctrine, she first agreed that authoritarian systems that the United States supported in Central and South America as well as in the Philippines featured oligarchical rule, corruption, and repression by the police and military. Thanks largely to the existence of a private sector economy, however, the systems held out the promise of future democratic reforms. Left-wing dictatorships, which lacked a market economy, offered less promise for change, and totalitarianism, by its very nature, presented the bleakest prospects for transformation. Any development of democracy in authoritarian states would come slowly, she cautioned, and under no circumstances should the United States withdraw its support from such a nation that was under siege, as President Carter had done in Iran and Nicaragua.

Late twentieth-century conservatives continued to hold disparate views on foreign policy matters. Some followed in the steps of such earlier figures as Henry Cabot Lodge or the political scientist Hans Morgenthau and argued for the primacy of realism and national self-interest in the conduct of the nation's foreign affairs. Others looked to the example of the America Firsters or Robert A. Taft and shunned overseas entanglements in favor of varying degrees of isolationism. What both groups resolutely opposed was a revivification of Wilsonian internationalism with its emphasis on morality and idealism and its penchant for utopianism. Jeane Kirkpatrick proposed a more nuanced foreign policy. By emphasizing the immorality of totalitarianism and the moral superiority of democracy, by asserting both the righteousness and necessity of the nation's global struggle against communism, and by insisting that America's promotion of democratic ideals abroad formed part of its national self-interest, she dextrously had managed to link ideals with realism as complementary forces in the achievement of goals. (*See Document 22.*)

Conservatism After the Reagan Presidency. With the apparent defanging of the Soviet threat, the neoconservative Francis Fukuyama boldly announced the "end of history." In *The End of History and the Last Man* (1992), he conceded that the United States still had to contend with international problems in the Mideast but that otherwise its role was to set a model for a benevolent order of liberal democracy and capitalism that the world could and would accept. But the 1990s failed to bring the peace and stability the young scholar anticipated. Problems remained in the Mideast, particularly with Iraq and with Muslim extremists. Although only a few communist nations remained, one of them, the People's Republic of China, became an increasing source of concern when in 1999 it was made public that Beijing had masterminded the theft of a number of American nuclear secrets.

Perceived as much less of a threat was North Korea, but still that nation had a small nuclear arsenal. Internecine ethnic fighting in the Balkans brought the threat of wider conflict; the genocidal practices both there and in Rwanda further undermined the hope for an "end to history."

Conservatives were divided in their response to global events. With American troops sent on various peacekeeping missions to Somalia, Haiti, Bosnia, and Kososvo during the nineties, and with the expansion of NATO to include new nations from Central and Eastern Europe, there were growing signs of a new isolationism. Pat Buchanan gave voice to this development as a media commentator and during his unsuccessful quest for the Republican party's presidential nomination in 1992 and 1996. He had been concerned with the Persian Gulf crisis of 1989 and President George Bush's subsequent call for a "New World Order," which was predicated upon an activist foreign policy. An economic nationalist unlike most neoconservatives, he has expressed strong reservations about the supposed benefits of free trade and global corporate capitalism. In 1993 he opposed the creation of the North American Free Trade Agreement (NAFTA), which eliminated most tariffs and trade barriers among the United States, Canada, and Mexico, for fear that ultimately it would diminish the wages of some American workers and eliminate the jobs of others. To date NAFTA has sizably increased the nation's trade deficit with Mexico.

While reflecting the views of the Old Right with regard to foreign policy and economic nationalism, Buchanan has persistently taken positions welcomed by the New Right and the Religious Right. Opposed to affirmative action, bilingual education, and abortion, he declared in 1999 when he launched his third try for the presidency that there existed the need for a moral reawakening to purge society of "a polluted and poisoned culture." Indeed, the jeremiad against contemporary social mores and attitudes has continued largely unabated among both religious and secular conservatives during the last decade of the century. The Religous Right, which had suffered some decline as previously noted, gained renewed strength, especially when the leadership of the Christian Coalition passed to energetic and affable Ralph Reed in 1989. An unsuccessful aspirant for the Republican presidential nomination in 1996, Gary Bauer also helped to reinvigorate the Religious Right with his Family Research Council, a politically active organization of more than 400,000 members.

Conservative secularists also have actively championed the crusade on behalf of the nation's morals and ethics. The title of Robert Bork's book *Slouching Towards Gomorrah* (1999) conveys the jurist's message, to wit, the nation is headed for catastrophe. Blaming radical individualism and radical egalitarianism, the two "defining characteristics of modern liberalism," for current problems, he gloomily predicted that only a religious revival, a serious discourse on morality, a major war, or a dire economic depression could induce regeneration. Less saturnine but highly popular with the reading public was *The Book of Virtues* (1993) by William J. Bennett, who had served under President Reagan as head of NEH and under President Bush as secretary of education and then as "drug czar." An anthology of moral uplift organized around ten "virtues," the work appeared on the best-seller list of the *New York Times* for more than eighty weeks and sold well over two million copies. Bennett continued to stress values both in *Body Count* (1996), in which he blamed welfare dependency, divorce, and poor parenting for the "moral poverty" that leads to crime among the young, and in *The Death of Outrage: Bill Clinton and the Assault on American Ideals* (1998).

Of all the moral and ethical questions of the 1990s none provoked more controversy among conservatives and others than the sexual involvement of President Bill Clinton with a young White House intern. The far Right was especially vocal in calling for the president's impeachment. Impeached on several counts in 1998, the president was found not guilty the following year. It was ironic that his chief legal counsel was the brother of William Bennett. More ironic was the fact that this two-term chief executive was elected as a committed liberal but, to the consternation of other liberals, appeared to espouse a conservative position on some issues, most notably his support for a welfare reform measure of 1996 that forced a number of recipients to seek employment or lose benefits. It also seemed incongruous that the liberal Clinton reduced the number of federal employees by fifteen percent in contrast to President Reagan, who, as noted, slightly increased their numbers.

Just before the congressional elections of 1994 the conservative Republican leaders in the House, led by majority leader Newt Gingrich, issued the *Contract with America*, which pledged a variety of changes that included fiscal responsibility, war on crime, tax cuts, social security reforms, term limits to office, and the refusal to place U.S. military forces under UN command. The ensuing election gave Republicans control of Congress and held out an oxymoronic promise of a "conservative revolution." The revolution has not materialized, but parts of the *Contract* have been enacted, including the transfer of broad authority to the states to regulate welfare policy and the abrogation of federal farm subsidy programs that dated back to the New Deal. What has emerged, moreover, has been a willingness born of necessity for nonconservatives to engage in serious discourse with conservatives. That the two leading aspirants—both liberals—for the Democratic presidential nomination in 2000 endorsed "empowerment zones" and tax and other incentives for businesses in poor urban neighborhoods—a pet scheme of former conservative Republican Representative Jack Kemp of New York—speaks to this development.

But who speaks for conservatives? Who are the conservatives whose viewpoints will carry the most weight in such vital public policy issues as those that affect social security, healthcare, welfare, education, gun control, and the environment? And foreign policy? As death and diminished activity continue to claim the philosophically diverse conservatives of the post–World War II generation, who will enunciate conservative principles and values, and which principles and values? Contemporary libertarians by and large have distanced themselves from conservatives, whom they accuse of betraying free market principles in economics and meddling in the private lives of individuals by trying to dictate the norms of personal and social behavior. Nonetheless, they continue to offer ideas which attract many conservatives, as with the Cato Institute's suggestion that social security funds be invested in the stock market.

Meanwhile Irving Kristol observed in 1995 that neoconservatism had ended as a separate movement and had largely merged with traditional conservatism. The offspring of neoconservatives, he explained, "are now all conservatives without adjectival modification." Not all conservatives, neo or otherwise, would agree that the merger had occurred, but they could not have failed to have witnessed the torch of conservatism being passed from parent to offspring: William Kristol, former aide to Vice President Dan Quayle and powerful Republican stategist; John Podhoretz, former White House staff member under President Bush and journalist. Still, distinguished conservative parentage has not been a requisite for a host of other contemporary conservatives who have also achieved prominence and who have made and are making their contribution to conservatism in words and in deeds. Having denounced the liberal establishment for so long, conservatives currently find themselves an establishment, one that is able to communicate its ideas readily through the press, television, and radio to widespread and sympathetic audiences. Moreover, conservative patrons have made Croesus-like contributions to help fund dozens of conservative think thanks and special programs to develop and disseminate conservative ideas and policies. Lionel Trilling's observation in 1950 on the scantness of conservative thought has lost what aptness it may once have possessed. As for the future . . . What will be the precise history of the conservative tradition, its emphases, its twists and turns, in the new millenium is impossible to discern. More likely than not, however, it will remain a coat of many colors—and a durable coat at that.

PART II

DOCUMENTS

DOCUMENT NO. 1

ALEXANDER HAMILTON BROADLY
INTERPRETS THE CONSTITUTION*

The interpretation of the powers granted to the federal government by the Constitution generated significant controversy during the first years of the new nation. Thomas Jefferson, President Washington's secretary of state, construed these powers narrowly, while Secretary of the Treasury Alexander Hamilton defined them broadly. Washington sided with Hamilton, with the result that the first Bank of the United States was established in 1791. Beginning with the Federalists but with important exceptions, conservatives usually supported the Hamiltonian interpretation of implied powers through the Civil War era.

γ   γ   γ

Now it appears to the Seretary of the Treasury that this *general principle* is *inherent* in the very *definition* of government, and *essential* to every step of the progress to be made by that of the United States, namely: That every power vested in a government is in its nature *sovereign*, and includes, by *force* of the *term*, a right to employ all the *means* requisite and fairly applicable to the attainment of the *ends* of such power, and which are not precluded by restrictions and exceptions specified in the Constitution, or not immoral, or not contrary to the *essential ends* of political society.

This principle, in its application to government in general, would be admitted as an axiom; and it will be incumbent upon those who may incline to deny it, to prove a distinction, and to show that a rule which, in the general system of things, is essential to the preservation of the social order, is inapplicable to the United States.

The circumstance that the powers of sovereignty are in this country divided between the National and State governments, does not afford the distinction required. It does not follow from this, that each of the portion of *powers* delegated to the one or to the other, is not sovereign with *regard to its proper objects*. It will only *follow* from it, that each has

* Alexander Hamilton, *Opinion as to the Constitutionality of the Bank of the United States*, in *The Works of Alexander Hamilton*, ed. Henry Cabot Lodge, Vol. III (New York: G. P. Putnam's Sons, 1904), pp. 446–448; 454; 457–458; 489.

sovereign power as to *certain things*, and not as to *other things*. To deny that the Government of the United States has sovereign power, as to its declared purposes and trusts, because its power does not extend to all cases, would be equally to deny that the State governments have sovereign power in any case, because their power does not extend to every case. The tenth section of the first article of the Constitution exhibits a long list of very important things which they may not do. And thus the United States would furnish the singular spectacle of a *political society* without *sovereignty*, or of a *people governed*, without *government*.

If it would be necessary to bring proof to a proposition so clear, as that which affirms that the powers of the Federal Government, as to *its objects*, were sovereign, there is a clause of its Constitution which would be decisive. It is that which declares that the Constitution, and the laws of the United States made in pursuance of it, and all treaties made, or which shall be made, under their authority, shall be the *supreme law of the land.* The power which can create the *supreme law of the land* in *any case,* is doubtless *sovereign* as to such case.

This general and indisputable principle puts at once an end to the *abstract* question, whether the United States have power to erect a *corporation*; that is to say, to give a *legal* or *artificial capacity* to one or more persons, distinct from the *natural.* For it is unquestionably incident to *sovereign power* to erect corporations, and consequently to *that* of the United States, in *relation* to the *objects* intrusted to the management of the government. The difference is this: where the authority of the government is general, it can create corporations in *all cases*; where it is confined to certain branches of legislation, it can create corporations *only* in those cases. . . .

It may be truly said of every government, as well as of that of the United States, that it has only a right to pass such laws as are necessary and proper to accomplish the objects intrusted to it. For no government has a right to do *merely what it pleases.* Hence, by a process of reasoning similar to that of the Secretary of State, it might be proved that neither of the State governments has the right to incorporate a bank. It might be shown that all the public business of the State could be performed without a bank, and inferring thence that it was unnecessary, it might be argued that it could not be done, becuase it is against the rule which has been just mentioned. A like mode of reasoning would prove that there was no power to incorporate the inhabitants of a town, with a view to a more perfect police. For it is certain that an incorporation may be dispensed with, though it is better to have one. It is to be remembered that there is no *express* power in any State constitution to erect corporations. . . .

The truth is, that difficulties on this point [implied powers] are inherent in the nature of the Federal Constitution; they result inevitably from a division of the legislative power. The consequence of this division is, that there will be cases clearly within the power of the National Government; others, clearly without its powers; and a third class, which will leave room for controversy and difference of opinion, and concerning which a reasonable latitude of judgment must be allowed.

But the doctrine which is contended for is not chargeable with the consequences imputed to it. It does not affirm that the National Government is sovereign in all respects, but that it is sovereign to a certain extent—that is, to the extent of the objects of its specified powers.

It leaves, therefore, a criterion of what is constitutional, and of what is not so. This criterion is the *end*, to which the measure relates as a *means*. If the *end* be clearly comprehended within any of the specified powers, and if the measure have an obvious relation to that *end*, and is not forbidden by any particular provision of the Constitution, it may safely be deemed to come within the compass of the national authority. There is also this further criterion, which may materially assist the decision: Does the proposed measure abridge a pre-existing right of any State or of any individual? If it does not, there is a strong presumption in favor of its constitutionality, and slighter relations to any declared object of the Constitution may be permitted to turn the scale. . . .

There is a sort of evidence on this point [that Congress can erect a corporation], arising from an aggregate view of the Constitution, which is of no inconsiderable weight: the very general power of laying and collecting taxes, and appropriating their proceeds—that of borrowing money indefinitely—that of coining money, and regulating foreign coins—that of making all needful rules and regulations respecting the property of the United States. These powers combined, as well as the reason and nature of the thing, speak strongly this language: that it is the manifest design and scope of the Constitution to vest in Congress all the powers requisite to the effectual administration of the finances of the United States. As far as concerns this object, there appears to be no parsimony of power.

To suppose, then, that the government is precluded from the employment for the administration of its finances as that of a bank, is to suppose what does not coincide with the general tenor and complexion of the Constitution, and what is not agreeable to impressions that any new spectator would entertain concerning it.

DOCUMENT NO. 2

A CONSERVATIVE DEFENDS A REPUBLICAN
FORM OF GOVERNMENT*

John Adams never doubted that a republican form of government best suited the new nation. But as he made clear in a letter to his cousin Samuel Adams, a republican government needed the services of a natural aristocracy.

γ   γ   γ

I am very willing to agree with you in fancying, that in the greatest improvements of society, government will be in the republican form. It is a fixed principle with me, that all government is and must be republican. But, at the same time, your candor will agree with me, that there is not in lexicography a more fraudulent word. Whenever I use the word *republic* with approbation, I mean a government in which the people have collectively, or by representation, an essential share in the sovereignty. The republican forms of Poland and Venice are each worse, and those of Holland and Bern very little better, than the monarchical form in France before the late revolution. . . . For, after a fair trial of its miseries, the simple monarchical form will ever be, as it has ever been, preferred to it by mankind. Are we not, my friend, in danger of rendering the word *republican* unpopular in the country by an indiscreet, indeterminate, and equivocal use of it? . . . If, in this country, the word *republic* should be generally understood, as it is by some, to mean a form of government inconsistent with a mixture of three powers, forming a mutual balance, we may depend upon it that such mischievous effects will be produced by the use of it as will compel the people of America to renounce, detest, and execrate it as the English do. With these explanations, restrictions, and limitations, I agree with you in your love of republican governments, but in no other sense.

With you, I have also the honor most perfectly to harmonise in your sentiments of the humanity and wisdom of promoting education in knowledge, virtue, and benevolence. But I think that these will confirm mankind in the opinion of the necessity of preserving and strengthen-

* John Adams, Letter to Samuel Adams, 18 October 1790, in *The Works of John Adams, Second President of the United States*, Vol. 6 (Boston: Charles C. Little and James Brown, 1851), pp. 415–417.

ing the dikes against the ocean, its tides and storms. Human appetites, passions, prejudices, and self-love will never be conquered by benevolence and knowledge alone, introduced by human means. The millennium itself neither supposes nor implies it. All civil government is then to cease, and the Messiah is to reign. That happy and holy state is therefore wholly out of this question. You and I agree in the utility of universal education; but will nations agree in it as fully and extensively as we do, and be at the expense of it? We know, with as much certainty as attends any human knowledge, that they will not. We cannot, therefore, advise the people to depend for either safety, liberty, and security, upon hopes and blessings which we know will not fall to their lot. If we do our duty then to the people, we shall not deceive them, but advise them to depend upon what is in their power and will relieve them.

. . . We have human nature, society, and universal history to observe and study, and from these we may draw all the real principles which ought to be regarded. Disciples will follow their masters, and interested partisans their chieftains; let us like it or not, we cannot help it. But if the true principles can be discovered, and fairly, fully, and impartially laid before the people, the more light increases, the more the reason of them will be seen, and the more disciples they will have. Prejudice, passion, and private interest, which will always mingle in human inquiries, one would think might be enlisted on the side of truth, at least in the greatest number; for certainly the majority are interested in the truth, if they could see to the end of all its consequences. "Kings have been deposed by aspiring nobles." True, and never by any other. "These" (the nobles, I suppose,) "have waged everlasting war against the common rights of men." True, when they have been possessed of the *summa imperii* in one body, without a check. So have the plebeians; so have the people; so have kings; so has human nature, in every shape and combination, and so it ever will. But, on the other hand, the nobles have been essential parties in the preservation of liberty, whenever and wherever it has existed. In Europe, they alone have preserved it against kings and people, wherever it has been preserved; or, at least, with very little assistance from the people. One hideous despotism, as horrid as that of Turkey, would have been the lot of every nation of Europe, if the nobles had not made stands. By nobles, I mean not peculiarly an hereditary nobility, or any particular modification, but the natural and actual aristocracy among mankind. The existence of this you will not deny.

DOCUMENT NO. 3

THE SUPREME COURT EXTENDS ITS POWERS*

Chief Justice John Marshall rendered decisions that greatly enhanced the powers of the Supreme Court and established vital precedents in constitutional law. A strong Federalist in his convictions, he advanced the cause of nationalism in various cases by subordinating state powers to those of the federal government. In the instance of Cohens v. Virginia *(1821), Marshall affirmed the appellate authority of federal courts over state courts.*

γ   γ   γ

The American States, as well as the American people, have believed a close and firm union to be essential to their liberty and to their happiness. They have been taught by the same experience that this government would be a mere shadow, that must disappoint all their hopes, unless invested with large portions of that sovereignty which belongs to independent States. Under the influence of this opinion, and thus instructed by experience, the American people, in the conventions of their respective States, adopted the present constitution.

If it could be doubted, whether, from its nature, it were not supreme in all cases where it is empowered to act, that doubt would be removed by the declaration, that "this constitution and the laws of the United States which shall be made in pursuance thereof, and all treaties made, or which shall be made under the authority of the United States, shall be the supreme law of the land; and the judges in every State shall be bound thereby, anything in the constitution or laws of any State to the contrary notwithstanding." This is the authoritative language of the American people; and, if gentlemen please, of the American States. It marks, with lines too strong to be mistaken, the characteristic distinction between the government of the Union, and those of the States. The general government, though limited as to its objects, is supreme with respect to those objects. This principle is a part of the constitution; and if there be any who deny its necessity, none can deny its authority.

To this supreme government ample powers are confided; and if it were possible to doubt the great purposes for which they were so con-

---

* *Cohens v. Virginia* (1821)

fided, the people of the United States have declared, that they are given "in order to from a more perfect union, establish justice, insure domestic tranquillity, provide for the common defense, promote the general welfare, and secure the blessings of liberty to themselves and to their posterity." With the ample powers confided to this supreme government for these interesting purposes are connected many express and important limitations on the sovereignty of the States; but in addition to these, the sovereignty of the States is surrendered in many instances where the surrender can only operate to the benefit of the people, and where, perhaps, no other power is conferred on Congress than a conservative power to maintain the principles established in the constitution. The maintenance of these principles in their purity is certainly among the great duties of government. One of the instruments by which this duty may be peaceably performed is the judicial department. It is authorized to decide all cases, of every description, arising under the constitution or laws of the United States. From this general grant of jurisdiction no exception is made of those cases in which a State may be a party. When we consider the situation of the government of the Union and of a State in relation to each other, the nature of our constitution, the subordination of the state governments to that constitution, the great purpose for which jurisdiction over all cases arising under constitution and laws of the Unite States is confided to the judicial department, are we at liberty to insert in this general grant, an exception of those cases in which a State may be a party? Will the spirit of the constitution justify this attempt to control its words? We think it will not. We think a case arising under the constitution or laws of the United States is cognizable in the Courts of the Union, whoever may be parties to the case. . . .

Different States may entertain different opinions on the true construction of the constitutional powers of Congress. . . .

But a constitution is framed for ages to come, and is designed to approach immortality as nearly as human institutions can approach it. Its course cannot always be tranquil. It is exposed to storms and tempests, and its framers must be unwise statesmen indeed, if they have not provided it, so far as its nature will permit, with the means of self-preservation from the perils it may be destined to encounter. No government ought to be so defective in its organization as not to contain within itself the means of securing the execution of its own laws against other dangers than those which occur every day. Courts of justice are the means most usually employed; and it is reasonable to expect that a government should repose on its own Courts, rather than on others. There is certainly nothing in the circumstances under which our constitution was formed, nothing in the history of the times, which would justify the opinion that the confidence reposed in the States was so implicit as to leave in them and their tribunals the power of resisting or defeating, in the form of law, the legitimate measures of the Union. . . .

That the United States form, for many and for most important purposes, a single nation, has not yet been denied. In war we are one people. In making peace we are one people. In all commercial regulations we are one and the same people. In many other respects the American people are one, and the government which is alone capable of controlling and managing their interests in all these respects, is the government of the Union. It is their government, and in that character they have no other. America has chosen to be, in many respects, and to many purposes, a nation; and for all these purposes her government is complete; to all these objects it is competent. The people have declared that in the exercise of all the powers given for these objects it is supreme. It can, then, in effecting these objects, legitimately control all individuals or governments within the American territory. The constitution and laws of a State, so far as they are repugnant to the constitution and laws of the United States, are absolutely void. These States are constituent parts of the United States. They are members of one great empire—for some purposes sovereign, for some purposes subordinate.

In a government so constituted is it unreasonable that the judicial power should be competent to give efficacy to the constitutional laws of the legislature? That department can decide on the validity of the constitution or law of a State, if it be repugnant to the constitution or to a law of the United States. Is it unreasonable that it should also be empowered to decide on the judgment of a State tribunal enforcing such unconstitutional law? Is it so very unreasonable as to furnish a justification for controlling the words of the constitution? We think it is not. We think that, in a government acknowledgedly supreme with respect to objects of vital interest to the nation, there is nothing inconsistent with sound reason, nothing incompatible with the nature of government, in making all its departments supreme, so far as is necessary to their attainment. The exercise of the appellate power over those judgments of the state tribunals which may contravene the constitution or laws of the United States, is, we believe, essential to the attainment of those objects. . . .

We are not restrained, then, by the political relations between the general and State governments from construing the words of the constitution defining the judicial power in their true sense. We are not bound to construe them more restrictively than they naturally import.

They give to the Supreme Court appellate jurisdiction in all cases arising under the constitution, laws, and treaties of the United States. The words are broad enough to comprehend all cases of this description, in whatever court they may be decided.

DOCUMENT NO. 4

A DEFENSE OF
PROPERTY QUALIFICATIONS FOR VOTING*

Conservatives, fearing that mob rule would undermine republican institutions and values, sought ways to block the rapid advance of democracy in the early years of the nineteenth century. The movement toward universal white male suffrage particularly troubled them, but their efforts to thwart the movement proved fruitless at the state constitutional conventions held in Massachusetts (1820–1821), New York (1821), and Virginia (1829–30). Chancellor James Kent, a justice of the New York State Supreme Court, led the conservative opposition in his state.

γ   γ   γ

. . . These are some of the fruits of our present government; and yet we seem to be dissatisfied with our present condition, and we are engaged in the bold and hazardous experiment of remodelling the constitution. Is it not fit and discreet: I speak as to wise men; is it not fit and proper that we should pause in our career, and reflect well on the immensity of the innovation in contemplation? Discontent in the midst of so much prosperity, and with such abundant means of happiness, looks like ingratitude, and as if we were disposed to arraign the goodness of Providence. Do we not expose ourselves to the danger of being deprived of the blessings we have enjoyed?

The senate has hitherto been elected by the farmers of the state—by the free and independent lords of the soil, worth at least $250 in freehold estate, over and above all debts charged thereon. The governor has been chosen by the same electors, and we have hitherto elected citizens of elevated rank and character. Our assembly has been chosen by freeholders, possessing a freehold of the value of $50, or by persons renting a tenement of the yearly value of $5, and who have been rated and actually paid taxes to the state. By the report before us, we propose to annihilate, at one stroke, all those property distinctions and to bow before the idol of universal suffrage. That extreme democratic principle, when applied

---

* Kent, "Remarks to the New York Constitutional Convention (1821)," N. H. Carter et al., *Reports of the Proceedings and Debates of the Convention of 1821* (Albany: E. E. Hosford, 1921), sec. 219ff.

143

to the legislative and executive departments of the government, has been regarded with terror, by the wise men of every age, because in every European republic, ancient and modern, in which it has been tried, it has terminated disastrously, and been productive of corruption, injustice, violence, and tyranny. And dare we flatter ourselves that we are a peculiar people, who can run the career of history, exempted from the passions which have disturbed and corrupted the rest of mankind? If we are like other races of men, with similar follies and vices, then I greatly fear that our posterity will have reason to deplore in sackcloth and ashes, the delusion of the day. . . .

Now, sir, I wish to preserve our senate as the representative of the landed interest. I wish those who have an interest in the soil, to retain the exclusive possession of a branch in the legislature, as a strong hold in which they may find safety through all the vicissitudes which the state may be destined, in the course of Providence, to experience. I wish them to be always enabled to say that their freehold cannot be taxed without their consent. The men of no property, together with the crowds of dependents connected with great manufacturing and commercial establishments, and the motley and undefinable population of crowded ports, may, perhaps, at some future day, under skilful management predominate in the assembly, and yet we should be perfectly safe if no laws could pass without the free consent of the owners of the soil. That security we at present enjoy; and it is that security which I wish to retain.

The apprehended danger from the experiment of universal suffrage applied to the whole legislative department, is no dream of the imagination. It is too mighty an excitement for the moral constitution of men to endure. The tendency of universal suffrage, is to jeopardize the rights of property, and the principles of liberty. There is a constant tendency in human society, and the history of every age proves it; there is a tendency in the poor to covet a share in the plunder of the rich; in the debtor to relax or avoid the obligation of contracts; in the majority to tyrannize over the minority, and trample down their right; in the indolent and profligate, to cast the whole burthens of society upon the industrious and the virtuous; and *there is a tendency in ambitious and wicked men, to inflame these combustible materials*. It requires a vigilant government, and a firm administration of justice, to counteract that tendency. Thou shalt not covet; thou shalt not steal; are divine injunctions induced by this miserable depravity of our nature. Who can undertake to calculate with any precision, how many millions of people, this great state will contain in the course of this and the next century, and who can estimate the future extent and magnitude of our commerical ports? The dispropor-tion between the men of property, and the men of no property, will be in every society in a ratio to its commerce, wealth, and population. We are no longer to remain plain and simple republics of farmers, like the New-England colonists, or the Dutch settlements on the Hudson. We are fast becoming a great nation, with great commerce, manufactures, population, wealth, luxuries, and with the vices and miseries that they engender. One seventh of the population of the city of Paris this day subsists on charity, and one third of the inhabitants of that city die in the hospitals; what would become of such a city with universal suffrage? France has upwards of four, and England upwards of five millions of manufacturing and commerical labourers without property. Could these Kingdoms sustain the weight of universal suffrage? The radicals in England, with the force of that mighty engine, would at once sweep away the property, the laws, and the liberties of that island like a deluge.

The growth of the city of New-York is enough to startle and awaken those who are pursuing the *IGNIS FATUUS* [delusive aim] of univer-sal suffrage. . . .

DOCUMENT NO. 5

AN ARGUMENT FOR LIBERTY
BALANCED BY ORDER*

Orestes Brownson undertook a spiritual quest that led him from various liberal Protestant sects to the hierarchically structured Roman Catholic Church. Similarly, he moved from a warm embrace of democracy to a more measured one. In his later years his emphasis upon order would become more pronounced.

γ   γ   γ

The ends the people seek to gain are, we willingly admit, for the most part just and desirable; but the justice and desirableness of the end, almost always blind them to the true character and tendency of the means by which they seek to gain it. They become intent on the end, so intent as to be worked up to a passion—and then in going to it, they break down everything which obstructs or hinders their progress. Now, what they break down, though in the way of gaining that particular end, may after all be our only guaranty of other ends altogether more valuable. Here is the danger. What more desirable than personal freedom? What more noble than to strike the fetters of the slave? Aye, but if in striking off his fetters, you trample on the constitution and law, which are your only guaranty of freedom for those who are now free, and also for those you propose to make free, what do you gain to freedom? Great wrong may be done in seeking even a good end, that in going to it, it tramples down more rights than it vindicates by success. We own, therefore, that the older we grow, and the longer we study in that school, the only one in which fools will learn, the more danger do we see in popular passions, and the less is our confidence in the wisdom and virtue of the people. . . .

"But what is our resource against all these evils? What remedy do you propose?" . . . Without an efficient Constitution, which is not only an instrument through which the people govern, but which is a power that governs them, by effectually confining their action to certain specific subjects, there is and can be no good government, no individual liberty.

* Orestes Brownson, "Democracy and Liberty." *United States Magazine and Democratic Review*. April 1843: 374–387, passim.

Without the influence of wise and patriotic statesmen, whose importance, in our adulation of the people as a mass, we have underrated, and without the Christian Church exerting the hallowed and hallowing influence of Christianity upon the people both as individuals and as the body politic, we see little hope, even with the best of constitution, of securing the blessings of freedom and good government. . . .

Democracy, in our judgment, has been wrongly defined to be a *form* of government; it should be understood of the *end*, rather than of the *means*, and be regarded as a principle rather than a form. The end we are to aim at, is the Freedom and progress of all men, especially of the poorest and most numerous class. He is a democrat who goes for the highest moral, intellectual, and physical elevation of the great mass of people, especially of the laboring population, in distinction from a special devotion to the interests and pleasures of the wealthier, more refined, or more distinguished few. But the means by which this elevation is to be obtained, are not necessarily the institution of the purely democratic form of government. Here has been our mistake. We have been quite too ready to conclude that if we only once succeed in establishing Democracy—universal suffrage and eligibility, without constitutional restraints on the power of the people—as a form of government, the end will follow as a matter of course. The considerations we have adduced, we think prove to the contrary.

In coming to this conclusion it will be seen that we differ from our friends not in regard to the end, but in regard to the means. We believe, and this is the point on which we insist, that the end, freedom and progress, will not be secured by this loose radicalism with regard to popular sovereignty, and these demagogical boasts of the virtue and intelligence of the people, which have begun to be so fashionable. They who are seeking to advance the cause of humanity by warring against all existing institutions, religious, civil, or political, do seem to us to be warring against they very end they wish to gain.

It has been said, that mankind are always divided into two parties, one of which may be called the Stationary Party, the other the Movement Party, or Party of Progress. Perhaps it is so; if so, all of us who have any just conceptions of our manhood, and of our duty to our fellow-men, must arrange ourselves on the side of the Movement. But the Movement itself is divided into two sections—one the radical section, seeking progress by destruction; the other the conservative section, seeking progress through and in obedience to existing institutions. Without asking whether the rule applies beyond our own country, we contend that the conservative section is the only one that a wise man can call his own. In youth we feel differently. We find evil around us; we are in a dungeon; loaded all over with chains; we cannot make a single free movement; and we utter one long, loud, indignant protest against whatever is. We feel then that we can advance religion only by destroying the Church; learning only be breaking down universities; and freedom only by abolishing the State. Well, this is one kind of progress; but we ask, has it ever been known to be successful? Suppose that we succeed in demolishing the old edifice, in sweeping away all that the human race has been accumulating for the last six thousand years, what have we gained? Why, we are back where we were six thousand years ago; and without any assurance that the human race will not re-assume its old course and rebuild what we have destroyed. . . .

As we grow older, sadder, and wiser, and pass from Idealists to Realists, we change all this, and learn that the only true way of carrying the race forward is through its existing institutions. We plant ourselves, if on the sad, still on the firm reality of things, and content ourselves with gaining what can be gained with the means existing institutions furnish. We seek to advance religion through and in obedience to the Church; law and social well-being through and in obedience to the State. Let it not be said that in adopting this last course, we change sides, leave the Movement, and go over to the Stationary Party. No such thing. We do not thus in age forget the dreams of our youth. It is because we remember those dreams, because young enthusiasm has become firm and settled principle, and youthful hopes positive convictions, and because we would realize what we dared dream, when we first looked forth on the face of humanity, that we cease to exclaim "Liberty *against* Order," and substitute the practical formula, "LIBERTY ONLY IN AND THROUGH ORDER." The love of liberty loses none of its intensity. In the true manly heart it burns deeper and clearer with age, but it burns to enlighten and to warm, not to consume.

Here is the practical lesson we have sought to unfold. While we accept the end our democratic friends see, while we feel our lot is bound up with theirs, we have wished to impress upon their minds, that we are to gain that end only through fixed and established order; not against authority, but by and in obedience to authority, and an authority competent to ordain and to guaranty it. Liberty without the guaranties of Authority, would be the worst of tyrannies.

DOCUMENT NO. 6

JOHN C. CALHOUN AND
THE CONCURRENT MAJORITY*

Considered by some to be America's most original political theorist, John C. Calhoun was torn between the increasingly irreconcilable forces of nationalism and sectionalism. Fearful that under majoritarian democracy the more populous North would make it impossible for the South to safeguard and pursue its interests, he conceived of a means by which the latter could protect those interests and at the same time promote national harmony. The South Carolinian also opposed democratic egalitarianism as hostile to individual freedom and progress.

γ　　　　　γ　　　　　γ

. . . For as the community becomes populous, wealthy, refined, and highly civilized, the difference between the rich and the poor will become more strongly marked; and the number of the ignorant and dependent greater in proportion to the rest of the community. With the increase of this difference, the tendency to conflict between them will become stronger; and, as the poor and dependent become more numerous in proportion, there will be, in governments of the numerical majority, no want of leaders among the wealthy and ambitious, to excite and direct them in their efforts to obtain the control.

The case is diffeent in governments of the concurrent majority. There, mere numbers have not the absolute control; and the wealthy and intelligent being identified in interest with the poor and ignorant of their respective portions or interests of the community, become their leaders and protectors. And hence, as the latter would have neither hope nor inducement to rally the former in order to obtain the control, the right of suffrage, under such a government, may be safely enlarged to the extent stated, without incurring the hazard to which such enlargement would expose governments of the numerical majority.

In another particular, governments of the concurrent majority have greatly the advantage. I allude to the difference in their respective tendency, in reference to dividing or unifying the community. That of the

* John C. Calhoun, "A Disquisition on Government," *The Works of John C. Calhoun*, ed. Richard K. Cralle, Vol. 1 (New York: D. Appleton & Company, 1863), 46–49; 56–57.

concurrent, as has been shown, is to unite the community, let its interests be ever so diversified or opposed; while that of the numerical is to divide it into two conflicting portions, let its interests be, naturally, ever so united and identified.

That the numerical majority will divide the community, let it be ever so homogeneous, into two great parties, which will be engaged in perpetual struggles to obtain the control of the government, has already been established. The great importance of the object at stake, must necessarily form strong party attachments and party antipathies;—attachments on the part of the members of each to their repective parties, through whose efforts they hope to accomplish an object dear to all; and antipathies to the opposite party, as presenting the only obstacle to success.

In order to have a just conception of their force, it must be taken in consideration, that the object to be won or lost apppeals to the strongest passions of the human heart,—avarice, ambition, and rivalry. It is not then wonderful, that a form of government, which periodically stakes all its honors and emoluments, as prizes to be contended for, should divide the community into two great hostile parties; or that party attachments, in the progress of the strife, should become so strong among the members of each respectively, as to absorb almost every feeling of our nature, both social and individual; or that their mutual antipathies should be carried to such an excess as to destroy, almost entirely, all sympathy between them, and to substitute in its place the strongest aversion. Nor is it surprising, that under their joint influence, the community should cease to be the common centre of attachment, or that each party should find that centre only in itself. It is thus, that, in such governments, devotion to party becomes stronger than devotion to country;—the promotion of the interests of party more important than the promotion of the common good of the whole, and its triumph and ascendency, objects of far greater solicitude, than the safety and prosperity of the community. It is thus, also, that the numerical majority, by regarding the community as a unity, and having, as such, the same interests throughout all its parts, must, by its necessary operation, divide it into two hostile parts, waging, under the forms of law, incessant hostilities against each other.

The concurrent majority, on the other hand, tends to unite the most opposite and conflicting interests, and to blend the whole in one common attachment to the country. By giving to each interest, or portion, the power of self-protection, all strife and struggle between them for ascendency is prevented and, thereby, not only every feeling calculated to weaken the attachment to the whole is suppressed, but the individual and the social feelings are made to unite in one common devotion to country. Each sees and feels that it can best promote its own prosperity by conciliating the goodwill, and promoting the prosperity of the others. And hence, there will be diffused throughout the whole community kind feelings between its different portions; and, instead of antipathy, a rivalry amongst them to promote the interests of each other, as far as this can be done consistently with the interest of all. Under the combined influence of these causes, the interests of each would be merged in the common interests of the whole; and thus, the community would become a unit, by becoming the common centre of attachment of all its parts. And hence, instead of faction, strife, and struggle for party ascendency, there would be patriotism, nationality, harmony, and a struggle only for supremacy in promoting the common good of the whole. . . .

There is another error, no less great and dangerous, usually associated with the one which has just been considered. I refer to the opinion, that liberty and equality are so intimately united, that liberty cannot be perfect without perfect equality.

That they are united to a certain extent,—and that equality of citizens, in the eyes of the law, is essential to liberty in a popular government, is conceded. But to go further, and make equality of *condition* essential to liberty, would be to destroy both liberty and progress. The reason is, that inequality of condition, while it is a necessary consequence of liberty, is, at the same time, indispensable to progress. In order to understand why this is so, it is necessary to bear in mind, that the main spring to progress is, the desire of individuals to better their condition; and that the strongest impulse which can be given to it is, to leave individuals free to exert themselves in the manner they may deem best for that purpose, as far at least as it can be done consistently with the ends for which government is ordained,—and to secure to all the fruits of their exertions. Now, as individuals differ greatly from each other, in intelligence, sagacity, energy, perseverance, skill, habits of industry and economy, physical power, position and opportunity,—the necessary effect of leaving all free to exert themselves to better their condition, must be a corresponding inequality between those who may possess these qualities and advantages in a high degree, and those who may be deficient in them. The only means by which this result can be prevented are, either to impose such restrictions on the exertions of those who may possess them in a high degree, as will place them on a level with those who do not; or to deprive them of the fruits of their exertions. But to impose such restrictions on them would be destructive of liberty,—while, to deprive them of the fruits of their exertions, would be to destroy the desire of bettering their condition. It is, indeed, this inequality of condition between the front and rear ranks, in the march of progress, which gives so strong an impulse to the former to maintain their position, and to the latter to press forward into their files. This gives to progress its greatest impulse. To force the front rank back to the rear, or attempt to push forward the rear into line with the front, by the interposition of the government, would put an end to the impulse, and effecutally arrest the march of progress.

DOCUMENT NO. 7

A SOUTHERNER DEFENDS SLAVERY*

The rapid growth of industrial capitalism, with its accompanying social and economic disruptions, deeply troubled some conservatives. Among them was the apologist for slavery, George Fitzhugh, who offered the highly unorthodox argument that the conditions of southern slaves were preferable to those of northern wage earners. Scoffing at abstract rights and utopian fantasies, he preferred order to the vicissitudes of change. That order, he reminded his readers, was ultimately grounded in force.

γ   γ   γ

Nothing written on the subject of slavery from the time of Aristotle, is worth reading, until the days of the modern Socialists. Nobody, treating of it, thought it worth while to enquire from history and statistics, whether the physical and moral condition of emancipated serfs or slaves had been improved or rendered worse by emancipation. None would condescend to compare the evils of domestic slavery with the evils of liberty without property. . . . It never occurred to either the enemies or the apologists for slavery, that if no one would employ the free laborer, his condition was infinitely worse than that of actual slavery—nor did it occur to them, that if his wages were less than the allowance of the slave, he was less free after emancipation than before. . . .

We do not conceive that there can be any other moral law in free society, than that which teaches "that he is most meritorious who most wrongs his fellow beings:" for any other law would make men martyrs to their own virtues. We see thousands of good men vainly struggling against the evil necessities of their situation, and aggravating by their charities the evils which they would cure, for charity in free society is but the tax which skill and capital levy from the working poor, too often, to bestow on the less deserving and idle poor. We know a man at the North who owns millions of dollars, and would throw every cent into the ocean to benefit mankind. But it is capital, and, place it where he will, it becomes an engine to tax and oppress the laboring poor.

It is impossible to place labor and capital in harmonious or friendly

* George Fitzhugh, *Cannibals All! or, Slaves without Masters* (Richmond, VA: A. Morris, 1857), pp. 33; 47–49; 53; 358–359; 361–362.

relations, except by the means of slavery, which identifies their interests. Would that gentleman lay his capital out in land and negroes, he might be sure, in whatever hands it came, that it would be employed to protect laborers, not to oppress them; for when slaves are worth near a thousand dollars a head, they will be carefully and well provided for. In any other investment he may make of it, it will be used as an engine to squeeze the largest amount of labor from the poor, for the least amount of allowance. We say allowance, not wages; for neither slaves nor free laborers get wages, in the popular sense of the term: that is, the employer or capitalist pays them from nothing of his own, but allows them a part, generally a very small part, of the proceeds of their own labor. Free laborers pay one another, for labor creates all values, and capital, after taking the lion's share by its taxing power, pays the so-called wages of one laborer from the proceeds of the labor of another. Capital does not breed, yet remains undiminished. Its profits are but its taxing power. Men seek to become independent, in order to cease to pay labor; in order to become masters, without the cares, duties and responsibilities of masters. Capital exercises a more perfect compulsion over free laborers, than human masters over slaves: for free laborers must at all times work or starve, and slaves are supported whether they work or not. Free laborers have less liberty than slaves, are worse paid and provided for, and have no valuable rights. Slaves, with more of actual practical liberty, with ampler allowance, and constant protection, are secure in the enjoyment of all the rights, which provide for their physical comfort at all times and under all circumstances. The free laborer must be employed or starve, yet no one is obliged to employ him. the slave is taken care of, whether employed or not. Though each free laborer has no particular master, his wants and other men's capital, make him a slave without a master, or with too many masters, which is as bad as none. It were often better that he had an ascertained master, instead of an irresponsible and unascertained one. . . .

We have said that laborers pay all taxes, but labor being capital in slave society, the laborers or slaves are not injured by increased taxes; and the capitalist or master has to retrench his own expenses to meet the additional tax. Capital is not taxed in free society, but *is taxed* in slave society, because, in such society, labor is capital.

The capitalist and the professional can, and do, by increased profits and fees, throw the whole burden of taxation on the laboring class.

Slaveholders cannot do so; for diminished allowance to their slaves, would impair their value and lessen their own capital. . . .

Looking to theory, to the examples of the Ancient Repubics, and to England under the Plantagenets, we shall find that Southern institutions are far the best now existing in the world.

We think speculations as to constructing governments are little worth; for all government is the gradual accretion of Nature, time and circumstances. Yet these theories have occurred to us, and, as they are conservative, we will suggest them. In slave-holding countries all freemen should vote and govern, because their interests are conservative. In free states, the government should be in the hands of the land-owners, who are conservative. A system of primogeniture, and entails of small parcels of land, might, in great measure, identify the interests of all; or, at least, those who held no lands would generally be the children and kinsmen of those who did, and be taken care of by them. The frequent accumulation of large fortunes, and consequent pauperism of the masses, is the greatest evil of modern society. Would not small entails prevent this? All cannot own lands, but as many should own them as is consistent with good farming and advanced civilization. The social institutions of the Jews, as established by Moses and Joshua, most nearly fulfill our ideas of perfect government.

A word, at parting, to Northern Conservatives. A like danger threatens North and South, proceeding from the same source. Abolitionism is maturing what Political Economy began. With inexorable sequence "Let Alone" is made to usher in No-Government. North and South our danger is the same, and our remedies, though differing in degree, must in character be the same. "Let Alone" must be repudiated, if we would have any Government. We must, in all sections, act upon the principle that the world is "too little governed." You of the North need not institute negro slavery; far less reduce white men to the state of negro slavery. But the masses require more of protection, and the masses and philosophers equally require more of control. . . . That country is "too little governed," where the best and most conservative citizens have to resolve themselves into mobs and vigilance committees to protect rights which government should, but does not, protect. . . .

Physical force, not moral suasion, governs the world. The negro sees the driver's lash, becomes accustomed to obedient, cheerful industry, and is not aware that the lash is the force that impels him. The free citizen fulfills . . . his round of social, political and domestic duties, and never dreams that the Law, with its fines and jails, penitentiaries and halters, or Public Opinion, with its ostracism, its mobs, and its tar and feathers, help to keep him revolving in his orbit. Yet, remove these physical forces, and how many good citizens would shoot, like fiery comets, from their spheres, and disturb society with their eccentricities and their crimes.

DOCUMENT NO. 8

AN ARGUMENT FOR
LAISSEZ-FAIRE CONSERVATISM*

Social Darwinism had little tolerance for tradition or sentiment. The race was to the swift and the strong; those who lagged behind deserved their fate. No publicist voiced this new laissez-faire conservatism more forcefully or persistently than William Graham Sumner. Despite his disavowal of sentimentality, his warm feelings for the "forgotten man" and "forgotten woman" are evident.

γ   γ   γ

. . . The truth is that cupidity, selfishness, envy, malice, lust, vindictiveness, are constant vices of human nature. They are not confined to classes or to nations or particular ages of the world. . . . All history is only one long story to this effect: men have struggled for power over fellow-men in order that they might win the joys of earth at the expense of others and might shift the burdens of life from their own shoulders upon those of others. It is true that, until this time, the proletariat, the mass of mankind, have rarely had the power and they have not made such a record as kings and nobles and priests have made of the abuses they would perpetrate against their fellow-men when they could and dared. But what folly it is to think that vice and passion are limited by classes, that liberty consists only in taking power away from nobles and priests and giving it to artisans and peasants and that these latter will never abuse it! They will abuse it just as all others have done unless they are put under checks and guarantees, and there can be no civil liberty anywhere unless rights are guaranteed against all abuses, as well from proletarians as from generals, aristocrats, and ecclesiastics.

. . . We have come, under the regime of liberty and equality before the law, to a form of society which is based not on status, but on free contract. . . . In a society based on free contract, men come together as free and independent parties to an agreement which is of mutual advantage. The relation is rational, even rationalistic. It is not poetical. It does

---

* William Graham Sumner, *The Forgotten Man and Other Essays*, ed. Albert Galloway Keller (New Haven, CT: Yale University Press, 1918), pp. 470; 475–476; 491–492; 494–495.

157

not exist from use and custom, but for reasons given, and it does not endure by prescripton but ceases when the reason for it ceases. There is no sentiment in it at all. The fact is that, under the regime of liberty and equality before the law, there is no place for sentiment in trade or politics as public interests. Sentiment is thrown back into private life, into personal relations, and if ever it comes into a public discussion of an impersonal and general public question it always produces mischief.

    . . . The paupers and the physically incapacitated are an inevitable charge on society. About them no more need be said. But the weak who constantly arouse the pity of humanitarians and philanthropists are the shiftless, the imprudent, the negligent, the impractical, and the inefficient, or they are the idle, the intemperate, the extravagant, and the vicious. Now the troubles of these persons are constatly forced upon public attention, as if they and their interests deserved especial consideration, and a great portion of all organized and unorganized effort for the common welfare consists in attempts to relieve these classes of people. I do not wish to be understood now as saying that nothing ought to be done for these people by those who are stronger and wiser. That is not my point. What I want to do is point out the thing which is overlooked and the error which is made in all these charitable efforts. The notion is accepted as if it were not open to any question that if you help the inefficient and vicious you may gain something for society or you may not, but that you lose nothing. This is a complete mistake. Whatever capital you divert to the support of a shiftless and good-for-nothing person is so much diverted from some other employment, and that means from somebody else. . . . Now this other man who would have got it but for the charitable sentiment which bestowed it on a worthless member of society is the Forgotten Man. . . .

    Now who is the Forgotten Man? He is the simple, honest laborer, ready to earn his living by productive work. We pass him by because he is independent, self-supporting, and asks no favors. He does not appeal to the emotons or excite the sentiments. He only wants to make a contract and fulfill it, with respect on both sides and favor on neither side. He must get his living out of the capital of the country. The larger the capital is, the better living he can get. Every particle of capital which is wasted on the vicious, the idle, and the shiftless is so much taken from the capital available to reward the independent and productive laborer. . . .

    Such is the Forgotten Man. He works, he votes, generally he prays—

but he always pays—yes, above all, he pays. He does not want an office; his name never gets into the newspaper except when he gets married or dies. He keeps production going on. He contributes to the strength of parties. He is flattered before election. He is strongly patriotic. He is wanted, whenever, in his little circle, there is work to be done or counsel to be given. He may grumble some occasionally to his wife and family, but he does not frequent the grocery or talk politics at the tavern. Consequently, he is forgotten. He is a commonplace man. He gives no trouble. He excites no admiration. He is not in any way a hero (like a popular orator); or a problem (like tramps and outcasts); nor notorious (like criminals); nor an object of sentiment (like the poor and weak); nor a burden (like paupers and loafers); nor an object out of which social capital may be made (like the beneficiaries of church and state charities); nor an object for charitable aid and protecton (like animals treated with cruelty); nor one over whom sentimental economists and statesmen can parade their fine sentiments (like inefficient workmen and shiftless artisans). Therefore, he is forgotten. All the burdens fall on him, or on her, for it is time to remember that the Forgotten Man is not seldom a woman. . . .

It is plain enough that the Forgotten Man and the Forgotten Woman are the very life and substance of society. . . . Whatever you do for any of the petted classes wastes capital. If you do anything for the Forgotten Man, you must secure him his earnings and savings, that is, you legislate for the security of capital and for its free employment; you must oppose paper money, wildcat banking and usury laws and you must maintain the inviolability of contracts. Hence you must be prepared to be told that you favor the capitalist class, the enemy of the poor man.

. . . Every step which we win in liberty will set the Forgotten Man free from some of his burdens and allow him to use his powers for himself and for the commonwealth.

DOCUMENT NO. 9

THE EFFECTS OF PUBLIC
OPINION ON DEMOCRACY*

Technological advances, commercialism and sensationalistic yellow journalism combined to create a mass readership for American newspapers in the late nineteenth century. This wider reading public in turn influenced politics—and not for the better, according to Edward Lawrence Godkin. Deploring the decline in serious reading as one of the "unforeseen tendencies of democracy," the journalist in his criticisms anticipated ones that are relevant a century later.

γ　　　　　γ　　　　　γ

Nothing is more striking in the reading public to-day, in our democracy, than the increasing incapacity for continuous attention. The power of attention is one that, just like muscular power, needs cultivation or training. The ability to listen to a long argument or exposition, or to read it, involves not only strength but habit in the muscles of the eye or the nerves of the ear. In familiar language, one has to be used to it, to do it easily.

There seems to be a great deal of reason for believing that this habit is becoming much rarer. Publishers complain more and more of the refusal of nearly every modern community to read books, except novels, which keep the attention alive by amusing incidents and rapid changes of situation. Argumentative works can rarely count on a large circulation. This may doubtless be ascribed in part to the multiplicity of the objects of attention in modern times, to the opportunities of simple amusement, to the large area of the world which is brought under each man's observation by the telegraph, and to the general rapidity of communication. But this large area is brought under observation through the newspaper; and that the newspaper's mode of presenting facts does seriously affect the way in which people perform the process called "making up their minds," especially about public questions, can hardly be denied. The nearest approach we can make to what people are think-

* Edward Lawrence Godkin, "The Growth and Expression of Public Opinion," *Unforeseen Tendencies of Democracy* (Westminster, England: Archibald Constable & Co., 1903), pp. 196–200; 212–215.

ing about any matter of public interest is undoubtedly by "reading the papers." It may not be a sure way, but there is no other. It is true, often, lamentably true, that the only idea most foreigners and observers get of a nation's modes of thought and standards of duty and excellence, and in short of its manners and morals, comes through reading its periodicals. . . .

In America more than in any other country, the collection of "news" has become a business within half a century, and it has been greatly promoted by the improvements in the printing-press. Before this period, "news" was generally news of great events,—that is, of events of more than local importance; so that if a man were asked, "What news?" he would try, in his answer, to mention something of world-wide significance. But as soon as the collection of it became a business, submitted to the ordinary laws of competition, the number of things that were called "news" naturally increased. Each newspaper endeavored to outdo its rival by the greater number of facts it brought to the public notice, and it was not very long before "news" became whatever, no matter how unimportant, which the reader had not previoulsy heard of. The sense of proporton about news was rapidly destroyed. Everything, however trifling, was considered worth printing, and the newspaper finally became, what it is now, a collection of the gossip, not only of the whole world, but of its own locality. . . .

The diligent newspaper reader, therefore, gets accustomed to passing rapidly from one to another of a series of incidents, small and great, requiring simply the tranfer, from one trifle to another, of a sort of lazy, uninterested attention, which often beomes sub-conscious; that is, a man reads with hardly any knowledge or recollection of what he is reading. . . . That this should have its effect on the editorial writing is what naturally might be expected. If the editorial article is long, the reader, used to the short paragraphs, is apt to shrink from the labor of perusing it; if it is brief, he pays little more attention to it than he pays to the paragraphs. When, therefore, any newspaper turns to serious discussion in its columns, it is difficult, and one may say increasingly difficult, to get a hearing. . . .

One might go over the civilized world in this way, and find that the public opinion of each country, on any given topic, had escaped from the philosophers, so to speak,—that all generalizing about it had become difficult, and that it was no longer possible to divide influences into categories.

The conclusion most readily reached about the whole matter is that authority, whether in religion or in morals, which down to the last century was so powerful, has ceased to exert much influence on the affairs of the modern world, and that any attempt to mould opinion on religious or moral or political questions, by its instrumentality, is almost certain to prove futile. . . . This is tantamount to saying that historic experience has not nearly the influence on political affairs it once had. The reason is obvious. The number of persons who have something to say about political affairs has increased a thousandfold, but the practice of reading books has not increased, and it is in books that experience is recorded. In the past, the governing class, in part at least, was a reading class. . . . Their successors rarely read anything but newspapers. This is increasingly true, also, of other democratic countries. The old literary type of statesmen, of which Jefferson and Madison and Hamilton, Guizot and Thiers, were examples, is rapidly disappearing, if it has not already disappeared.

The importance of this in certain branches of public affairs is great, —the management of currency, for example. All we know about currency we learn from the experience of the human race. What man will do about any kind of money,—gold, silver, or paper,—under any given set of conditions, we can predict only by reading of what man has done. . . . The loss of influence or weight by the reading class is therefore of great importance, for to this loss we undoubtedly owe most of the prevalent wild theories about currency. They are the theories of men who do not know that their experiments have been tried already and have failed. In fact, I may almost venture the assertion that the influence of history on politics was never smaller than it is to-day, although history was never before cultivated with so much acumen and industry. So that authority and experience may fairly be ruled out of the list of forces which seriously influence the government of democratic societies. In the formation of public opinion they do not greatly count.

DOCUMENT NO. 10

A CULTURAL
CONSERVATIVE'S AMBIVALENCE*

Few men of letters sought to assess the positive and negative qualities of American life and manners more thoughtfully or impartially than Charles Eliot Norton. Generally pleased for its material advances, he lamented the nation's cultural shortcomings. As the nineteenth century gave way to the twentieth, he grew increasingly concerned for the future but still found hopeful signs. Unlike the poet Edward Arlington Robinson's Minver Cheevey, he did not long to return to an imagined golden age—except perhaps for the New England of his youth.

γ   γ   γ

To J. B. Harrison

13 March 1894

. . . I agree with your view of the character of our people, but it makes me less despondent than it seems to make you. I do not wonder at their triviality, their shallowness, their materialism. I rather wonder that, considering their evolution and actual circumstances, they are not worse. Here are sixty or seventy millions of people of whom all but a comparatively small fraction have come up, within two or three generations, from the lower orders of society. They belong by descent to the oppressed from the beginning of history, to the ignorant, to the servile class or to the peasantry. They have no traditions of intellectual life, no power of sustained thought, no developed reasoning facultly. But they constitute on the whole as good a community on a large scale as the world has ever seen. Low as their standards may be, yet taken in the mass they are higher than so many millions of men ever previously attained. They are seeking material comfort in a brutal way, and securing in large measure what they seek, but they are not inclined to open robbery or cruel extortion. On the whole they mean "to do about right." I marvel at their self-restraint. That they are getting themselves and us all into dangerous difficulties is clear, but I believe they will somehow,

---

* *Letters of Charles Eliot Norton*, eds. Norton, Sara and M. A. De Wolfe Howe, Vol. 2 (Boston and New York: Houghton Mifflin, 1913), pp. 219–220; 236–237; 243–244; 304–305.

with a good deal of needless suffering, continue to stumble along without great catastrophe.

The world has never been a pleasant place for a rational man to live in. I doubt if it is a worse place for him now than it has been in past times. . . .

To Leslie Stephen

8 January 1896

. . . But there is a deeper consideration. The rise of the democracy to power in America and in Europe is not, as has been hoped, to be a safeguard of peace and civilization. It is the rise of the uncivilized, whom no school education can suffice to provide with intelligence and reason, It looks as if the world were entering on a new stage of experience, unlike anything heretofore, in which there must be a new discipline of suffering to fit men for the new conditions. I fear that America is beginning a long course of error and of wrong, and is likely to become more and more a power for disturbance and for barbarism. The worst sign is the lack of seriousness in the body of the people; its triviality, and its indifference to moral principle. . . .

To Samuel G. Ward

26 April 1896

. . . You say that Democracy insures a teachable people; in a sense, yes. But I do not feel sure that it is not becoming less open to any teaching but that of its own experience. The scorn of wisdom, the rejection of authority, are part and parcel of the process of development of the democracy. The rapid growth of its prosperity and power in this country has given to it an extravagant self-confidence, and disposes it to make self-will the rule of conduct. It seems to me not unlikely that for a considerable time to come there will be an increase of lawlessness and of public folly,—and that the calamities resulting from these conditions are to be the hammers by which better dispositions and better conditions are to be slowly beaten out on the anvils of time.

Democracy, ideally, means universal public spirit; practically it exhibits itself in its acute phase as general selfishness and private spirit. Universal suffrage proves not a means of increasing the sense of individual responsibility, but a distinct source of moral corruption. . . . Men are not worse than they were, but they are exposed in larger numbers to temptations which they are not prepared to resist, and which are threatening to the public welfare.

At any rate there is one consoling reflection, that there are far more human beings materially well off to-day than ever before in the history of the world, and if you and I could have the choice, there is no period at which we would have rather lived, and none in which we could have lived with so much satisfaction in the condition of the generality of our fellows. I believe, indeed, that the very pleasantest little oasis of space and time was that of New England from about the beginning of the century to about 1825. The spirit of that time was embodied in Emerson, in Longfellow, in Holmes and in Lowell. It was an inexperienced and youthful spirit, but it was a happy one; it had the charm of youth, its hope, its simplicity, its sweetness.

How interesting our times have been and still are! None ever so interesting, or so full of change and of problems!

To S. G. Ward

14 April 1901

. . . Certainly the religious, the political, the financial condidtions of our country are extraordinary, and I am at a loss as to the proportion of the good and evil auguries to be drawn from them. Such wide-spread and immense material prosperity is a novelty in the world's history. . . .

There is no force to counteract its influence; for Protestantism as a religion has completely failed. It is not the mere breaking down of its dogma, but the fact of its having become, with the progress of science, vacant of spiritual significance, and a church of essentially insincere profession, that is the ruin of Protestantism. It has no spiritual influence with which to oppose the spirit of materialism. If Rome were but a trifle more enlightened, and instead of opposing, would support and strengthen the American Catholic interpretation of Romanism, the Catholic church in this countlry would rapidly gain in spiritual power, and would render an enormous service in standing against the anarchic irreligion of the unchurched multitude. In spite of Roman obscurantism, it seems to me likely that Catholicism will gain strength among us. For science has obviously nothing but a stone to offer to the ignorant and dependent masses who are always longing for bread, and the Roman church offers a convenient and, for those who like it, a wholesome substitute for the bread. . . .

DOCUMENT NO. 11

A CONSERVATIVE LOOKS TO MEDIEVALISM*

Alienation from modernism afflicted many persons who lived during the late nineteenth and early twentieth centuries. Escapism took such forms as migration to exotic lands, religious conversion, the decadent movement in art and literature, militarism, and medievalism, to name several. Like Charles Eliot Norton and Henry Adams—but much more so—the noted architect Ralph Adams Cram looked to the Middle Ages for guidance. More than cultural, his conservatism envisioned a revivification of medieval traditions and values.

γ　　　　　γ　　　　　γ

. . . To me all that we are doing in architecture indicates the accuracy of the deduction we draw from myriad other manifestations, that we are at the end of an epoch of materialism, rationalism, and intellectualism, and at the beginning of a wonderful new epoch, when once more we achieve a just estimate of comparative values; when material achievement becomes the slave again, and no longer the slave-driver; when spiritual intuition drives mere intellect back into its proper and very circumscribed sphere; and when religion, at the same time dogmatic, sacramental, and mystic, becomes, in the ancient and sounding phrase, "One, Holy, Catholic, and Apostolic," and assumes again its rightful place as the supreme element in life and thought, the golden chain on which are strung, and by which are bound together, the varied jewels of action.

Everywhere, and at the very moment when our material activity and our material triumphs seem to threaten the high stars, appear the evidences that this wonderful thing is coming to pass, and architecture adds its modicum of proof. What else does it mean, that on every hand men now demand in art better things than ever before, and get them, from an ever increasing number of men, whether they are Pagans, Goths, or Vandals? What is the meaning of the return to Gothic, not only in form, but "in spirit and truth"? Is it that we are pleased with its forms and wearied of others? Not at all. It is simply this, that the

---

* Ralph Adams Cram, *The Ministry of Art* (Boston and New York: Houghton Mifflin Company, 1914), pp. 44–46; 55; 62.

166

Renaissance-Reformation-Revolution [French] having run its course, and its epoch having reached its appointed term, we go back, deliberately, or instinctively,—back, as life goes back, as history goes back, to restore something of the antecedent epoch, to win again something we had lost, to return to the fork in the roads, to gain again the old lamps we credulously bartered for new. Men laugh (or did; I think they have given it over of late) at what they call the reactionary nature and the affectation of the Gothic restoration of the moment, and they would be right if it meant what they think it means. Its significance is higher than their estimate, higher than the conscious impulses of those who are furthering the work, for back of it all lies the fact that what we need to-day in our society, in the State, in the Church, is precisely what we abandoned when, as one man, we arose to the cry of the leaders and abettors of the Renaissance. We lost much, but we gained much; now the time has come for us to conserve all that we gained of good, slough off the rest, and then gather up once more the priceless heritage of mediaevalism, so long disregarded.

And that is what the Gothic restoration means, a returning to other days—not for the retrieving of pleasant but forgotten forms, but for the recovery of those impulses in life which made these forms inevitable. . . .

Whether we know it or not,—and some of us act by instinct rather than conviction,—we are fighting the battles of a new civilization, which, like all true civilization, is also the old. . . .

Shall we rest there? Shall we restore a style and a way of life, and a mode of thought? Shall we re-create an amorphous mediaevalism and live listlessly in that fool's paradise? On the contrary. When a man finds himself confronting a narrow stream, with no bridge in sight, does he leap convulsively on the very brink and then project himself into space? If he does he is very apt to fail of his immediate object, which is to get across. No; he retraces his steps, gains his running start, and clears the obstacle at a bound. This is what we architects are doing when we fall back on the great past for our inspiration; this is what, specifically, the Gothicists are particularly doing. We are getting our running start, we are retracing our steps to the great Christian Middle Ages, not that there we may remain, but that we may achieve an adequate point of departure; what follows must take care of itself.

DOCUMENT NO. 12

A NEW HUMANIST URGES ARISTOCRACY*

*Relatively few in number and reaching only a limited audience, the New
Humanists offered a searching critique of early twentieth-century society.
Paul Elmer More, like his friend and fellow New Humanist Irving Babbitt,
was especially concerned by the shortcomings of democracy. His plea for an
aristocracy based on moral character and talent was reminiscent of that
voiced by other conservatives since the earliest years of the republic.*

γ γ γ

. . . The remedy for the evils of licence is not in the elimination of
popular restraint, but precisely in bringing the people to respect and
follow their right leaders. The cure of democracy is not *more* democracy,
but *better* democracy.

Nor is such a cure dependent on the appearance in a community of
men capable of the light, for these the world always has, and these we
too have in abundance; it depends rather on so relating these select natures to the community that they shall be also men of leading. The
danger is, lest, in a State which bestows influence and honours on its
demagogues, the citizens of more refined intelligence, those true philosophers who have discourse of reason, and have won the difficult citadel of their own souls, should withdraw from public affairs and retire
into that citadel as it were into an ivory tower. . . . In such a State distinction becomes the sorry badge of isolation. The need is to provide for
a natural aristocracy.

Now it must be clearly understood that in advocating such a measure,
at least under the conditions that actually prevail today, there is involved
no futile intention of abrogating democracy, in so far as democracy
means government by and of the people. A natural aristocracy does not
demand the restoraton of inherited privilege or a relapse into the crude
dominion of money; it is not synonymous with oligarchy or plutocracy.
It calls rather for some machinery or some social consciousness which
shall ensure both the selection from among the community at large of
the "best" and the bestowal on them of "power"; it is the true consum-

* Paul Elmer More, *Shelburne Essays*, Ninth Series: *Aristocracy and Justice* (Boston and
New York: Houghton Mifflin Company, 1915), pp. 29–32; 35–38.

mation of democracy. . . . No one supposes that the "best" are a sharply defined class moving about among their fellows with a visible halo above them and a smile of beatific superiority on their faces. Society is not made of such classifications, and governments have always been of a more or less mixed character. A natural aristocracy signifies rather a tendency than a conclusion, and in such a sense it was taken, no doubt, by my sociological friend of radical ideas who pronounced it the great practical problem of the day.

The first requisite for solving this problem is that those who are designed by nature, so to speak, to form an aristocracy should come to an understanding of their own belief. There is a question to be faced boldly: What is the true aim of society? Does justice consist primarily in levelling the distribution of powers and benefits, or in proportioning them to the scale of character and intelligence? Is the main purpose of the machinery of government to raise the material welfare of the masses, or to create advantages for the upward striving of the exceptional? Is the state of humanity to be estimated by numbers..? Shall our interest in mankind begin at the bottom and progress upward, or begin at the top and progress downward? To those who feel that the time has come for a reversion from certain present tendencies, the answer to this question cannot be doubtful. Before anything else is done we must purge our minds of the current cant of humanitarianism. This does not mean that we are to deny the individual appeals of pity and introduce a wolfish egotism into human relations. On the contrary, it is just the preaching of false humanitarian doctrines that results practically in weakening the response to rightful obligations . . . In the end the happiness of the people also, in the wider sense, depends on the common recognition of the law of just subordination. But, whatever the ultimate effect of this sort may be, the need now is to counterbalance the excess of emotional humanitarianism with an injection of the truth—even the contemptuous truth. Let us, in the name of a long-suffering God, put some bounds to the flood of talk about the wages of the bricklayer and the trainman, and talk a little more about the income of the artist and teacher and public censor who have taste and strength of character to remain in opposition to the tide. Let us have less cant about the great educative value of the theatre for the people and less humbug about the virtues of the nauseous problem play, and more consideration of what is clean and nourishing food for the larger minds. Let us forget for a while our absorbing desire to fit schools to train boys for the shop and the counting-room, and concern ourselves more effectvely with the dwindling of those disciplinary studies which lift men out of the crowd. . . .

One hears a vast deal these days about a class consciousness, and it is undoubtedly a potent social instrument. Why should there not be an outspoken class consciousness among those who are in advance of civilizatin as well as among those who are in the rear? . . .

Now there is to-day a vast organization for manipulating public opinion in favor of the workingman and for deluding it in the interest of those who grow fat by pandering in the name of emancipation to the baser emotions of mankind; but of organization among those who suffer from the vulgarizing trend of democracy there is little or none. . . .

The instrument by which this control of public opinion is effected is primarily the imagination; and here we meet with a real difficulty. It was the advantage of such a union of aristocracy and inherited oligarchy as Burke advocated that it gave something visible and definite for the imagination to work upon, whereas the democratic aristocracy of character must always be comparatively vague. But we are not left wholly without the means of giving to the imagination a certain sureness of range while remaining within the forms of popular government. The opportunity is in the hands of our higher institutions of learning. . . . In brief the need is to restore to their predominance in the curriculum those studies that train the imagination, not, be it said, the imagination in its purely aesthetic function, though that aspect of it also has been sadly neglected, but the imagination in its power of grasping in a single firm vision, so to speak, the long course of human history and of distinguishing what is essential therein from what is ephemeral. The enormous preponderance of studies that deal with the immediate questions of economics and government inevitably results in isolating the student from the great inheritance of the past; the frequent habit of dragging him through the slums of sociology, instead of making him at home in the society of the noble dead, debauches his mind with a flabby, or inflames it with a fanatic, humanitarianism. He comes out of college, if he has learnt anything, a *nouveau intellectuel*, bearing the same relation to the man of genuine education as the *nouveau riche* to the man of inherited manners; he is narrow and unbalanced, a prey to the prevailing passion of the hour, with no feeling for the majestic claims of that within us which is unchanged from the beginning. . . . There is truth in the Hobbesian maxim that "imagination and memory are but one thing" by their union in education alone shall a man acquire the uninvidious equivalent in character of those broadening influences which came to the oligarch through prescription—he is moulded indeed into the true aristocrat. And with the assertion of what may be called a spiritual prescription he will find among those over whom he is set as leader and guide a measure of respect which springs from something in the human breast more stable and honourable and more conformable to reason than the mere stolidity of unreflecting prejudice. For, when everything is said, there could be no civilized society were it not that deep in our hearts, beneath all the turbulences of greed and vanity, abides the instinct of obedience to what is noble and of good repute. It awaits only the clear call from above.

DOCUMENT NO. 13

A SOUTHERN AGRARIAN TAKES HIS STAND*

Rebelling against the progressive American ethos of the 1920s, the Southern Agrarians stressed the distinctiveness of their regional culture, much as had southerners during the antebellum era. That culture, argued these twentieth-century agrarians, who included the poet and essayist John Crowe Ransom, was a conservative one that drew upon a European heritage, preferred agriculture to industry and commerce, and cherished communal and family ties. While agriculture has increasingly diminished as an economic force in American life, the values of the agrarians have retained their appeal for many conservatives.

γ   γ   γ

The Southerner must know, and in fact he does very well know, that his antique conservatism does not exert a great influence against the American progressivist doctrine. The Southern idea today is down, and the progressive or American idea is up. But the historian and the philosopher, who take views that are thought to be respectively longer and deeper than most, may very well reverse this order and find that the Southern idea rather than the American has in its favor the authority of example and the approval of theory. And some prophet may even find it possible to expect that it will yet rise again.

I will propose a thesis which seems to have about as much cogency as generalizations usually have: The South is unique on this continent for having founded and defended a culture which was according to the European principles of culture; and the European principles had better look to the South if they are to be perpetuated in this country.

. . . The Southern problem is complicated, but at its center is the farmer's problem, and this problem is simply the most acute version of that general agrarian problem which inspires the despair of many thoughtful Americans today.

* Reprinted with the permission of Louisiana State University Press from John Crowe Ransom, "Reconstructed but Unregenerate," in *I'll Take My Stand: The South and the Agrarian Tradition* by Twelve Southerners. Paperback edition, 1977. Pp. 3; 18–22. Copyright 1930 by Harper & Brothers. Copyright renewed 1958 by Donald Davidson. Introduction copyright © 1962, 1977 by Louis D. Rubin, Jr. Biographical essays copyright © 1962, 1977 by Virginia Rock.

The agrarian discontent in America is deeply grounded in the love of the tiller for the soil, which is probably, it must be confessed, not peculiar to the Southern specimen, but one of the more ineradicable human attachments, be the tiller as progressive as he may. In proposing to wean men from this foolish attachment, industrialism sets itself against the most ancient and the most humane of all the modes of human livelihood. Do Mr. Hoover and the distinguished thinkers at Washington see how essential is the mutual hatred between the industrialists and the farmers, and how mortal is their conflict? The gentlemen at Washington are mostly preaching and legislating to secure the fabulous "blessings" of industrial progress; they are on the industrial side. The industrialists have a doctrine which is monstrous, but they are not monsters personally; they are forward-lookers with nice manners, and no American progressivist is against them. The farmers are boorish and inarticulate by comparison. Progressivism is against them in their fight, though their traditional status is still so strong that soft words are still spoken to them. All the solutions recommended for their difficulties are really enticements held out to them to become a little more cooperative, more mechanical, more mobile—in short, a little more industrialized. But the farmer who is not a mere laborer, even the farmer of the comparatively new places like Iowa and Nebraska, is necessarily among the more stable and less progressive elements of society. He refuses to mobilize himself and become a unit in the industrial army, because he does not approve of army life.

I will use some terms which are hardly in the vernacular. He identifies himself with a spot of ground, and this ground carries a good deal of meaning; it defines itself for him as nature. He would till it not too hurriedly and too mechanically to observe in it the contingency and the infinitude of nature; and so his life acquires its philosophical and even its cosmic consciousness. A man can contemplate and explore, respect and love, an object as substantial as a farm or a native province. But he cannot contemplate nor explore, respect nor love, a mere turnover, such as an assemblage of "natural resources," a pile of money, a volume of produce, a market, or a credit system. It is into precisely these intangibles that industrialism would translate the farmer's farm. It means the dehumanization of his life.

However that may be, the South at last, looking defensively about her in all directions upon an industrial world, fingers the weapons of industrialism. There is one powerful voice in the South which, tired of a long status of disrepute, would see the South made at once into a section second to none in wealth, as that is statistically reckoned, and in progressiveness, as that might be estimated by the rapidity of the industrial turnover. This desire offends those who would still like to regard the South as, in the old sense, a home; but its expression is loud and insistent. The urban South, with its heavy importation of regular American ways and regular American citizens, has nearly capitulated to these novelties. It is the village South and the rural South which supply the resistance, and it is lucky for them that they represent a vast quantity of inertia.

Will the Southern establishment, the most substantial exhibit on this continent of a society of the European and historic order, be completely crumbled by the powerful acid of the Great Progressive Principle? Will there be no more looking backward but only looking forward? Is our New World to be dedicated forever to the doctrine of newness?

It is in the interest of America as a whole, as well as in the interest of the South, that these questions press for an answer. I will enter here the most important items of the situation as well as I can; doubtless they will appear a little over-sharpened for the sake of exhibition.

(1) The intention of Americans at large appears now to be what it was always in danger of becoming: an intention of being infinitely progressive. But this intention cannot permit of an established order of human existence, and of that leisure which conditions the life of intelligence and the arts.

(2) The old South, if it must be defined in a word, practiced the contrary and European philosophy of establishment as the foundation of the life of the spirit. The ante-bellum Union possessed, to say the least, a wholesome variety of doctrine.

(3) But the South was defeated by the Union on the battlefield with remarkable decisiveness, and the two consequences have been dire: the Southern tradition was physically impaired, and has ever since been unable to offer an attractive example of its philosophy in action; and the American progressive principle has developed into a pure industrialism without any check from a Southern minority whose voice ceased to make itself heard.

(4) The further survival of the Southern tradition as a detached local remnant is now unlikely. It is agreed that the South must make contact again with the Union. And in adapting itself to the actual state of the

Union, the Southern tradition will have to consent to a certain indus-trialization of its own.

(5) The question at issue is whether the South will permit herself to be so industrialized as to lose entirely her historic identity, and to re-move the last substantial barrier that has stood in the way of American progressivism; or will accept industrialism, but with a very bad grace, and will manage to maintain a good deal of her traditional philosophy.

DOCUMENT NO. 14

A CONSERVATIVE OPPOSES UNIVERSAL
MILITARY TRAINING*

A strong isolationist bent characterized numerous conservatives before Pearl Harbor, especially midwestern conservatives like Senator Robert A. Taft. After World War II, Taft, widely known as "Mr. Republican," adopted a cautious approach to the nation's involvement in the Cold War. This three-time unsuccessful candidate for his party's presidential nomination carefully weighed the prospect of global confrontation with communism against the cost to individual liberties and the nation's economic well-being.

γ   γ   γ

. . . The President has requested a budget for the ensuing 12 months of approximately $11,000,000,000, and now there is a demand for an additional three or four billion dollars.

Certainly I am in favor of a military force which will be wholly adequate to defend the United States. But is such a large sum necessary? Are we organizing our armed forces to get full value from every dollar? What kind of weapons and what kind of forces do we need in order that we may get most value out of every dollar spent?

We are met at the outset by the suggestion that we civilians can know nothing of the problem, that every decision must be made by military authorities who are experts on these problems. Of course, this argument cannot be true. The ultimate decision on over-all questions of defense and even military policy must be made by a civilian government. If we admit the final authority of the military to decide these problems, it means that they will soon have in their hands the entire economic and political future of the United States. No student of government can be found who advocates the leaving of final decisions in time of peace, or even perhaps in time of war, to a military commander. We would lose our personal liberties and our worth-while national existence. Of course we must ask and heed their advice, but the ultimate decision is a decision

---

* U.S., Congress, Senate, Senator Robert A. Taft speaking on "Universal Military Training and National Defense," 80th Cong., 2d sess., 20 April 1948, *Congressional Record* 94: 2359–2360.

to be made by the people themselves through their elected representatives. Otherwise there will be no liberty or equality under law.

In the first place, the perfectionist in military defense would insist
on such a complete military force that there would be no possibility
whatever of any attack from abroad. But such a force might cost from
50 to 100 billion dollars a year, as it did during the war, and would make
impossible any reasonable standard of living, or any freedom of this Nation to develop the destinies of its people in a free life and an improved
material well-being.

The conclusion is that we must get a defense which will make this
country substantially safe without destroying the possibility of the improvement of civilian life. We must be selective therefore among the
various means of defense which are proposed. We must not duplicate
services in the Army, the Navy, and the Air Force. We must abandon
those activities which seem of secondary importance and perhaps no
longer in accord with the new situations which have arisen in military
strategy.

I belive further that we should remember that success in war has ap-
parently depended more on the existence of a great civilian productive
power, developed primarily to improve the conditions of the civilian
population. It was our great industrial capacity and our industrial know-
how which made it possible for us, without an Army trained in advance, to conquer the greatest and most powerful technically trained
and equipped armies in the history of the world.

We must realize that the main purpose of any foreign policy should
be the freedom of the United States, and the second guiding policy
should be the maintenance of the peace. The first line of national defense, in fact, consists of keeping the peace, so that there may be no
need to test the adequacy of our defense forces. . . .

Regardless of our will to peace, of course, we must recognize that in
this modern world we may be attacked. We must recognize that a modern attack with weapons which have been developed may be more sudden, swift, and effective than anything the world has ever seen. We must
under all circumstances be prepared to meet such an attack. While the
Russian attitude remains what it is, we had better retain the atomic
bomb. . . .

It seems obvious to me today that the next war will be fought predominantly in the air. The only complete protection that we can give to

this country against modern weapons is to have an air force able to dominate the air over this continent. . . .

I cannot understand, however, the value of universal military training as a means of defense. And whatever one may think of it as a permanent provision, it certainly seems to have no value as a solution of the present emergency. . . .

UMT would undertake to train approximately 1,000,000 boys every year to provide about 10,000,000 men of military age with such one-year training. It would be a tremendously espensive operation . . . I am basically opposed to it because it seems to me literally the very regimentation which we are trying to avoid.

There can be no greater limitation of freedom than to take men from their education, their homes and their occupations and force them into a camp to be trained according to the dictates of some War Department bureau in Washington. "Indoctrination" is the term which has been common in Army circles during the war. It means the educating of boys by a Federal bureau according to the ideologies which dominate that bureau. We have just passed a Federal-aid-to-education bill, but it prohibits completely any direct Federal interference or any direct Federal education. I certainly am opposed to the Federal Government interfering in education, because I think that it presents a real danger to the whole philosophy of American government. . . .

If we want an effective reserve it ought to be a much smaller number of men, much more highly trained and technically trained. It ought to be organized on the basis of the National Guard and the ROTC and kept constantly in touch with the developments of the Regular Army. Men should be paid for the time which they have to give. If the armed forces once abandoned the dream of a perpetual draft of involuntary manpower and turned to the problem of maintaining proper reserve components with high morale, they would get a much better reserve and they can get it on a voluntary basis.

In this whole field there is no reason why our approach should not be governed by the same principles of liberty as must guide other Government programs. UMT is a return to the New Deal belief that results can only be accomplished by Government complulsion, and power given to Government bureaus. The New Dealers have scoffed at the idea that the people can work out their own salvation, or work out their own problems without Government direction. Their every move has supported the idea of more power for the state and less power for the individual.

Those methods have failed in the field of economic control. They have failed even to provide the education and social security which is the greatest promise of the New Deal. I believe very strongly that economic and intellectual progress in this country can only result from the restoration of the liberty of the people. And even more strongly I believe that in providing a defense against possible foreign attacks on the liberty of our people we cannot adopt methods by which we ourselves destroy our own liberty.

DOCUMENT NO. 15

WILLIAM F. BUCKLEY, JR. SPEAKS OUT FOR CONSERVATISM*

No person contributed more to the revival of conservatism during the post–World War II era than William F. Buckley, Jr. Despite confessing that he was less sure of who was a conservative than who was a liberal, he has usually made the distinction abundantly clear in his diverse writings and speaking engagements. In Up from Liberalism *he elaborated on this distinction and articulated the principles and practical concerns of many mid-twentieth century conservatives.*

γ   γ   γ

. . . Conservatives do not deny the existence of undiscovered truths, but they make a critical assumption, which is that those truths that have *already* been apprehended are more important to cultivate than those undisclosed ones close to the liberal grasp only in the sense that the fruit was close to Tantalus, yet around whose existence virtually the whole of modern academic theory revolves. Conservatism is the tacit acknowledgement that all that is finally important in human experience is behind us; that the crucial explorations have been undertaken, and that it is given to man to know what are the great truths that emerged from them. Whatever is to come cannot outweigh the importance to man of what has gone before.

There is nothing so ironic as the nihilist or relativist (or the believer in the kind of academic freedom that postulates the equality of ideas) who complains of the anti-intellectualism of American conservatives. Such is *our* respect for the human mind that we pay it the supreme honor: we credit it with having arrived at certain great conclusions. We believe that millenniums of intellect have served an objective purpose. Certain problems have been disposed of. Certain questions are closed: and with reference to that fact the conservative orders his life and, to the extent he is called upon by circumstances to do so, the life of the community . . .

* William F. Buckley, Jr., *Up from Liberalism* rev. ed. (New Rochelle, NY: Arlington House, 1968), pp. 182–183; 218–221; 223–224; 228–229. Reprinted with the kind permission of the author.

Up where from liberalism? There is no conservative political manifesto which, as we make our faltering way, we can consult, confident that it will point a sure finger in the direction of the good society. Indeed, sometimes the conservative needle appears to be jumping about on a disoriented compass. . . .

Still, for all the confusion and contradiction, I venture to say it is possible to talk about "the conservative position" and mean something by it. At the political level, conservatives are bound together for the most part by negative response to liberalism; but altogether too much is made of that fact. Negative action is not necessarily of negative value. Political freedom's principal value is negative in character. The people are politically stirred principally by the necessity for negative affirmations. Cincinnatus was a farmer before he took up his sword, and went back to farming after wielding some highly negative strokes upon the pates of those who sought to make positive changes in his way of life.

. . . A navigator for whom two lighthouses can mark extreme points of danger relative to his present position, knows that by going back and making a wholly different approach, the two lighthouses will fuse together to form a single object to the vision, confirming the safety of his position. They are then said to be "in range."

There is a point from which opposition to the social security laws and a devout belief in social stability are in range; as also a determined resistance to the spread of world Communism—and a belief in political non-interventionism; a disgust with the results of modern education—and sympathy for the individual educational requirements of the individual child; a sympathetic understanding of the spiritual essence of human existence—and a desire to delimit religous influence in political affairs; a patriotic concern for the nation and its culture—and a genuine respect for the integrity and differences of other peoples' culture; a militant concern for the Negro—and a belief in decentralized political power even though, on account of it, the Negro is sometimes victimized; a respect for the onmicompetence of the free marketplace—and the knowledge of the necessity for occupational interposition. There is a position from which these views are "in range"; and that is the position, generally speaking, where conservatives now find themselves on the political chart. Our most serious challenge is to restore principles—the right principles; the principles liberalism has abused, forsaken, and replaced with "principles" that have merely a methodological content—our challenge is to restore principles to public affairs. . . .

Conservatism must insist that while the will of man is limited in what it can do, it can do enough to make over the face of the world; and that the question that must always be before us is, What shape should the world take, given modern realities? How can technology hope to invalidate conservatism: Freedom, individuality, the sense of community, the sanctity of the family, the supremacy of the conscience, the spiritual view of life—can these verities be transmuted by the advent of tractors and adding machines? These have had a smashing social effect upon us, to be sure. They have created a vortex into which we are being drawn as though irresistibly; but that, surely, is because the principles by which we might have made anchor have not been used, not because of their insufficiency or proven inadaptability. . . .

Freedom and order and community and justice in an age of technology: that is the contemporary challenge of political conservatism. . . .

Conservatives do not deny that technology poses enormous problems; they insist only that the answers of liberalism create worse problems than those they set out to solve. Conservatives cannot be blind, or give the appearance of being blind, to the dismaying spectacle of unemployment, or any other kind of suffering. But conservatives can insist that the statist solution to the problem is inadmissible. It is not the single conservative's responsibility or right to draft a concrete program —merely to suggest the principles that should frame it.

What then *is* the indicated course of action? It is to maintain and wherever possible enhance the freedom of the individual to acquire property and dispose of that property in ways that he decides on. To deal with unemployment by eliminating monopoly unionism, featherbedding, and inflexibilities in the labor market, and be prepared, where residual unemployment persists, to cope with it locally, placing the political and humanitarian responsibility on the lowest feasible political unit. Boston can surely find a way to employ gainfully its 136 textile specialists—and its way would be very different, predictably, from Kentucky's with the coal miners; and let them be different. Let the two localities experiment with different solutions, and let the natural desire of the individual for more goods, and better educcation, and more leisure, find satisfaction in individual encounters with the marketplace, in the growth of private schools, in the myriad economic and charitable activities which, because they took root in the individual imagination and impulse, take organic form. And then let us see whether we are better off than we would be living by decisions made bewween nine and five in

Washington office rooms, where the oligarchs of the Affluent Society sit, allocating complaints and solutions to communities represented by pins on the map.

Is that a program? Call it a No-Program, if you will, but adopt it for your very own. I will not cede more power to the state. I will not willingly cede more power to anyone, not to the state, not to General Motors, not to the CIO. I will hoard my power like a miser, resisting every effort to drain it away from me. I will then use *my* power, as *I* see fit. I mean to live my life an obedient man, but obedient to God, subservient to the wisdom of my ancestors; never to the authority of political truths arrived at yesterday at the voting booth. That is a program of sorts, is it not?

It is certainly program enough to keep conservatives busy, and liberals at bay. And the nation free.

DOCUMENT NO. 16

YOUNG CONSERVATIVES AFFIRM
THEIR PRINCIPLES*

Meeting at the home of their intellectual mentor, William F. Buckley, Jr., in Sharon, Connecticut, a small group of young conservatives calling themselves Young Americans for Freedom (YAF) enunciated their beliefs and pledged themselves to political activism. They strongly supported Barry Goldwater's presidential race in 1964. Later, a number of them became influential conservative figures.

γ   γ   γ

Adopted by the Young Americans for Freedom
in conference at Sharon, Conn., September 9–11, 1960

In this time of moral and political crisis, it is the responsibility of the youth of America to affirm certain eternal truths.

We, as young conservatives, believe:

That foremost among the transcendent values is the individual's use of his God-given free will, whence derives his right to be free from the restrictions of arbitrary force;

That liberty is indivisible, and that political freedom cannot long exist without economic freedom;

That the purposes of government are to protect these freedoms through the preservation of internal order, the provision of national defense, and the administration of justice;

That when government ventures beyond these rightful functions, it accumulates power which tends to diminish liberty;

That the Constitution of the United States is the best arrangement yet devised for empowering government to fulfill its proper role, while restraining it from the concentration and abuse of power;

That the genius of the Constitution—the division of powers—is summed up in the clause which reserves primacy to the several states, or to the people, in those spheres not specifically delegated to the Federal Government;

* *The Sharon Statement* (1960). Reprinted with the kind permission of William F. Buckley, Jr.

That the market economy, allocating resources by the free play of supply and demand, is the single economic system compatible with the requirements of personal freedom and constitutional government, and that it is at the same time the most productive supplier of human needs;

That when government interferes with the work of the market economy, it tends to reduce the moral and physical strength of the nation; that, when it takes from one man to bestow on another, it diminishes the incentive of the first, the integrity of the second, and the moral autonomy of both;

That we will be free only so long as the national sovereignty of the United States is secure: that history shows periods of freedom are rare, and can exist only when free citizens concertedly defend their rights against all enemies;

That the forces of international Communism are, at present, the greatest single threat to these liberties;

That the United States should stress victory over, rather than coexistence with, this menace; and

That American foreign policy must be judged by this criterion: does it serve the just interests of the United States?

DOCUMENT NO. 17

BARRY GOLDWATER OPPOSES
THE CIVIL RIGHTS ACT OF 1964*

The Civil Rights Act of 1964 outlawed racial discrimination in public accommodations and segregation in state-supported institutions. Additionally, it empowered the Justice Department to pursue civil rights violations and the Fair Employment Practices Commission to fight discrimination in the private sector of the economy. Concerned for the broad powers it gave the federal government and for the police-state atmosphere it might create, Senator Barry Goldwater opposed the measure. This opposition was as principled as it was politically unwise.

γ   γ   γ

I am unalterably opposed to discrimination or segregation on the basis of race, color, or creed, or on any other basis; not only my words, but more importantly my actions through the years have repeatedly demonstrated the sincerity of my feeling in this regard.

This is fundamentally a matter of the heart. The problems of discrimination can never be cured by laws alone; but I would be the first to agree that laws can help—laws carefully considered and weighed in an atmosphere of dispassion, in the absence of political demagogery, and in the light of fundamental constitutional principles.

For example, throughout my 12 years as a member of the Senate Labor and Public Welfare Committee, I have repeatedly offered amendments to bills pertaining to labor that would end discrimination in unions, and repeatedly those amendments have been turned down by the very members of both parties who now so vociferously support the present approach to the solution of our problem. Talk is one thing, action is another, and until the members of this body and the people of this country realize this, there will be no real solution to the problem we face.

To be sure, a calm environment for the consideration of any law dealing with human relationships is not easily attained—emotions run high,

* U.S., Congress, Senate, Senator Barry Goldwater speaking against the Civil Rights bill of 1964, 88th Cong., 2d sess., 18 June 1964, *Congressional Record* 110: 14318–14319.

political pressures become great, and objectivity is at a premium. Nevertheless, deliberation and calmness are indispensable to success. . . .

It is with great sadness that I realize the nonfulfillment of these high hopes. My hopes were shattered when it became apparent that emotion and political pressure—not persuasion, not commonsense, not deliberation—had become the rule of the day and of the processes of this great body.

One has only to review the defeat of commonsense amendments to this bill—amendments that would in no way harm it but would, in fact, improve it—to realize that political pressure, not persuasion or commonsense, has come to rule the consideration of this measure.

I realize fully tht the Federal Government has a responsibility in the field of civil rights. I supported the civil rights bills which were enacted in 1957 and 1960, and my public utterances during the debates on those measures and since reveal clearly the areas in which I feel that Federal responsibility lies and Federal legislation on this subject can be both effective and appropriate. Many of those areas are encompassed in this bill and to that extent, I favor it.

I wish to make myself perfectly clear. The two portions of this bill to which I have constantly and consistently voiced objections, and which are of such overriding significance that they are determinative of my vote on the entire measure, are those which would embark the Federal Government on a regulatory course of action with regard to private enterprise in the area of so-called public accommodations and in the area of employment—to be more specific—titles II and VII of the bill. I find no constitutional basis for the exercise of Federal regulatory authority in either of these areas; and I believe the attempted usurpation of such power to be a grave threat to the very essence of our basic system of government; namely, that of a constitutional republic in which 50 sovereign States have reserved to themselves and to the people those powers not specifically granted to the Central or Federal Government.

If it is the wish of the American people that the Federal Government should be granted the power to regulate in these two areas and in the manner contemplated by this bill, then I say that the Constitution should be so amended by the people as to authorize such action in accordance with the procedures for amending the Constitution which that great document itself prescribes. I say further that for this great legislative body to ignore the Constitution and the fundamental concepts of our governmental system is to act in a manner which could ultimately destroy the freedom of all American citizens, including the freedoms of the very persons whose feelings and whose liberties are the major subject of this legislation.

My basic objection to this measure is, therefore, constitutional. But, in addition, I would like to point out to my colleagues in the Senate and to the people of America, regardless of their race, color, or creed, the implications involved in the enforcement of regulatory legislation of this sort. To give genuine effect to the prohibitions of this bill will require the creation of a Federal police force of mammoth proportions It also bids fair to result in the development of an "informer" psychology in great areas of our national life—neighbors spying on neighbors, workers spying on workers, business spying on businessmen—where those who would harass their fellow citizens for selfish and narrow purposes will have ample inducement to do so. These, the Federal police force and an "informer" psychology, are the hallmarks of the police state and landmarks in the destruction of a free society. . . .

If my vote is misconstrued, let it be, and let me suffer the consequences. Just let me be judged in this by the real concern I have voiced here and not by words that others may speak or by what others may say about what I think. . . .

It is the general welfare that must be considered now, not just the special appeals for special welfare. This is the time to attend to the liberties of all.

DOCUMENT NO. 18

IRVING KRISTOL ON CONSERVATISM
AND CAPITALISM*

Neoconservatives made important intellectual and practical contributions to conservatism during the last three decades of the twentieth century. A leading figure among them has been Irving Kristol, whose diverse writings helped greatly to disseminate neoconservative ideas. In this document, written in 1975, he points to important differences between conservatism and liberalism, and examines the relationship between capitalism and culture.

γ   γ   γ

These days, Americans who defend the capitalist system, i.e., an economy and a way of life organized primarily around the free market, are called "conservative." If they are willing to accept a limited degree of government intervention for social purposes, they are likely to be designated as "neoconservative." Under ordinary circumstances these labels would strike me as fair and appropriate. . . .

But the circumstances surrounding the use of such labels today are *not* ordinary; they are almost paradoxical. To begin with, the institutions which conservatives wish to preserve are, and for two centuries were called, *liberal* institutions, i.e., institutions which maximize personal liberty vis-à-vis a state, a church, or an official ideology. On the other hand, the severest critics of these institutions—those who wish to enlarge the scope of governmental authority indefinitely, so as to achieve ever greater equality at the expense of liberty—are today commonly called "liberals." It would certainly help to clarify matters if they were called, with greater propriety and accuracy, "socialists" or "neosocialists." And yet we are oddly reluctant to be so candid. . . .

Why does this happen? And why, especially, do conservatives permit it to happen? . . .

The answer, I think, has to do with the fact that the idea of "liberty" which conservatives wish to defend, and which our liberal institutions are supposed to incarnate, has become exceedingly nebulous in the course of the past century. This puts conservatives in the position of

* Irving Kristol, *Neoconservatism: The Autobiography of an Idea* (New York: The Free Press, 1995), pp. 230–234. Reprinted with the kind permission of the author.

being, or seeming to be, merely mindless defenders of the status quo. Indeed, to many they seem merely intransigent defenders of existing privilege, issuing appeals to "liberty" for such an ulterior purpose alone. This, in turn, has permitted "liberals" to impress their own definition of "liberty" on public opinion.

This "liberal" definition has two parts. First, it entails ever-greater governmental intervention in certain areas—economics, educational administration, the electoral process, etc.—to achieve greater equality, itself now identified with "true liberty." Second, it entails less intervention in those areas—religion, school curricula, culture, entertainment, etc.—which have to do with the formation of character, and in which it is assumed that "the marketplace of ideas" will "naturally" produce ideal results. . . .

Ever since the beginnings of modern capitalism in the eighteenth century, two very different conceptions of liberty have emerged. The first was the "libertarian" idea. It asserted that God and/or nature had so arranged things that, by the operations of an "invisible hand," individual liberty, no matter how self-seeking, could only lead ultimately to humanity's virtuous happiness. "Private vices, public benefits" was its motto—and still is.

The second idea of liberty may be called the "bourgeois" idea. It asserted that liberty implied the right to do bad as well as the right to do good, that liberty could be abused as well as used—in short, that a distinction had to be made between liberty and "license." The making of this distinction was the task of our cultural and religious institutions, especially the latter. It was these institutions which infused the idea of liberty with positive substance, with "values," with an ethos. The basic belief was that a life led according to these values would maximize personal liberty in a context of social and political stability, would ensure—insofar as this is humanly possible—that the exercise of everyone's personal liberty would add up to a decent and good society. The practical virtues implied by the "bourgeois" values were not very exciting: thrift, industry, self-reliance, self-discipline, a moderate degree of public-spiritedness, and so forth. On the other hand, they had the immense advantage of being rather easily attainable by everyone. You didn't have to be a saint or a hero to be a good bourgeois citizen.

It did not take long for the culture emerging out of bourgeois society to become bored with, and hostile to, a life and a social order based on such prosaic bourgeois values. Artists and intellectuals quickly made it apparent that "alienation" was their destiny, and that the mission of this culture was to be antibourgeois. But so long as religion was a powerful force among ordinary men and women, the disaffection of the intellectuals was of only marginal significance. It is the decline in religious belief over the past 50 years—together with the rise of mass higher education, which popularized the culture's animus to bourgeois capitalism —that has been of decisive importance.

ADAM SMITH'S MISTAKE. The defenders of capitalism were, and are, helpless before this challenge. Businessmen, after all, had never taken culture seriously. They have always rather agreed with Adam Smith when he wrote:

> Though you despise that picture, or that poem, or even that system of philosophy which I admire, there is little danger of our quarreling on that account. Neither of us can reasonably be much interested about them.

He could not have been more wrong. What rules the world is ideas, because ideas define the way reality is perceived; and, in the absence of religion, it is out of culture—pictures, poems, songs, philosophy—that these ideas are born.

It is because of their indifference to culture, their placid philistinism, that businessmen today find themselves defending capitalism and personal liberty in purely amoral terms. They are "libertarians"—but without a belief in the providential dispensations of God or nature. Capitalism, they keep insisting, is the most *efficient* economic system. This may be true if you agree with Adam Smith when he said: "What can be added to the happiness of man who is in health, who is out of debt, and has a clear conscience?" But if you believe that a comfortable life is not necessarily the same thing as a good life, or even a meaningful life, then it will occur to you that efficiency is a means, not an end in itself. Capitalist efficiency may then be regarded as a most useful precondition for a good life in a good society. But one has to go beyond Adam Smith, or capitalism itself, to discover the other elements that are wanted.

It was religion and the bourgeois ethos that used to offer this added dimension to capitalism. But religion is now ineffectual, and even businessmen find the bourgeois ethos embarrassingly old-fashioned. This leaves capitalism, and its conservative defenders, helpless before any moralistic assault, however unprincipled. And until conservatism can give its own moral and intellectual substance to its idea of liberty, the "liberal" subversion of our liberal institutions will proceed without hindrance.

DOCUMENT NO. 19

A JURIST CALLS FOR JUDICIAL RESTRAINT*

Conservatives vigorously opposed the activism of the Supreme Court under Chief Justice Earl Warren. The Court, they charged, assumed unto itself legislative powers. Robert H. Bork spoke for many conservatives in opposing such extended powers. Advocating that judges should construe the "original intent" of the framers of the Constitution, he argued that "good results" stemming from legal decisions were subordinate to the "legitimate process" of decision making.

γ   γ   γ

The most common charge leveled against the idea of interpreting each provision of the Constitution according to the understanding of the generation of Americans who ratified and endorsed it is that better results can be, and have been, produced by ignoring what was intended. Often the accusation is stronger: The actual Constitution would allow *that* statute to stand, which would be intolerable.

This is the classic form of eternal temptation: to trade the right of self-government for protection by benevolent judges. They are wiser and more humane than your fellow citizens, as shown by the fact that those citizens produced the statute which you and the judges abhor. What does legal reasoning matter if the judges know a good result when they see one? . . .

Consider the inversion of legal reasoning now in vogue. The orthodox style was to listen to a controversy between people, ascertain the facts, and then determine which side of the dispute was better supported by the relevant body of legal doctrine, whether that doctrine was expressed in judicial opinions, statutes, or the Constitution. The lawyer, judge, or professor asked what words were in the texts of these materials and what was the best interpretation of those words. The object was to frame a rule that was correct and that decided the case. A universal form of legal education and reasoning was to frame hypothetical situations to test the limits of the rule and to discover whether in such situations the rule

* Reprinted with the permission of The Free Press, a Division of Simon & Schuster from *The Tempting of America: The Political Seduction of the Law* by Robert H. Bork. Copyright © 1990 by Robert H. Bork. Pp. 261–262; 264–265.

embodied a sensible reading of the underlying text. This form of analysis makes sense only if the object is to carry the intended meaning of the legal text forward into the decision of real controversies. The rule comes out of the Constitution.

The person who judges constitutional law by results reverses this process. He asks what decision in each case is politically or morally attractive to him, devises a rule that achieves that result, and then works backward. The rule does not come out of, but is forced into, the Constitution. There is nothing that can be called legal reasoning in this. It is a process of personal choice followed by rationalization; the major and minor premises do not lead to a result, the result produces the major and minor premises. There is, furthermore, no point in testing those premises by hypotheticals to determine what results they might produce in the future, because the future results will be chosen by personal desire and the premises will be abandoned or reshaped to fit the new desired outcome. . . .

Well, why not? Aren't results more important to people than processes? Isn't the insistence upon reasoning from the actual principles of the Constitution an arid intellectualism that ignores human yearnings? An adherence to logical systems at the expense of social justice? One answer is that the result that is "good," though not justified by the Constitution, is not the result that the elected representatives of the people thought good. Thus, the ultimate answer is that legal reasoning is an intellectual enterprise essential to the preservation of freedom and democracy.

When a court strikes down a statute, it always denies the freedom of a people who voted for representatives who enacted the law. We accept that more readily when the decision is based upon a fair reading of a constitutional provision. The Constitution, after all, was designed to remove a number of subjects from democratic control, subjects ranging from the composition of the Houses of Congress to the freedoms guaranteed by the Bill of Rights. But when the Court, without warrant in the Constitution, strikes down a democratically produced statute, that act substitutes the will of a majority of nine lawyers for the will of the people. That is what is always involved when constitutional adjudication proceeds by a concern for results rather than by concern for reasoning from original understanding. That is what is approved by law professors and politicians, two groups that are not as distinct as they once were, who assess decisions by sympathy or lack of sympathy with the results.

For such people, a judicial nominee's character, professionalism, and intellectual capacity are far less important than that he follow the politically correct line.

Legal reasoning, which is rooted in a concern for legitimate process rather than preferred results, is an instrument designed to restrict judges to their proper role in a constitutional democracy. That style of analysis marks off the line between judicial power and legislative power, which is to say that it preserves both democratic freedom and individual freedom. Yet legal reasoning must begin with a body of rules or principles or major premises that are independent of the judge's preferences. That, as we have seen, is impossible under any philosophy of judging other than the view that the original understanding of the Constitution is the exclusive source for those exterior principles.

The person who understands these issues and nevertheless continues to judge constitutional philosophy by sympathy with its results must, if he is candid, also admit that he is prepared to sacrifice democracy in order that his moral views may prevail. He calls for civil disobedience by judges and claims for the Supreme Court an institutionalized role as a perpetrator of limited *coups d'etat*. He believes in the triumph of the will. It is not clear why he does not advocate rioting or physical force, so long, of course, as the end is good as he sees the good. Such a man occupies an impossible philosophic position. What can he say of a Court that does not share his politics or morality? What can an admirer of the Warren Court say if the Supreme Court should become dominated by conservative activists? What can he say of the Taney Court's *Dred Scott* decision? He cannot say that the decision was the exercise of an illegitimate power because he has already conceded that power. There seems nothing he can say except that the Court is politically wrong and that he is morally justified in evading its rulings whenever he can and overthrowing it if possible in order to replace it with a body that will produce results he likes. In his view, the Court has no legitimacy as a legal institution. This being the case, the advocate of a political, value-choosing (rather than value-implementing) Court must answer another difficult question. Why should the Court, a committee of nine lawyers, be the sole agent for overriding democratic outcomes? The man who prefers results to processes has no reason to say that the Court is more legitimate than any other institution capable of wielding power. If the Court will not agree with him, why not argue his case to some other group, say the Joint Chiefs of Staff, a body with rather better means for enforcing its decisions? No answer exists.

DOCUMENT NO. 20

THE MORAL MAJORITY AND ITS GOALS*

Alarmed by what they considered to be the spiritual and social decay of the nation, the Reverend Jerry Falwell and others organized the Moral Majority. Its membership quickly ballooned, the result of a deep-seated belief that moral decline was both widespread and pernicious. More than twenty years later most of the issues that the Moral Majority confronted remain controversial and unresolved.

γ   γ   γ

ORGANIZING THE MORAL MAJORITY

Facing the desperate need in the impending crisis of the hour, several concerned pastors began to urge me to put together a political organization that could provide a vehicle to address these crucial issues. Men like James Kennedy (Fort Lauderdale, Florida), Charles Stanley (Atlanta, Georgia), Tim La Haye (San Diego, California), and Greg Dixon (Indianapolis, Indiana) began to share with me a common concern. They urged that we formulate a nonpartisan political organization to promote morality in public life and to combat legislation that favored the legalization of immorality. Together we formulated the Moral Majority, Inc. Today Moral Majority, Inc., is made up of millions of Americans, including 72,000 ministers, priests, and rabbis, who are deeply concerned about the moral decline of our nation, the traditional family, and the moral values on which our nation was built. We are Catholics, Jews, Protestants, Mormons, Fundamentalists—blacks and whites—farmers, housewives, businessmen, and businesswomen. We are Americans from all walks of life united by one central concern: to serve as a special-interest group providing a voice for a return to moral sanity in these United States of America. Moral Majority is a political organization and is not based on theological considerations. We are Americans who share similar moral convictions. We are opposed to abortion, pornography, the drug epidemic, the breakdown of the traditional family, the establishment of homosexuality as an accepted alternate life-style,

---

* *The Fundamentalist Phenomenon: The Resurgence of Conservative Christianity*, ed. Jerry Falwell with Ed Dolson and Ed Hendson (New York: Doubleday, 1981), pp. 188–190. Reprinted with the kind permission of the author.

and other moral cancers that are causing our society to rot from within. Moral Majority strongly supports a pluralistic America. While we believe that this nation was founded upon the Judeo-Christian ethic by men and women who were strongly influenced by biblical moral principles, we are committed to the separation of Church and State.

Here is how Moral Majority stands on today's vital issues:

1. *We believe in the separation of Church and State.* Moral Majority, Inc., is a political organization providing a platform for religious and nonreligious Americans who share moral values to address their concerns in these areas. Members of Moral Majority, Inc., have no common theological premise. We are Americans who are proud to be conservative in our approach to moral, social, and political concerns.

2. *We are pro-life.* We believe that life begins at fertilization. We strongly oppose the massive "biological holocaust" that is resulting in the abortion of one and a half million babies each year in America. We believe that unborn babies have the right to life as much as babies that have been born. We are providing a voice and a defense for the human and civil rights of millions of unborn babies.

3. *We are pro-traditional family.* We believe that the only acceptable family form begins with a legal marriage of a man and a woman. We feel that homosexual marriages and common-law marriages should not be accepted as traditional families. We oppose legislation that favors these kinds of "diverse family forms," thereby penalizing the traditional family. We do not oppose civil rights for homosexuals. We do oppose "special rights" for homosexuals who have chosen a perverted life-style rather than a traditional life-style.

4. *We oppose the illegal drug traffic in America.* The youth in America are presently in the midst of a drug epidemic. Through education, legislation, and other means we want to do our part to save our young people from death on the installment plan through illegal drug addiction.

5. *We oppose pornography.* While we do not advocate censorship, we do believe that education and legislation can help stem the tide of pornography and obscenity that is poisoning the American spirit today. Economic boycotts are a proper way in America's free-enterprise system to help persuade the media to move back to a sensible and

reasonable moral stand. We most certainly believe in the First Amendment for everyone. We are not willing to sit back, however, while many television programs create cesspools of obscenity and vulgarity in our nation's living rooms.

6. *We support the state of Israel and Jewish people everywhere.* It is impossible to separate the state of Israel from the Jewish family internationally. Many Moral Majority members, because of their theological convictions, are committed to the Jewish people. Others stand upon the human and civil rights of all persons as a premise for support of the state of Israel. Support of Israel is one of the essential commitments of Moral Majority. No anti-Semitic influence is allowed in Moral Majority, Inc.

7. *We believe that a strong national defense is the best deterrent to war.* We believe that liberty is the basic moral issue of all moral issues. The only way America can remain free is to remain strong. Therefore we support the efforts of our present administration to regain our position of military preparedness—with a sincere hope that we will never need to use any of our weapons against any people anywhere.

8. *We support equal rights for women.* We agree with President Reagan's commitment to help every governor and every state legislature to move quickly to ensure that during the 1980s every American woman will earn as much money and enjoy the same opportunities for advancement as her male counterpart in the same vocation.

9. *We believe ERA is the wrong vehicle to obtain equal rights for women.* We feel that the ambiguous and simplistic language of the Amendment could lead to court interpretations that might put women in combat, sanction homosexual marriage, and financially penalize widows and deserted wives.

10. *We encourage our Moral Majority state organizations to be autonomous and indigenous.* Moral Majority state organizations may, from time to time, hold positions that are not held by the Moral Majority, Inc., national organization.

DOCUMENT NO. 21

CULTURAL MODERNISM AND CAPITALISM*

Contemporary conservatives, like the custodians of culture during the late nineteenth and early twentieth centuries, generally have preferred traditionalism to experimentation in the arts and have looked askance at modernism. Not so the critic Hilton Kramer, who has vigorously defended the works of high modernism while at the same time denigrating the trivia and tastelessness produced by radical culture. Moreover, Kramer views capitalism beneficently, noting how it has fostered modernism.

γ   γ   γ

American cultural life in the early 1980s was characterized by an odd combination of social euphoria and critical entropy. In many fields, we were confronted with the dismaying spectacle of rapid institutional growth taking place in an environment of creative inertia. In the visual arts, for example, the atmosphere of public celebration generated by new museum construction, the hurly-burly surrounding "blockbuster" exhibitions, the expansion of the art audience and the art market, and the runaway vogue for "postmodern" skyscraper architecture was everywhere accompanied by an accelerating sense that standards had collapsed and art had entered upon a period of decadence. In the literary world, the impulse to elevate a handful of mediocre writers to an unearned stardom while ignoring the calamitous decline of literary culture in the educated classes became a firmly established practice, and in the world of serious music there was likewise a widespread tendency to look for salvation in celebrity performance and the writing of spuriously romantic ("popular") compositions. Even in the realm of television, which had never been noted for its intellectual standards, it was no longer possible to speak seriously of "educational TV"—clearly a lost cause—as the vulgarities of Public Broadcasting Service, an enterprise increasingly devoted to popular entertainment and political journalism, made

* Reprinted with the permission of The Free Press, a Division of Simon & Schuster, from *The New Criterion Reader: The First Five Years*. Edited with an introduction by Hilton Kramer. Copyright © 1988 by The Foundation for Cultural Review, Inc. Pp. xi; xiii–xiv.

a mockery of the few artistic or "highbrow" subjects it condescended to program. . . .

The howls of protest that greeted *The New Criterion* varied, of course, both in the intensity of their wrath and in the kind of abuse they heaped upon the magazine and its writers. For some of our critics, our worst offense lay in our energetic defense of modernism—which, because of the disfavor it now met with in radical circles, had itself become a political issue. Coming at a time when widespread manifestations of a "postmodern" temper had acquired the momentum of an irresistible fashion, this defense of modernism caused considerable shock and indignation. In the academy, in the museums, and in the media, modernism was in the process of being unmasked and "deconstructed" as either a bourgeois plot or an outmoded aesthetic idea or both, and anything said in its defense—especially anything that claimed, as *The New Criterion* often did, that modernism continued to represent our most vital and essential cultural tradition—was taken to be a threat to the prevailing orthodoxy.

For others, it was our commitment to capitalism that could not be forgiven. Not only on the extreme Left but even among many liberals, capitalism is so firmly established in the demonology of intellectual debate as the enemy of an enlightened culture that all questions having to do with the relation obtaining between capitalism and contemporary cultural life are regarded as settled—settled, that is, in the judgment that capitalism is to be regarded as the primary obstacle to whatever it is we may wish to achieve in both society and art. With this view—an essentially Marxist view that had come to occupy a sacrosanct place in the new cultural orthodoxy—*The New Criterion* categorically disagreed, and we left our readers in no doubt as to where we stood on this crucial issue.

From certain of our critics, however, what drew the fiercest response was precisely an espousal of the idea that modernism and capitalism, notwithstanding the tensions that had marked their past history, had now evolved in a way that had made them natural and inevitable allies in a modern democratic society; and that it is indeed upon the survival and prosperity of both, no matter how troubled their relation to each other might sometimes be, that the future vitality of a democratic society and a free cultural life is henceforth likely to depend.

It was to be expected that this idea would meet with opposition from the hard-line opponents of capitalism, and there was no shortage of opposition from that quarter. More interesting (because of what it signified) was the critical response this idea met with among liberals who had more or less reconciled themselves, however warily, to an acceptance of capitalism but who were unprepared to modify their view of modernism. For liberals of this persuasion, capitalism might somehow be accommodated, if only because it guaranteed their own prosperity and freedom, but certain myths—or should we call them pieties?—surrounding the modernist movement were not on that account to be surrendered simply because they had been rendered obsolete by history. For these liberals, the very conception of modernism has remained so inextricably bound up with the idea of insurrection and revolution that they cannot bring themselves to think about modernism in any other terms. Modernism-as-insurrection is the last remaining remnant of radicalism they forfeited when they made their uneasy peace with capitalism, and it is all the more precious, of course, as a token of the *révolté* impulse they have largely abandoned. . . .

Was Impressionism a mode of insurrection? Was Cubism? Can we find in the achievements of the modern masters—in the paintings of Cézanne, Matisse, and Miró; in the poetry of Eliot, Stevens, and Valéry; in the fiction of Proust, Joyce, and Mann; in the music of Schoenberg and Stravinsky; or in the architecture of Wright, Corbusier, and Mies—any warrant to support this notion of insurrection? We cannot, and it is the sheerest sentimentality to believe otherwise. It is also bad history to suppose that modernism can somehow be isolated, as if by political quarantine, from the high culture of capitalism and the middle class. . . .

It is precisely in the autonomy accorded to art by the tradition of modernism that we find the freedom of spirit that is the cultural analogue of the political freedoms guaranteed to us by capitalist democracy. This is one of the reasons why all attempts to establish the culture of modernism in nondemocratic, anti-capitalist societies have proved to be tragically short-lived. To deny modernism its aesthetic autonomy is to deny its very essence. Like it or not, it is only in democratic capitalistic societies—which is to say, in the world of bourgeois democracies—that modernism has flourished *as* a cultural tradition. No doubt the relation in which modernism stands to these bourgeois societies will continue at times to be a troubled one. It is in the nature of modernism to be critical of its own conventions. But to characterize that critical impulse as insurrectionist is to misunderstand it in the most fundamental way.

On this subject, at least, the radicals who reject modernism as insufficiently revolutionary are actually a good deal closer to the truth than the liberals. That modernism has proved not to be a mode of insurrection is a matter the radicals understand very well, which is why they have labored so diligently to discredit the whole modernist enterprise.

DOCUMENT NO. 22

A NEOCONSERVATIVE'S VIEWS
ON FOREIGN POLICY*

*Neoconservatives played an important role in the formulation and enact-
ment of foreign policy during the presidency of Ronald Reagan. No administration figure articulated that foreign policy more clearly or persuasively
than Jeane Kirkpatrick. Rejecting the either/or antinomies of realism and
idealism, she urged a foreign policy that both protected the nation's self-
interests and abetted democratic prospects abroad.*

γ   γ   γ

. . . It seems to me that there are four distinctions that are crucial to
thinking about human rights and human rights policy—distinctions
often overlooked in our time. This first is the distinction between ideas
and institutions. The second is the distinction between rights and goals.
The third is between intentions and consequences. And the fourth,
finally, is the distinction between private and public morality.

First the distinction between ideas and institutions. It is terribly important to bear in mind at all times, I think, that ideas and words are
far more manipulable than are institutions. Ideas have only to be conceived in order to exist. The idea of a right is very easy to conceive of;
and we can claim any right that we can think of. . . .

Institutions on the other hand are stabilized patterns of human
behavior. Institutions involve millions of other real, living, flesh-and-
blood people. Institutions involve the subjectivities of other people.
They rest on the expectations of other people. They are shaped by the
experience of other people. They are made up of habits and internalized
values and beliefs. From time to time, of course, they also rest on coer-
cion. These internalized expectations become inextricably bound up
with the identity of the people who hold them; they are reinforced with
habit and are extremely resistant to change. This is one of the reasons
why revolutionaries are frequently prepared to write off a generation

* Jeane J. Kirkpatrick, *The Reagan Phenomenon—And Other Speeches on Foreign Policy*
(Washington and London: American Enterprise Institute for Public Policy Research,
1983), pp. 39–45. Reprinted with the permission of The American Enterprise Institute
for Public Policy Research, Washington, D.C.

when they seek genuine change: they know the internalized expectations of mature people will prove so resistant to change that such people will never acquire the new identifications and expectations necessary to consummate the revolution.

Rights, then, are easy to claim and extremely difficult to translate into reality. . . .

The second distinction I want to emphasize is the distinction between rights and goals. In our time, as everybody knows, rights proliferate at an extraordinary rate. To the familiar old eighteenth-century rights of life, liberty, security of persons, and property have been added the right to nationality, the right to privacy, equal rights in marriage, the right to education, the right to culture, the right to leisure, the right to full development of one's personality and powers, the right to self-determination, self-goverment, to adequate standards of living.

. . . For every goal toward which human beings have worked there is, in our time, a right. Neither nature nor experience nor probability informs these lists of entitlements. The fact that they are without any possibility of realization, however, does not mean that they are without consequences. There are important consequences.

Treating goals as rights is, I think, grossly misleading about the way in which real goals are achieved in life. Rights are vested in persons or groups, but goals are achieved by human effort. . . .

Utopian expectations concerning the human condition, which are grounded in that failure to distinguish between ideas and institutions, are compounded then by a vague sense that Utopia is one's due, one's right. When the belief that one has a right to devolop coincides with the facts of primitive psychology, of caste systems, social hierarchies, societies based on ascription, on dictatorship—and those are, of course, the characteristics of many societies in the world that claim the right to development—then the tendency to blame someone is almost overwhelming.

The third distinction that I think has special relevance to human rights and foreign policy is the distinction between intention and consequence. In political philosophy, as in ethics, there are theories that emphasize motives and there are theories that emphasize consequences. Preoccupation with motives is a well-known characteristic of the political purist.

Political purists have multiplied in our time, almost as rapidly as rights. Their distinguishing characteristic is, above all, an emphasis on internal criteria for action, on conforming behavior to what one feels is right. Doing what one knows is right becomes more important than producing any given desirable result. In human rights and foreign policy the tendency to prefer an ethic of motives to an ethic of consequences leads to an overweening concern with the purity of the intentions as embodied in our policies. When our motives are viewed as more important than the consequences of our actions, then whether our policies have in fact contributed to the creation of a new form of tyranny in a place like Iran seems to matter less than whether our intentions were good. The principal function of a human rights policy that emphasizes motives rather than consequences is, I believe, to make us feel good about ourselves. It feels good to feel good, to be sure. But one wonders about that as a goal of foreign policy.

The fourth distinction important to thinking about human rights and foreign policy is the distinction between personal morality and political morality. Personal morality derives from the characteristics of individuals and depends on the cultivation of personal virtues like faith, hope, charity, discipline, and reliability. Political morality, on the other hand, depends not on the personal morality of individuals but on the juxtaposition and interrelation of parts of a society.

This is a fact that is well known in political philosophy and has been at least since Plato, who defined justice in terms of the relationship among the parts of a society. It was just as clear to the Founding Fathers of this country. Justice, democracy, liberty are all the products of an arrangement of offices, a distribution of power, embodied in a constitution. Constitutions produce political goods by respecting and harmonizing the diverse parts of the political community. All the important political goods—democracy, due process, protection of rights to free speech, assembly—are, as the Founding Fathers understood, the consequence of a wisely structured constitution. . . .

If these distinctions are important and must be taken into account by a sound foreign policy, where does this leave us in relation to human rights? It seems to me, first of all, that it does not at all diminish the importance of human rights as a factor in our foreign policy. Human rights can be, should be, must be, will be taken into account by U.S. foreign policy. The end of a foreign policy that takes acccount of human rights will be, and should be, to enhance the lives of others. The end of a foreign policy should be to produce positive consequences for the actor and potential beneficiary. Such a policy will, I think, take careful account of context as well as motives. It will calculate the means available and appropriate for achieving the desired end. It will assess the interrelationships between means and ends, remembering always that human society is as complex as human nature itself. We have had enough of rationalism in our foreign policy, enough of purism, and of purely private virtues in public policies. It is my hope that in its approach to human rights and foreign policy, this administration will take the cure of history. . . .

If we take the cure of history, I think we will also find that in the real world force is sometimes necessary to defend human rights and that American power is necessary to protect and expand the frontiers of human rights in our time. In this administration, we believe we have a more adequate perception of the relationship among force, freedom, morality, and power. We have, we believe, a more adequate conception of the relationship between abstract rights and concrete societies, between blueprints and institutions. We think that by attempting less sweeping programs we can produce more progress in human rights. Time, of course, will tell whether our more modest expectations will prove more productive in human freedom and well-being.

SELECT BIBLIOGRAPHY

The following include works that were most useful in the preparation of this book as well as ones that offer further insights into American conservatism. Given the limitations of space, works that are primary rather than secondary sources, were cited in the text, or appeared as Documents have been omitted.

Andrew, John A. III. *The Other Side of the Sixties: Young Americans for Freedom and the Rise of Conservative Politics*. New Brunswick, NJ: Rutgers University Press, 1997.

Bartlett, Irving H. *The American Mind in the Mid-Nineteenth Century*. 2nd ed. Arlington Heights, IL: Harlan Davidson, 1982.

Bernhard, Winfred E. *Fisher Ames: Federalist and Statesman, 1758–1808*. Chapel Hill: University of North Carolina Press, 1965.

Bode, Carl. *Mencken*. Carbondale: Southern Illinois University Press, 1969.

Brennan, Mary C. *Turning Right in the Sixties: The Conservative Capture of the GOP*. Chapel Hill: University of North Carolina Press, 1995.

Brookhiser, Richard, *Alexander Hamilton, American*. New York: Free Press, 1999.

Conkin, Paul K. *The Southern Agrarians*. Knoxville: University of Tennessee Press, 1988.

Crunden, Robert. *The Mind and Art of Albert Jay Nock*. Providence, RI: Brown University Press, 1972.

Curtis, William. *William Graham Sumner*. Boston: Twayne, 1981.

Diggins, John P. *Up from Communism: Conservative Odysseys in American Intellectual History*. New York: Harper & Row, 1975.

D'Souza, Dinesh. *Illiberal Education*. New York: Free Press, 1991.

———. *Ronald Reagan: How an Ordinary Man Became an Extraordinary Leader*. New York: Free Press, 1997.

Duggan, Francis X. *Paul Elmer More*. New York: Twayne, 1966.

Dunn, Charles W. and J. David Woodward. *American Conservatism from Burke to Bush: An Introduction*. Lanham, MD: Madison Books, 1991.

Eastland, Terry. *Ending Affirmative Action: The Case for Colorblind Justice*. New York: Basic Books, 1996.

Edwards, Lee. *The Conservative Revolution: The Movement That Remade America*. New York: Free Press, 1999.

Ehrman, John. *The Rise of Neoconservatism: Intellectuals and Foreign Affairs, 1945–1994*. New Haven, CT: Yale University Press, 1995.

Frederickson, George M. *The Inner Civil War: Northern Intellectuals and the Crisis of the Union*. New York: Harper & Row, 1965.

Genovese, Eugene. *The Southern Tradition: The Achievement and Limitations of an American Conservatism*. Cambridge, MA: Harvard University Press, 1994.

Gerson, Mark. *The Neoconservative Vision: From the Cold War to the Culture Wars*. Lanham, MD: Rowman & Littlefield, 1995.

Goldberg, Robert Alan. *Barry Goldwater*. New Haven, CT: Yale University Press, 1995.

Gottfried, Paul. *The Conservative Movement*. 2nd ed. New York: Twayne, 1993.

Herrera, R. A. *Orestes Brownson: Sign of Contradiction*. Wilmington, DE: ISI Books, 1999.

Hoeveler, David J., Jr. *The New Humanism: A Critique of Modern America, 1900–1940*. Charlottesville: University Press of Virginia, 1977.

———. *Watch on the Right: Conservative Intellectuals in the Reagan Era*. Madison: The University of Wisconsin Press, 1991.

Hofstadter, Richard. *Social Darwinism in American Thought*. Rev. ed. Boston: Beacon Press, 1992.

Judis, John B. *William F. Buckley: Patron Saint of the Conservatives*. New York: Simon & Schuster, 1988.

Kens, Paul. *Justice Stephen Field: Shaping Liberty from the Gold Rush to the Gilded Age*. Lawrence: University of Kansas Press, 1997.

Kimball, Roger. *Tenured Radicals: How Politics Has Corrupted Our Higher Education*. New York: Harper & Row, 1990.

Kirk, Russell. *The Conservative Mind: From Burke to Eliot*. 7th ed. Washington, DC: Regnery, 1995.

Labaree, Leonard Woods. *Conservatism in Early American History*. Ithaca, NY: Cornell University Press, 1959.

Livermore, Shaw, Jr. *The Twilight of Federalism: The Disintegration of the Federalist Party, 1815–1930*. New York: Gordian Press, 1972.

Lora, Ronald. *Conservative Minds in America*. Westport, CT: Greenwood Press, 1980.

McCloskey, Robert G. *American Conservatism in the Age of Enterprise, 1865–1910*. Cambridge, MA: Harvard University Press, 1951.

———. *The American Supreme Court*. Chicago: University of Chicago Press, 1960.

McDonald, Forrest. *Novus Ordo Seclorum: The Intellectual Origins of the Constitution*. Lawrence: University of Kansas Press, 1985.

Mallan, John P. "Roosevelt, Brooks Adams, and Lea: The Warrior Critique of Business Civilization." *American Quarterly*, Vol. VIII, No. 3 (1956): 216–230.

Miles, Michael. *The Odyssey of the American Right*. New York: Oxford University Press, 1980.

Morgan, H. Wayne. *Keepers of Culture: The Art-Thought of Kenyon Cox, Royal Cortissoz, and Frank Jewett Mather, Jr.* Kent, OH: Kent State University Press, 1989.

Muccigrosso, Robert. *American Gothic: The Mind and Art of Ralph Adams Cram.* Washington, DC: University Press of America, 1980.

Nash, George. *The Conservative Intellectual Movement in the United States since 1945.* Rev. ed. Wilmington, DE: ISI Books, 1998.

Nevin, Thomas R. *Irving Babbitt.* Chapel Hill: University of North Carolina Press, 1984.

Nisbet, Robert. "Conservatives and Libertarians." *Modern Age* XXIV (Winter 1980): 2–8.

———. *The Quest for Community.* New York: Oxford University Press, 1953.

Osterweis, Rollin G. *Romanticism and Nationalism in the Old South.* New Haven, CT: Yale University Press, 1949.

Patterson, James T. *Mr. Republican: A Biography of Robert A. Taft.* Boston: Houghton Mifflin, 1972.

Peele, Gillian. *Revival and Reaction.* Oxford: Clarendon Press, 1984.

Person, James E., Jr. *Russell Kirk: A Critical Biography of a Conservative Mind.* Lanham, MD: Madison Books, 1999.

Peterson, Merrill D. *The Great Triumvirate: Webster, Clay, and Calhoun.* New York: Oxford University Press, 1987.

Rossiter, Clinton. *Conservatism in America: The Thankless Persuasion.* 2nd ed. Cambridge, MA: Harvard University Press, 1982.

Samuels, Ernest. *Henry Adams.* 3 vols. Cambridge, MA: Harvard University Press, 1948–1964.

Schlafly, Phyllis. *The Power of the Positive Woman.* New Rochelle, NY: Arlington House, 1977.

Sproat, John. *"The Best Men": Liberal Reformers in the Gilded Age.* New York: Oxford University Press, 1968.

Smith, Jean Edward. *John Marshall: Definer of a Nation.* New York: Henry Holt, 1998.

Sowell, Thomas. *Civil Rights: Rhetoric or Reality?.* New York: William Morrow, 1984.

Steinfels, Peter. *The Neoconservatives: The Men Who Are Changing American Politics.* New York: Simon & Schuster, 1979.

Stone, Brad Lowell. *Robert Nisbet: Communitarian Traditionalist.* Wilmington, DE: ISI Books, 2000.

Thompson, C. Bradley. *John Adams and the Spirit of Liberty.* Lawrence: University Press of Kansas, 1998.

Tomsich, John A. *A Genteel Endeavor: American Culture and Politics in the Gilded Age.* Stanford, CA: Stanford University Press, 1971.

Vanderbilt, Kermit. *Charles Eliot Norton: Apostle of Culture in a Democracy*. Cambridge, MA: Harvard University Press, 1959.

Wall, Joseph. *Andrew Carnegie*. New York: Oxford University Press, 1970.

Wish, Harvey. *George Fitzhugh: Propagandist for the Old South*. Baton Rouge: Louisiana State University Press, 1943.

Wolfskill, George. *The Revolt of the Conservatives: A History of the American Liberty League, 1934–1940*. Boston: Houghton Mifflin, 1962.

INDEX